OUTRAGEOUS!

*The Fine Life
and Flagrant Good Times
of Basketball's Irresistible Force*

CHARLES BARKLEY
and ROY S. JOHNSON

SIMON & SCHUSTER
New York • London • Toronto • Sydney • Tokyo • Singapore

SIMON & SCHUSTER
Simon & Schuster Building
Rockefeller Center
1230 Avenue of the Americas
New York, New York 10020

Designed by Irving Perkins Associates
Manufactured in the United States of America

10 9 8 7 6 5 4 3 2 1

Library of Congress Cataloging in Publication Data
Barkley, Charles, date.
    Outrageous! : the fine life and flagrant good times of
  basketball's irresistible force / Charles Barkley and Roy S.
  Johnson.
        p.   cm.
      1. Barkley, Charles, date   . 2. Basketball players—United
  States—Biography.   3. Philadelphia 76ers (Basketball team)
  I. Johnson, Roy S.   II. Title.
  GV884.B28A3   1992
  796.323′092—dc20
  [B]   91-40301
                                                              CIP
ISBN: 0-671-73799-6

Photo Credits:

William Archie/*Detroit Free Press,* 11; Rich Clarkson, 8; Les King, 5; Heinz
Kluetmeier, 7; Manny Millan, 12, 13; Bob Moore Photography, 4; George
Reynolds/*Philadelphia Daily News,* 9; George Tiedemann, 6; Jerry Wachter,
10. All other photos courtesy of the author.

Photo Research by George Washington.

To the city of Leeds, Alabama, for allowing me to be raised where I didn't have to worry about the life-and-death pressures of the big city; and to my brothers, Darryl and John, who had to endure the pressures of growing up as the younger siblings of a professional athlete.

—C.W.B.

Thanks, Mom. Bye.

—R.S.J.

ACKNOWLEDGMENTS

More than anyone, I would like to thank Frank Mikens, Adolphus Edwards, and Simon Barkley—my fathers by committee.

—C.W.B.

Playing a supportive second fiddle to Charles is no easy task. Playing a supportive second fiddle to a temperamental writer can be even worse. Many thanks to those who tried, and succeeded: the two Johns, Cirillo of the Knicks and Mertz of the Nets, two of the NBA's PR men extraordinaire; my agent, Michael Carlisle, and editor, Jeff Neuman; Glenn Guthrie, a man with the patience of Job; Maureen Barkley, a woman with the tolerance of a saint; Charcey Mae Glenn and Johnnie Mae Edwards, the architects; my nitpicky researchers, Desmond Wallace and Joy Duckett Cain; photo editor George Washington; Dave Hardee in Auburn's sports information office; Charles's numerous friends; the Boyz 'n the 'Hood—Greg, Jim, Branford, Reggie, and Carlo; my beautiful new wife, Barbara; and of course, Norman, who still only cares that I'm home when it's time for a walk.

—R.S.J.

CONTENTS

I'm down at Auburn watching practice when Tevester Anderson, one of coach Sonny Smith's assistants, calls me over. "See that kid down there?" he says. "Yeah, the fat one. He won't practice. He's lazy. He's a terrible example for our other kids. I can't do a thing with him."

Now, Tevester's a great coach, and if he can't work with this kid, hey, I'm wondering who this kid can be. You know what I'm saying? And the kid must weigh 300 pounds!

So, now they start scrimmaging. Freshmen against the varsity. On one play the kid comes down on a fast break. Off the dribble now, he throws the ball off the backboard, swoops in—the ball's at the top of the square now, easily eleven feet off the floor. He catches it, cups it in his hand, and—wham!—throws it down. All in one motion!

I said, "Holy cow, we got a lot of guys in our league who can't do that." Then, he gets something like 25 points and about 20 rebounds in just twenty-five minutes of scrimmaging. The freshmen kill the varsity. Hammer 'em. I turned to Tevester and said, "My advice to you, my man, is to get to like the kid." That was my introduction to Charles Barkley.

—Hubie Brown
CBS analyst and former NBA coach

INTRODUCTION

By Roy S. Johnson

"Good evening, you're on WCAU."

"Hi, this is Mary from Trenton. I'm a longtime Sixers fan, and I'd like to talk about Charles Barkley."

"What's on your mind, Mary?"

"Well, I think he hogs the ball and plays selfish all the time. And another thing . . ."

Charles Barkley sits up in his chair in the living room at his town house in suburban Philadelphia. He is listening to the radio as Mary from Trenton speaks her mind. At first, he simply shakes his head and mutters to himself. "Another critic," he says. But then, Barkley grins.

As always, Barkley would have the last word. He was, after all, the gregarious forward for the Philadelphia 76ers who was once fined $5,000 by National Basketball Association commissioner David Stern for placing a "friendly" side bet with Mark Jackson of the New York Knicks during a game. Charles was summoned to New York, where he admitted his guilt in a meeting with Stern. But later, he was somewhat less than contrite. "I went to bed as Charles Barkley," he said. "But I woke up as Pete Rose."

For good measure, Charles walked into the Sixers locker room at the Spectrum in Philadelphia on the night after meeting with Stern and posed a question: "Does anybody know the line on tonight's game?"

He's also the player who, prior to the start of the 1989–90

season, challenged his teammates to wear earrings if they won ten straight games. When they reached the milestone early in the year, Barkley decorated his menacing facade with a tiny diamond in his right ear. Many of his teammates followed suit.

And he's also the player who once telephoned a man in Phoenix, also named Charles Barkley, who had written a letter to his bombastic namesake in Philadelphia. It stated, "Every time you mess up, get a technical, or get thrown out of a game, I have trouble here when I use my credit cards or try to write a check." A few days later in Phoenix, a telephone rang. It was Barkley. "Is this Charles Barkley?" he said. "I just wanted you to know that every time you screw up on your job in Phoenix, I have trouble here in Philadelphia when I go to write a check."

Imagine having to live with this man.

"Being a father is something every man should experience, especially in the delivery room," he says. "My wife was calling me every name in the book during labor. But I just told her, 'Come on, honey. It can't hurt that badly. I've played with sprained ankles before. It can't hurt worse than that.'"

And yet, despite an explosive exterior, Charles has demonstrated time and time again during his seven-year NBA career that he has a sense of responsibility about his prominent status in society.

He once intervened when a distraught mother in Florida called the Sixers offices, explaining to anyone who would listen that her son, who idolized Barkley, was threatening to quit school because he had been cut from the basketball team. Soon, Charles was on the telephone. He not only convinced the kid to stay in school, but he also admonished him to direct his adulation toward his parents. They are his true role models, Barkley said, not an athlete.

But if you believe anyone on the Sixers' payroll is spared the sting of Barkley's wrath, think again. In 1990–91, he challenged head coach Jimmy Lynam's authority directly in front of the team's bench; he fought with Manute Bol; he screamed at Armon Gilliam for not rebounding enough. During one lull in the season when some of the players weren't performing to their potential, Barkley, the team captain, took it upon himself to stir things up a bit. "I don't ever want to steal any money from the Sixers," he said. "But I've played with guys who need a mask to go pick up their checks."

Still, it is not a perfect world. And Barkley has often crossed the line he normally strides so deftly. Arenas throughout the NBA are littered with witnesses to his wrath, and victims of the explosiveness that is the trademark of his performances on the court. He has his enemies, none more so than in late March 1991 when Barkley's rage went too far: he spit toward a fan who had practically run onto the court to challenge him, and inadvertently hit an eight-year-old girl.

Still, there was Mary from Trenton.

Barkley picks up the telephone and is eventually connected to the host of the call-in show. He tapes a message for Mary that is aired on the station throughout the night: "Mary from Trenton, where are you? This is Charles Barkley and I'm not really a bad guy. But you'll never know until you call WCAU."

Mary turned out to be Mary Walsh, a seventy-three-year-old grandmother. She had turned off her radio immediately after her call, so she didn't hear Charles's message until the following morning when her son told her to tune in because she was being summoned. Mary had to be convinced by her son to respond. She had, after all, trashed Barkley on the radio, so she should at least answer his public plea.

A few days later, Charles dispatched a limousine to Trenton and had Mary, her two sons, and a daughter-in-law chauffeured to the Spectrum where Mary was feted with flowers and doused with kindness during a Sixers game. "Oh my," Mary says now. "What a nice man."

The last word.

AT THE AGE of twenty-eight, and years from an upbringing in the projects of Leeds, Alabama, Charles Wade Barkley has reached a level of athletic excellence that no one believed he was capable of achieving when he decided to leave Auburn University following his junior season in order to provide for his family. He was too short, too fat—once weighing nearly 300 pounds, Barkley (he's listed as 6′5″, but is actually closer to 6′4″) has at various times been called a blimp, a soda machine, a bread truck, Porky Pig on a trampoline, and my favorite, a runaway float from the Macy's Thanksgiving Day parade—and just too damned harebrained, it was said, to recast the Sixers into his own robust image and carry them to an NBA title. When Barkley was chosen as the fifth pick in the 1984 NBA draft, the Sixers were still Doc's team, and after Julius Erving's retirement in 1987 they would labor under the expectations of quiet elegance and consistent achievement that had been the trademarks of Erving's eleven-year tenure with the team.

And yet, in what has been a stormy, iconoclastic career, Barkley has thrived. He is at once outspoken, fearsome, overpowering, graceful, outlandish, and one of the most dominant players in the game. Inch for inch—a 6'4″ cannonball amid men much larger—he may be *the* most dominant player in the game.

And the Sixers, for better or worse, are now Charles Barkley's team, a squad reflective of their leader's indomitable yet enigmatic spirit. They have won one Atlantic Division title (in 1990) during what will surely be known as the Barkley Era, and have consistently been one of the formidable teams in the Eastern Conference. "Nobody," says Barkley, "wants to play us." Yet the Sixers have never reached the NBA Finals during Barkley's career, and due to the incessant maneuverings of team owner Harold Katz, their roster has been a cast of ever-changing faces.

Through it all, Charles has been a clean-headed, fist-pumping, loose-lipped Weight Watchers Worst Nightmare for the NBA. And he's loved most every minute of it.

PEOPLE LOOK AT Charles Barkley and wonder how he can do the things that he does on the basketball court. (Writer Jeff Coplon dubbed him "the Square Bear of Mid-Air" in a 1991 cover story in *The New York Times Magazine*.) They follow the rhythm of his unique physique—now a sculpted 255 pounds—and are in absolute awe. Yet fans of Barkley's style do not marvel at his inspired court vision, as they do when watching Earvin (Magic) Johnson or Larry Bird. Nor are they left breathless by his flights of incandescent brilliance, gifts to us from Michael Jordan.

In Barkley, rather, people see the struggle. They see an undaunted, unrelenting effort to overcome obstacles—too short, too fat, too emotional . . . you get the idea—that are not unlike the barriers that they also confront in their lives. And they are inspired by his emphatic, unabashed response. They see the hurdles that have marked the paths of their own lives, and they cheer his unbowed bravado.

He was born in 1963, a year that proved to be a watershed period in the civil rights movement. It was the year in which Dr. Martin Luther King, in celebrating the hundredth anniversary of the Emancipation Proclamation, delivered the historic "I Have a Dream" speech on the steps of the Lincoln Memorial before the largest gathering of civil rights demonstrators in U.S. history. It was also the year in which a young antiapartheid activist named Nelson Mandela was imprisoned in South Africa for trying to free his nation's black majority from the grip of white-minority rule.

It was a time when blacks throughout the U.S. were swelling with a newfound sense of freedom. There were renewed visions of a brighter future rife with unencumbered opportunity for all people, regardless of their ethnicity. In music, sports, politics, and business, it was a time when the gates that had long barred blacks from enjoying the fruits of their talents and labors were thrown open with a dynamic flourish.

Charles Barkley is just one of the hundreds of thousands of African Americans who crashed through those gates. Yet he must still contend with unfulfilled expectations, and an imperfect world.

The guess here is that he will continue to do just as he has: full tilt and with an explosive and reckless disregard for whoever or whatever stands in his way.

And we'll love every minute.

At least most of us will.

PROLOGUE: AN APOLOGY

WHO IS THIS jerk anyway?

I saw him out of the corner of my eye. He was running down the center aisle not long after my teammate Rick Mahorn and I had finished another chest-butt late in the final period against the New Jersey Nets at the Meadowlands Arena. It was March 26, 1991, and Rick had just fouled rookie forward Derrick Coleman—fouled him *hard!* I *loved* it!—as Derrick tried to score on a break with only 1:38 left on the clock. The game shouldn't have been close because the Nets are terrible; they've got no business beating anybody whose uniforms don't read "Kings" or "Clippers" across the front. But if Derrick had scored on the play, the Nets would've taken a 1-point lead. That's why Rick blasted him, after which I ran toward Rick near the baseline and charged him up with our patented Bump 'n' Thump routine, just to show him how much I appreciated his effort.

Derrick was just about to hit the first free throw to tie the game at 86 when this asshole started up again. He had been hassling me throughout the game from his seat in the section behind the baseline. He was cussin' and calling me all sorts of names—like "fatass" and "asshole." Contrary to what most people think, we can hear most of what fans scream to us from the stands, especially in a god-awful place like the Meadowlands, where nobody's ever there. When you play New Jersey, it's just you, the Nets, and a few of your very closest friends.

I usually try to ignore most of the things I hear. If I reacted every time someone called me a vulgar name, I might as well have my paycheck direct-deposited into an account at the Na-

tional Basketball Association's main office in New York. But this
guy was crossing the line. He was nonstop vulgarity, and when
he came all the way down the aisle and started messing with me
even more, I had finally had enough. I was lined up alongside
the lane, waiting for Derrick's free throws, and he was just a few
feet away from the baseline, close enough for me to grab him
around the neck and tell him what I really thought about him.

My first thought was, "This clown must be crazy! He's in my
face! *My* face! He must have lost his fuckin' mind!"

To be honest, the guy's lucky to be alive. But rather than toss
him back to his seat—which is what he deserved—I just
screamed right back at him, matched him name for name, vulgar
for vulgar. Finally, just as Derrick's first free throw fell through
the net, I gathered every bit of foam I had in my mouth and let
it fly—in his general direction but mainly toward the floor.

I wasn't really aiming at him, or anyone. I just wanted to make
a point.

What point?

That this asshole wasn't worth shit.

Trouble was, I was tired and dehydrated after playing most of
the game, so my mouth was dry. I had no control over where
my spit went, and unfortunately it hit someone, the kind of
person I would never have spit on in a thousand years: an eight-
year-old girl.

I'll never forget her name: Lauren Rose. She was an elementary student from New Jersey. She and her parents, Dr. and
Mrs. Robert Rose, were sitting in the first row behind the baseline, right next to the center aisle where the heckler had been
standing.

And Lauren, unfortunately, was in the wrong place at the
wrong time.

After I spit, I looked around to see if I'd hit anyone. When I
looked over where Lauren and her parents were sitting, it didn't
seem like anything was wrong. No one even moved. Lauren and
her mom sat there like nothing happened. Dr. Rose was actually
laughing. But later, an usher filed a complaint with the NBA.
Just like that, the lowest moment of my entire career was well
on its way to becoming a national story.

We lost the game in overtime, 98–95. Afterward, as I sat in

the locker room with a towel around my waist, I didn't feel like I'd done anything wrong out on the floor, but I was pretty subdued. I was tired, and I was confused about what had actually happened out there along the baseline. I replayed it in my mind a few times—even while I answered questions about the game from reporters, not one of whom asked me about the incident—before I finally stood up and walked to the shower. Maybe I suspected something was going to happen, but I don't think so.

It wasn't until the next day in Charlotte that I found out I had spit on Lauren. I got the news at the Charlotte Coliseum before our morning shootaround. It made me sick. Hearing that I had spit on an eight-year-old girl affected me more than anything I've every done in the NBA.

More than fighting with Bill Laimbeer.

More than arguing with the league office.

More than criticizing my teammates.

More than offending any of the many groups I offended during my first seven years in the NBA.

Why?

Because I had spit on a kid.

Kids are the best. They're usually right on when it comes to reading people. They're honest, and they treat the people they run into like they deserve to be treated. With kids, there's no bullshit. I've never had any problems with kids. They're sweet and innocent, and they just enjoy life, at least until grown-ups screw it up.

Now that I have a child of my own—Christiana was born on May 15, 1989—I'm even more in love with children. No matter whether the Sixers win or lose, no matter how badly I play, and no matter what I do on or off the court. Christiana is always there waiting for me, smiling with her arms spread wide, ready with a kiss. How can you not return that kind of love? I've even taught Christiana how to head-butt. She's one reason I never want to do anything bad to a kid.

The next couple of days were unbelievable.

It was a snowball that became a mountain, and I got caught in the avalanche. I was suspended for one game—that night while the team beat the sorry Hornets, I was in my hotel room, still feeling like shit—and fined $10,000. By itself, the fine was the largest I've ever received, and with the suspension the whole incident cost me a total of $49,000. But I never thought about the money I lost. I thought, for once, about the kinds of things that were being said about me—by people all around the country.

It was as if I had done something criminal. People went crazy. I was blasted in newspapers and on radio and television stations throughout the country. Not that I'm not used to people saying things about me—and I usually don't give a shit about it anyway—but in this case, criticizing me for what a lot of people thought was intentionally spitting on a child, they were wrong. Absolutely wrong.

At first, I rebelled. I mean, compared to some of the things that other players in the league had done earlier in the season, I was a saint! James Worthy of the Los Angeles Lakers had been arrested for hiring two prostitutes to come to his hotel in Houston before a game against the Rockets, and when he arrived at the game later that night he was given a standing ovation! He was greeted with another rousing ovation in Los Angeles. Give me a damn break!

And what about my former teammate David Wingate, who now plays for the Washington Bullets (and before that he played for the San Antonio Spurs)? Before the start of the season, he was arrested and charged with aggravated sexual assault by a woman in Philadelphia. He wasn't allowed to play for several months, not until the case was resolved. He was eventually cleared of the charges, and when he checked in for his first game at the HemisFair Arena in San Antonio, where he played for the Spurs, he was also given a standing ovation.

Here were two guys who were charged with crimes that are an affront to women everywhere—to people everywhere—and they were treated like damn war heroes! Meanwhile, I was treated like shit, like I'd committed an unpardonable sin. I was booed and cursed and crucified almost everywhere I went. It's not like I haven't been booed before, or even cursed by some of the crazy assholes who call themselves fans, people who think that their ticket entitles them to say any damn thing they want to say. But this was different.

This time, it hurt.

For once, I was ashamed of the nasty words that were starting to follow my name, as in, "Charles Barkley is a (fill in the blank)." And I was stung by the accusations being made about my character by people in every city.

For once, I was sorry for something I had done on the basketball court.

There was nothing I could do to change people's opinions about me. There was even some talk following the 1990–91 season that the incident had cost me the Most Valuable Player award. That's garbage. I didn't deserve it. (Now, the 1990 MVP award, that's another story.) Michael Jordan won it, and he deserved it. After that, I would have voted for David Robinson before voting for me.

I wasn't concerned about my image. (I never have been.) But I was concerned about Lauren, who had been the unintended victim of my stupidity. I called her and told her that I was really, really sorry for what happened. I apologized to both her and her father, and they both made me feel a lot better. They accepted my apology, as well as my offer to pay for their tickets for the 1991–92 season. (That's something you're reading here first. It was a private thing, unlike a certain apology faxed by Dennis Rodman to the Chicago Bulls' office, probably on the advice of his agent, after he mugged Scottie Pippen in the '91 playoffs.) I know it doesn't make up for what I did, but at least the Roses will be able to do something else with the money they would have spent for season tickets. And Lauren and her family were my guests when I was roasted at an Easter Seals dinner in July.

They're nice people, and for that I'm thankful. They were nothing like the asshole whose tirade had tripped my switch in the first place. People like him don't belong at NBA games, or at any other sporting event for that matter. Sports is entertainment, family entertainment. But some fans want to turn the games into their own form of entertainment, letting loose with taunts, insults, and words that would get them killed if they said them to someone out on the street.

What does the NBA do about this kind of behavior? Not a damn thing, except fine any player who responds to being treated like an animal. Commissioner David Stern has more respect for the assholes who taint the game than he does for the players the real fans pay to see. Instead of punishing the player, the league should throw the vulgar fans out of the arena and if they're season-ticket holders, revoke their seats. But the league is only concerned about profits. As long as they get their little money—from the fans, television, and at least in my case, the players, too—they're happy. It's not right.

As much as the spitting incident might have hurt my reputation—at least among people who weren't already convinced that I'm a jerk—it also helped me. A lot. I'm not promising that I'll never do something like that again, but I don't think I will. I never want to do anything like that again.

From now on, Homey won't play that! If I do anything that stupid again, people will be on my ass. Again. Even the people who have always stood by me. Maybe the most difficult thing I had to do after the incident was to call my mother, Charcey Mae Glenn, back home in Leeds, Alabama, and hear her tell me what I already knew—that this time, I had gone too far. This time, I was wrong.

If I commit another misdeed even remotely close to the spitting incident, the reaction will be even worse than before. And I'll have to be ready to take it. I'll deserve it.

Most importantly, though, the incident helped me to learn about limits—it's about time, huh?—and the extent to which my actions can cause so many people to think that Charles Barkley's an idiot or some asshole who has no respect for kids and doesn't care about what anybody thinks about him.

That couldn't be any further from the truth, though it took my doing something really over the line in order to realize it. It doesn't mean I'm going to stop being who or what I am. But I sure don't ever want to hurt someone innocent like Lauren again. The guilty had still better watch themselves.

In March, I apologized publically for what I did that night in New Jersey, and I'd like to apologize again. What I did was wrong, and I'm truly sorry it happened.

Now let's get on with it.

1

I DON'T MIND BEING A JERK

"HEY, FATHEAD, WELCOME to the team."

That was my introduction to pro basketball. As a rookie, an unsigned rookie for the Philadelphia 76ers, I figured that the best thing for me to do was to keep my mouth shut when I heard someone shouting in my direction. It was a hot and sticky July afternoon when I walked into the Fonde Recreation Center in downtown Houston, just a few weeks after I'd been picked by the Sixers in the first round of the 1984 NBA draft. I was the fifth player picked overall, so according to the guys who were supposed to be the experts, I was the fifth-best collegiate player in the country.

What the hell did they know? I thought I was even better than that, even though I'd played only three years at Auburn University before leaving for the NBA after my junior season.

I was feeling pretty good about myself. But at that moment, I was pretty scared—though that might be hard to believe—because I had no idea about what I was getting into by coming to play at the legendary Fonde.

Everybody in Houston who knew anything about basketball knew that this old, run-down rec center in the city's toughest area was the best place to find real competition: NBA players who didn't care if they knocked your head off and guys who wanted nothing more than to be able to say that they'd kicked an NBA player's ass. This was true basketball: no refs, no uniforms, no halftime. It was shirts and skins, and the only thing on the line was pride. It was For Men Only.

I was in town to meet with my newly signed agent, Lance Luchnick, who lived in Houston. He had told me not to be afraid of matching my skills with Fonde's best. Me, scared? Forget it. I was mortified. And it didn't help matters any when I walked into the hot, humid gym and heard this deep voice with the heavy Southern accent booming through the gym.

" 'Hey, fathead,' I said, 'welcome . . .' "

That's how I met Moses Malone.

How did I respond? Was I cocky? Arrogant? Just who was this nut calling me fathead? Was he crazy? Moses Malone? So what! Who cares that he's one of the best basketball players ever to play the game and probably the very best rebounder ever? Big deal! You think I gave a shit? I was coming to Fonde to kick some ass, just like I was going to do after signing my NBA contract. So what did I say?

"Thank you."

There might even have been a "Mr." or a "sir" thrown in there somewhere, too. I don't remember. Fear can be a humbling thing, especially the fear of having to live up to someone else's expectations. Or the fear of getting your own ass kicked. Take your pick.

I had just been drafted behind four college players everybody described as being legitimate "franchise" players, guys who were supposed to be the centerpiece around which a whole team could be built into a contender.

Houston used the first pick in the draft to select Hakeem— back then, he was known as Akeem—Olajuwon of the University of Houston, a shot-blocking Nigerian who's turned out to be one of the most frightening centers in the league, even though he's only 6'10", short for a pro center. He's one of the few guys who makes me cringe when I drive down the lane because I know that if he's anywhere in the vicinity, I might not only get my shot blocked, but I might also get my head blocked at the same time. Hakeem doesn't care what he blocks, as long as it's round and smooth—so my head qualifies.

Portland had fallen on hard times since its glory days in the midseventies when it dominated the league and won the 1977 NBA title. The Trail Blazers had the second pick in the draft and were faced with one of the easiest decisions in the history of the draft. Boy, did they screw it up! They believed all that bullshit about how teams should build around centers and not guards, so they picked Sam Bowie of Kentucky, a 7'2" center with a long history of leg problems. Five seasons, zero championships, and four leg operations later, Portland traded him to New Jersey, along with a first-round draft pick, for power forward Buck Williams, one of the most underappreciated players in the game.

(I was happy to see Buck shipped out to the Western Conference because he tried to beat me up every time we played the Nets. Actually, I love playing against him because I know it's going to be a war. With Buck, you don't have to worry about whether or not he's going to come to play. He was just what the sissy Blazers needed, as they proved when Portland reached the 1990 NBA Finals during his first season with the team. They went down to the Los Angeles Lakers in the Western Conference Finals the following season, but they'll be back. They've got more talent than any team in the league. For the Nets, of course, it was the kind of trade they always seem to make—the kind that makes them regulars in the NBA lottery.)

The Trail Blazers would have become contenders much sooner if management hadn't drafted Bowie instead of a skinny guard from the University of North Carolina who, like me, was leaving school after his junior season—a guy named Jordan.

That's how Christmas came in June that year for Chicago, which, with the third pick in the '84 draft, had the best damn basketball player on the planet just fall into their laps. Talk about a no-brainer—as in no brains in Portland. With the talent the Bulls management team, led by general manager Jerry Krause, slowly placed around Michael over the next few years, it was only a matter of time before the Bulls won the NBA title. They finally achieved that goal in June 1991, when they stomped the five-time-champs-under-Magic Lakers four games to one in the NBA Finals. It was a true no-contest, with the Bulls sweeping the final four games of the series pretty much at will, winning the last three *in Los Angeles*.

To reach the Finals, the Bulls had embarrassed the Knicks in three straight ass-whippings in the first round, manhandled us to win four games to one in the conference semifinals, then flat out kicked the shit out of the defending champion Detroit Pistons in four straight—it couldn't have happened to a more deserving bunch—before beating the Lakers so badly that Magic Johnson, at the age of thirty-two, went delirious between games four and five and hinted that he was thinking about retiring. He later said he wasn't serious. I, for one, never thought he was.

That the Bulls didn't win a title during Michael's first seven years in the league had nothing to do with Michael—John Paxson, Horace Grant, and Cliff Levingston, someone whom the Sixers should have tried to sign prior to the 1991 season when he was a free agent, made the difference against the Lakers— just as the reason the Sixers haven't won a championship since my arrival has nothing to do with me.

You don't win the NBA title with tradition, like people claimed the Boston Celtics did when they were hanging banners during the late fifties and throughout the sixties.

You also don't win the NBA title simply by having a fancy fast break, like some people think the Los Angeles Lakers did when they dominated the eighties by winning five championships.

And you don't win NBA titles by being bullies, either, no matter what the Pistons would like you to believe.

The only way to win the NBA title is to have the best *team* in the league. The most talent. The best players. Nine guys who can flat play their asses off. (You *can* have too much talent, though, especially at the end of the bench. The sixth through ninth man should be able to play; after that, the last three guys should just sit there and never complain. It's impossible to find enough playing time for everyone. Besides, these guys make a lot of money to keep their mouths shut. They should just be happy to be in the league.) No one man can do it alone. Not Michael. Not Magic. Not Hakeem. Not David. Not me. Not anybody. The Celtics, Lakers, Pistons, and Bulls have already figured that out. The Blazers, San Antonio Spurs, and Phoenix Suns are learning fast. (Note to Sixers owner Harold Katz: Time is running out. I've got three more good seasons left. So, get a clue.)

Ever since they came into the league as an expansion team in 1980, the Dallas Mavericks have been scratching their heads like village idiots when it comes to the draft. Rather than drafting talented players, they've usually been more concerned with drafting "nice" guys. Problem is, most of their "nice" guys couldn't play. The summer of 1984 was a classic: Dallas had the fourth pick in the draft, but I knew they weren't going to draft me. No way in hell were they going to draft an overweight, outspoken 6'6" center (who was really 6'4") from what they probably thought was a nowhere college basketball program.

Instead, they played it safe. They took clean-cut all-American Sam Perkins, a 6'9", long-armed forward from Dean Smith's all-American rah-rah program at North Carolina. Big mistake. It was one of the worst draft picks in franchise history—which is saying a lot, considering the likes of Bill Garnett and other stiffs who've passed through Dallas as first-round picks—and maybe one of the worst picks ever.

Why?

Because six years later, in August 1990, the Mavericks lost Perkins without getting even a dirty jockstrap for him in return when he became an unrestricted free agent—meaning the Mavs didn't have the right to match the offer, so about all they could do was drive him to the airport on the way out of town—and signed with the Lakers for an unbelievable $19.2 million over six years. For its trouble, Dallas suddenly had no championship banners, no Sam Perkins, no nothing. Hell, on most nights during the 1990–91 season, they didn't even have a damn team! They were a nonfactor all year, a lottery team that not long ago was a legitimate contender.

I sometimes wonder how many times those good old all-American guys in the Mavs' front office have kicked themselves in the butt with their pointy-toed cowboy boots because of their 1984 draft-day blunder.

Actually, you can't blame the Mavericks for passing me up. When draft day rolled around, I was just what they thought I was. None of the league's so-called "great basketball minds" thought I was a franchise player. I played postup basketball, close to the basket in the paint, in the trenches. Basically, I was a power forward in a small forward's body. Hell, I was a power

forward in a guard's body. At my height, everybody thought I
would get killed by the NBA's 6'8", 6'9", and 6'10" behemoth
power forwards, and that I wouldn't be able to score inside against
teams with big centers who blocked shots. I also wasn't a great
shooter from more than a few feet away from the basket. Another
negative. And while I had better-than-average ball-handling
skills, I was no guard. So, what was I? In NBA jargon, I was a
" 'tweener," which meant that after Hakeem, Sam, Michael, and
the other Sam, I was a major risk, a player who might not fit in
at any position. Or so most teams thought—most teams except
the Sixers.

I didn't care what the Mavs did because I knew the 76ers were
going to draft me. Katz told me so during my predraft interview
in Philadelphia, assuming I was still there when their turn came
at No. 5, and barring something strange happening—like Chicago and Dallas also going brain dead and passing up Michael.
I was real happy at first about the prospect of going to a good
team, and the Sixers were a *great* team, having just won the
1983 NBA title with legends like Julius Erving, Moses, and Maurice Cheeks as starters, and bench players like Bobby Jones. They
were also hungry again after being upset by the Nets—go figure—in the first round of the 1983–84 playoffs. Who wouldn't
have wanted to play for that team?

Well, me.

What changed my mind about playing for the Sixers was a
nightmare tale from my agent. (Hiring Lance would later become
a nightmare of its own for me, the single biggest and costliest
mistake I ever made, but that's another story.) Two days before
the draft, Lance dropped a bombshell: he said that because the
76ers' payroll placed them over the league's salary cap—a complicated system designed to keep the wealthiest teams, those
located in the largest television markets, from hoarding the most
talented and expensive players—the team would only be able
to sign me to a one-year contract for the league's minimum salary,
which at the time was $65,000. In short, I freaked.

"You mean I left college early for a stupid sixty-five grand
when guys drafted behind me will be getting millions?" I
screamed.

Lance didn't have to respond.

•   •   •

THE SALARY CAP was created on March 31, 1983, when several franchises were in danger of folding. That would have been a disaster for the league, which was still contending with a general perception that a lot of players—particularly black players—used drugs. And teams in the smallest markets, like Indiana, Milwaukee, and Utah, feared that they wouldn't be able to keep up financially with the teams from the larger, richer cities, teams that could afford to pay the new, higher salaries because of potentially higher local television, gate, and advertising revenues.

If even one team had gone into bankruptcy, it would have cost a dozen players their jobs and put the entire league on shaky financial ground. So the players' union and the owners came up with a plan that would basically keep the league from eating itself alive: the salary cap. One of the provisions of the agreement was that teams over the cap could only sign rookies to one-year contracts at the league minimum—unless they shipped someone out. Needless to say, the prospect of playing for the Sixers, championships and all, seemed a lot less exciting once I learned of the financial consequences. All of a sudden, even the Nets were looking pretty good to me.

Lance tried to cheer me up by saying that signing a one-year contract would let me be a restricted free agent at the end of my rookie season. At that point, I would be able to sign with any team in the league for the best deal I could get, and the Sixers would either have to match it or let me go. But I was still depressed. What if I got hurt? What if I didn't play well? What if the coach didn't give me enough minutes to prove myself? So much of a rookie's success, especially a rookie who's drafted by a good team, is out of his control.

I also had other concerns. One of the main reasons I left school, rather than playing one more year and getting my degree, was to be able to provide financial security for my family—my mother, grandmother, and two brothers back in Leeds, Alabama. Signing a multimillion-dollar NBA contract would have allowed me to do just that; signing a contract worth $65,000 wouldn't.

Suddenly, leaving Auburn didn't seem like such a good idea.

Suddenly, being drafted by the Sixers didn't seem like such a good idea.

If a player today found himself in the same predicament, he might threaten to take his game to Europe, particularly Italy where teams are now paying million-dollar salaries for players who are still in their prime—and for players like ninety-seven-year-old Bob McAdoo, the Nolan Ryan of basketball. Before the start of the 1989–90 season, Danny Ferry, a first-round draft pick of the Los Angeles Clippers and the second player taken overall, signed a five-year, $10-million contract with Il Messaggero of the Italian League because he wanted no part of the pitiful Clippers.

(Danny had every right to do what he did, but some of the things he said about the Clippers, and what he ultimately did to them by going to Europe rather than helping them build into a winner, was nothing short of gutless. Every rookie would like to go to a well-respected organization and compete for the title right away. But it doesn't always work out that way. Very few of the best players have ever gone to great teams.

When Isiah Thomas was drafted by the Pistons in 1981, the Bad Boys were just bad.

When Buck Williams became a Net that same year, most fans thought the team still played in Piscataway, New Jersey, wherever that is.

When Michael Jordan arrived in Chicago in 1984, the Bulls sucked.

When Patrick Ewing was picked by the Knicks the following year, New York was pitiful.

And when Brad Daugherty was picked by Cleveland in 1986, the Cavs were still the laughingstock of the league.

A lot of great players, All-Stars, have gone to teams that were terrible when they arrived. They accepted it and worked their asses off to make their teams better. And for most of them, it's paid off. It's the price you pay for having talent. Danny Ferry wasn't willing to pay that price and it diminished him in the eyes of a lot of NBA players—including me.)

At the time I came out of school, European teams were only interested in NBA players who were near the end of their careers. (Or guys who didn't really have much of a career, like Joe Barry

Carroll.) So, for me, playing in Europe wasn't a real option. Besides, I wanted to play in the NBA—end of discussion. But that didn't mean I didn't have any options. In fact, Lance and I agreed that in order to get out of this mess, I had only one choice: force the Sixers to draft someone else.

How?

Easy. In what I consider my first officially outrageous act as a pro, I decided to get fat.

At the end of my last interview with the Sixers, Katz had offered me a challenge. "I'm going to give you a little test," he said. "I want to see what kind of person you are. I want you down to 275 pounds when you come back to Philadelphia on the day before the draft."

"Okay," I said. "No problem."

I weighed about 282 at the time, which I thought was a perfect weight for me. (I've always said that my "playing weight" is whatever I happen to weigh when I'm playing.) Losing seven pounds would be easy. I went back home to Leeds and began working out, lifting a few weights—something I've rarely done, and never on a regular basis—and jogging, though nothing too strenuous, except playing basketball. Mostly, I just stopped eating. Two days before the draft, when Lance gave me the bad news about the salary cap, I was sleek and slim, 272 pounds on the nose. But that was going to change in a hurry.

Over the next forty-eight hours, I ate and drank anything and everything I could get to my face, everything that wasn't nailed down or poison. Biscuits. Rolls. Steak. Lobster. Dessert. Then after about my twentieth meal in two days, Lance and I went drinking at a Houston bar. I downed beers like Prohibition was coming back the following day. The next morning, the day I was supposed to fly to Philadelphia, I woke up and had a humongous breakfast. Finally, I ate and drank on the plane. By the time we landed, I thought I was going to explode. More importantly, I also thought that as far as the Sixers were concerned, I was as good as gone.

When I stepped on the scale at the Sixers' offices, I didn't want to look because I was afraid I hadn't eaten enough. But I peeked. It read 291 pounds! "Yes!" I said to myself. I couldn't have been happier.

Katz was stunned. He couldn't believe it. I thought his eyes were going to pop out of his head. He looked at me—I was doing the best pitiful-puppy-dog look you've ever seen, good preparation for my future commercial gigs—but couldn't say a word. He was furious. Finally, he exploded.

"Are you fuckin' crazy, or what?"

"I don't know what happened, Mr. Katz," I said, still struggling to hide the smile that was threatening to take over my face. "I really don't know."

He was so mad he just walked out of the room.

Pat Williams, the team's general manager, was also in the room. He was stunned, almost tongue-tied—which, if you know Pat, is just about as close as you're going to get to a miracle on earth. All he could say was, "Thanks for coming, Charles."

Lance and I hopped on the next Amtrak train to New York and celebrated all the way. I was convinced the Sixers would pass on me, leaving me to either Washington, San Antonio, or the Los Angeles Clippers, the next three teams in the draft. Avoiding the minimum-wage Sixers would have been worth the money it would cost me by being picked lower in the draft, especially if I went to a team that could pay me what I was worth.

The following day at the Felt Forum at Madison Square Garden, I leaned back in my chair and relaxed as Hakeem, Sam Bowie, Michael, and Sam Perkins were called to the stage by NBA commissioner David Stern, who announced the first round of the draft. I was so relaxed, in fact, that I was only half-listening when Stern started to name the Sixers' first-round draft pick. Then I heard: "The Philadelphia 76ers select Charles"—my stomach felt sick. My heart started racing—"Barkley, six-foot-six-inch forward from Auburn University."

All I could think of was "sixty-five thousand dollars per year." I was crushed. "Damn," I said under my breath. I was happy to get drafted, but in the back of my mind, I thought, "Shit, I blew it."

I don't remember much about the next few moments. I walked to the stage in a stupor, shook the commissioner's hand, and spent about an hour answering questions from reporters, who wanted to know how I felt about being able to play with Julius Erving. "Like shit," I wanted to say, but didn't.

I do know one thing. If I ever decide to get into acting, I'll know I have the talent. On Draft Day 1984 I learned that I could play any role. That day, I played a starring role in "Thankful to Be a Sixer." I smiled. I said all the right things. Inside, I thought I was going to throw up.

"Oh, my God," I thought. "What have I done?"

As it turned out, all my fears were groundless. The Sixers opened up a salary slot for me by cutting a second-year forward from Syracuse named Leo Rautins, who would have made about $150,000 for the 1984–85 season. I slipped right into his spot and signed a four-year, $2-million deal. Sorry, Leo.

That unsuccessful eating binge may have been the first really outrageous thing I did as a professional athlete, but it wasn't the last. Over the years, I've blasted my teammates, as well as the 76ers' management. I've fought with other players, cursed officials, fought opponents, and gotten into it with fans at several arenas. I've criticized the league office and the players' union. (At least I can't ever be accused of favoritism.) I've insulted whites, blacks, and women's groups. In fact, if there's someone out there I haven't offended at one time or another, please raise your hand.

That's what I thought.

I've never really intended to offend anyone, and yet I've managed to create controversy with amazing regularity—by word or deed. So what? I don't mind being a jerk.

I HAVEN'T ALWAYS been this way, you know. Big? Oh, I was always big. At least bigger, pudgier, huskier, and basically much larger than anyone else my age. When I started getting some national pub during my sophomore season at Auburn, when I was kicking asses all over the Southeast Conference, people outside of Alabama started picking up on the nicknames that had been created for me by the school's athletic department in its efforts to get some attention for the basketball program. There was Fatboy, the Leaning Tower of Pizza, Boy Gorge (I *really* hated that one), and of course, the Round Mound of Rebound.

I was upset at first by the names because they made people more interested in my physical appearance—my weight was the

most popular game-show question in Alabama—than my talent.
I was the best player in the SEC for three years straight between
1981 and 1984, but the only thing anyone cared about was how
many pizzas or chickens I could eat. That really pissed me off.

Looking back, I can say now that I didn't enjoy much of my
experience at Auburn, and having to endure those nicknames
was one of the main reasons.

While I'll confess that there's always been a lot of Charles
Barkley to go around, I wasn't always so vocal, so bold, and yes,
so obnoxious when it came to speaking my mind. I was actually
a pretty quiet kid. I listened to and watched the people around
me in Leeds, particularly my mother, Charcey Mae Glenn, and
my grandmother, Johnnie Mae Edwards. My father, Frank Barkley, abandoned us when I was only a year old. After that, my
mom and grandmother became the most important people in my
life. They taught me everything I would ever know about survival, pride, and character. They were my role models.

My grandmother was a workaholic. She was a beautician, a
nurse, and an assembly-line worker at a packinghouse for most
of her life and provided me with the foundation I've tried to live
my life on. Not a single day passes when I don't think of her
words: "When it all comes down to the final day, you'll have to
look in the mirror at yourself and God, and only then will you
be judged."

My grandmother had a deep impact on me in more ways than
one, but particularly when it comes to my faith in God. People
sometimes ask me how I can be religious and still play the way
I do and act the way I do. Well, I've got no problem with it.
God doesn't hold my talent against me. He gave it to me, and
He only wants me to reach my potential.

Now, before I go to bed every night, if I know in my heart
that I haven't been true to myself, I feel as if I've let Him down.
And Granny. What's most important to me is the truth, just like
it is for anyone who claims to know right from wrong, honesty
from deceit.

That's why I don't usually apologize for anything I've said or
done that might have offended someone or hurt some feelings—
except, of course, for what happened in New Jersey. So if that's

what you want to hear, then you might as well close this book right now and go read the comics.

Once I began to live by my grandmother's words, I became more like the person I am today. At Auburn, my outbursts were usually confined to closed-door meetings and practices, where I had plenty of differences with coach Sonny Smith. They started when I was a freshman, and Coach Smith was bullheaded about not starting me because of my "poor practice habits," even though I was by far the best player on his sorry team.

For the most part, only my teammates and coaches got to hear my tirades, and they mostly ignored me. "That's just Charles," they said. Now, much of my reputation is based on statements I've made during my career, or things I've done that have nothing to do with playing the game of basketball—from saying that I think all players should be tested for drugs (the players' union went crazy over that one) to joking that a player might "go home and beat [his] wife" after a particularly frustrating loss (most feminists didn't even know who I was until then), to throwing a roundhouse left to the head of Bill Laimbeer (tell me you wouldn't have loved to do the same thing), to having it out with one of my own teammates, Manute Bol.

Controversial is the word I often hear associated with me, and quite frankly, it offends me. What some might call controversial, I call telling the truth. I don't create controversies; they're there long before I open my mouth. I just bring them to your attention. If that's controversial, then so be it.

I wasn't brought up to believe that telling the truth would get me into trouble and cause some people to label me a buffoon— or even insane, like NBA vice president Rod Thorn insinuated when, after the spitting incident, he said that I might need psychological help. But over the years I've come to realize that a lot of people don't really want to hear the turth. Not about themselves, their associates, their lives, society, anything.

A lot of people in the NBA recognize that they have more to gain, especially financially, by saying what the people around them want to hear, and acting like those same people believe they should act—anything but be true to themselves. Quite simply, they're phonies. They've convinced themselves that they're the smartest general manager—like: Jack McCloskey of the Pistons, who said my teammate Hersey Hawkins didn't deserve to make the 1991 All-Star team when he should have been minding his own business—the shrewdest owner, or one of the best players in the league. And they expect everyone to kiss their feet because of it.

Well, they're all full of shit. But rather than be truthful with themselves and the fans, they put on airs and act like they can do no wrong, that they're above saying or doing anything that might be construed as controversial.

It doesn't do any good to name them here, mainly because a few of these people are my friends. I just wish they'd get off their air, I mean, soapbox every once in a while and join the honest folks.

MICHAEL JORDAN: *Sometimes Charles will say things everyone else might want to say, but won't have the courage to say. He speaks for the frustration in all of us.*

What's particularly frustrating to me is that some pro athletes go out of their way to portray themselves as "good" people—you know who they are; they smile on billboards and they sell cereal on television—so that their subtle message is that people like me (those who speak their minds no matter the consequences and try to be honest with the public) are "bad" people. They say the "right" things rather than saying what they feel in their hearts, what they know to be the truth. They create a squeaky-clean image, one that seems to tell the public that they've never done anything wrong, that they're without fault. Are they lying? Not exactly, but some of what we see from a lot of professional athletes these days is lying without lying. After all, no one is without faults. I'm a human being; I know I've done things that are wrong, things that I could never deny. So have a few other athletes who might have you think otherwise. No one's an angel. We've all got skeletons in our closets.

As a kid, I was a petty thief. I stole merchandise from local grocery and convenience stores, mostly because I was bored.

In college, I smoked marijuana. I'm not proud of these moments in my past, but I won't lie about them, either.

Unfortunately, skirting the truth is very marketable these days. It's great business for agents and athletes who are driven by the endorsement dollar. Some fans, some consumers, love halo-wearing athletes who seem close to perfection. Those fans want us to bow at their feet, and to talk about what wonderful lives we lead and how much we love their support. It's all trash.

I'd like to think that the majority of fans respect honesty. They're the ones who supported me in 1988 when I told Katz I was underpaid; in February 1987, when I called a couple of my teammates—World B. Free and Kenny Green—whiners and complainers (I didn't name the guilty players at the time, but they knew who they were, and they needed to hear what I had to say); and numerous other times when I've spoken out or done something that would have been viewed as heresy for most other high-profile athletes.

It's unfortunate that most of the honest athletes—guys like Eric Dickerson, Dave Winfield, Andrew Toney, and myself— are labeled controversial. Because we go against the system by asking for a raise when we know we deserve it, or by giving blunt answers to reporters' questions, we get branded. Most fans don't want their athletes to cause ripples. We're not allowed to be human beings with different opinions and thoughts, we're expected to be robots. Pieces of meat.

There are times when I don't understand it, either. Almost everyone, at some point in their lives, would love to be able to express their true feelings to those who need to be butt-kicked into reality. But because our lives have become so political, very few people can afford to take such a risk. It could cost them their job, their family, their friends, or their livelihood, so they simply accept the situation. But those same people should still respect honesty from people who are able—and most importantly, willing—to speak their minds, despite the potential damage to their images. My contract with the Sixers is guaranteed through the 1994–95 season, so no matter what I say, Katz can never fire me—as much as I'm sure he's wished that he could have on more than one occasion.

There have always been ways around telling the truth, of course, plenty of times when I could easily have avoided saying what I knew in my mind was right.

In October 1988, when I said I thought every NBA player should be tested for drugs, you'd have thought that I said we should all be castrated from the uproar it created. Random drug testing is against the rules outlined in the drug agreement between the league and the players' union. But we're paid a lot of money. If I were an owner, I would want drug testing as a way to protect my investment. The league does not have a rampant drug problem—alcohol problem? Yes. But no drug problem— so the vast majority of players have nothing to be afraid of. But did anyone back me up? Hell no. Not one player. Not the union. No one. They left me hanging, and my idea died a slow death.

There was also the time when I was unfairly labeled as the Pete Rose of the NBA—a gambler. It really pissed me off because the league, once again, made a big deal out of something that was really nothing, nothing but an honest joke between two friends. Here's what happened:

Near the end of the 1988-89 season, I made an imaginary $5,000 bet with Mark Jackson of the Knicks before our teams met in the first round of the playoffs. They swept us three games to none, but I never paid Mark a single dime because we never considered it a real bet. That fact alone should've let the league know that we weren't serious bettors. The original bet became a running joke between us, a running challenge between two friends having a good time.

Eight months after the initial bet, the Knicks were in Philadelphia trailing by a point with 22.4 seconds left in the game. I was on the free-throw line for two shots. Mark was standing nearby.

"You're gonna miss," he said, smiling.

"Wanna bet?" I responded.

"Bet."

I made both shots to put us ahead by 3.

We were both laughing as we came up the floor. Mark said, "I'll make the next shot."

"Bet you don't."

He does, a 3-pointer no less, with 15.4 seconds left. Just like that, the game is tied, and Mark and I were cracking up.

Finally, I say, "Okay, I'll make the next shot."

"Okay," says Mark. "Bet."

I put us ahead again by hitting a 15-footer with 2.7 on the clock. After the shot we slapped hands like we were back on the playground. Friends having a good time.

The Knicks called time-out to set up a play. I don't know what play their coach at the time, Stu Jackson, had designed, but Mark took the final shot as the buzzer went off. He missed, so the Sixers won. After the game, we both joked about the bet to reporters. I was into my best Muhammad Ali imitation, screaming, "Tell Mark, I want my money!"

It was all a joke until the next day when I was told that I had to go to New York to speak with Commissioner David Stern. He wanted to talk about gambling.

"What?" I said. "You've got to be kiddin' me."

Stern wasn't kidding. Steam must have been coming out of my ears the following day as I sat in his office overlooking Fifth Avenue. He started talking about the league's image, about how with the Pete Rose case still fresh on everybody's mind the NBA couldn't afford any talk of gambling. "Even when two good friends are just playing around, it doesn't look good," he said. I sat quietly and listened, even though I thought Stern was talking bullshit. Anybody could tell the difference between Pete Rose using a bookie to bet on baseball and two guys joking around on the basketball court.

Stern talked about how the league was suing the Oregon lottery, which wanted to allow people in the state to pick NBA games. (They didn't settle the lawsuit until December, when the state agreed to drop the NBA games.) I told him I thought he was overreacting.

Now, I'm going to gamble. But my game is craps. I'll play it for hours in Atlantic City, Las Vegas, Puerto Rico, and the Bahamas, no matter who likes or dislikes it. I've lost thousands of dollars at tables all over the world, and I enjoy it. It's my money, and I'm not breaking any laws.

But I don't bet on sports events. Betting on sports is crazy because you never know what little games are going on among the players at the end of the game, who's trying to outdo whom in some way that won't affect the outcome of the game but might affect whether or not a team covered the point spread. I wouldn't want my money resting on some twelfth man trying to score his career high.

I told all of this to Commissioner Stern. But he didn't care. He talked about how what Mark and I were doing that night might have affected the outcome of the game. "What if one of your teammates was wide open under the basket? Would you take the shot rather than give it up to the guy for an easy lay-up—just to win a friendly bet?" he asked.

"Give me a break," I said. "You'd have to be a nitwit to think that way."

MOST ATHLETES ADDRESS such controversial issues as drugs and gambling by kissing ass, although sooner or later they have to feel guilty about lying to themselves, as well as the public. Meanwhile, I get into trouble for being honest. I get criticized for telling the truth.

I'm not the first, or only, professional athlete with an image problem, of course. Some of my predecessors in the NBA on the "bad guy" list were guys like Wilt Chamberlain. Bill Walton, Kareem Abdul-Jabbar, Rick Barry, and Maurice Lucas, the original enforcer. No one can question their status as great players, but they were also criticized for being too outspoken and some-times rebellious. Those labels affected the way a lot of people perceived them and probably even cost them some of the honors and endorsements that went to athletes who were less contro-versial and as a result, more popular.

How many former baseball and football players are not in the Hall of Fame because they didn't grant interviews, were rude to the media, or were otherwise controversial?

I've generally had a good relationship with the media, except for a couple of guys in Philadelphia who haven't written anything fair about me since I came to this city. I consider most of the guys who work for the *Philadelphia Daily News*—including Phil Jasner and Stan Hochman—to be in this category. They go over-board with just about everything I do. But I don't let it affect me anymore. Once, it did. I took everything that was written about me personally. I would throw tantrums at home and hold grudges against any writer I perceived to be my enemy.

But then I realized something: newspaper reporters didn't make me, and they can't break me. That's how I came to grips with the media. Now, the only time I worry about what they write is when I play badly, and even then I'll always be honest about my performances. Maybe they'll bury me in the future, in two or three years when I won't be the same player I am now. But until then, I'll enjoy my relationship with the media. And as long as I'm playing well and doing my thing, I'll have the advantage.

But I have to admit I was truly hurt at the end of the 1989–90 season when I heard the news that I had lost the MVP award by one of the closest margins ever. Three different players could have won the award without any argument from me: Magic Johnson, Michael Jordan, or myself. That didn't even include guys like David Robinson, Patrick Ewing, Clyde Drexler, Kevin Johnson, Karl Malone, Hakeem Olajuwon, Isiah Thomas, and a handful of other players who were MVPs for their teams almost every night, but who were overshadowed by the three front-runners. So I had no problem with Magic winning the award, the third of his career. What hurt me, though, was that it seemed as if I had lost the award not because of anything having to do with my performance but because of some petty vendettas on the part of a few writers around the country, particularly two guys who didn't even list me in any of the five places on their ballots. That was bullshit!

How could anyone who covered the NBA on a regular basis that season, or at least pretended they were covering the league, not think that I was one of the top five players in the league in the 1989–90 season? Forget the second-tier guys; there was Michael, Magic, and myself, and then everybody else. I ranked sixth in the league in scoring (25.2 points), third in rebounding (11.5), and second in field-goal percentage (.600), while also getting 307 assists and 148 steals. I was voted Player of the Year by *The Sporting News*, which is selected by the players, and *Basketball Weekly*. The league's MVP voting was the closest it's been since sportswriters began voting for the award in 1981.

Magic finished with 636 points, including 27 first-place votes, 38 second-place votes, and 15 third-place votes from the 92 reporters who voted. I received 38 first-place votes, 15 second-place votes, and 16 third-place votes. I totaled 614 points, just 22 behind Magic. If the two jerks who left me off their ballots completely would have voted for me—like most of the voters—I would have been the league's 1990 MVP. Even if those two guys hated me, how could they have not put me second or third?

Playing in the NBA is a business, and because of some of the things I've said and done during my career, I'm not the most popular "businessman" in the league. I don't always toe the company line, and this time it cost me the most prestigious award in the business.

I honestly don't think I'll ever win the award because it seems like the league always wants to give it to someone with a squeaky-clean image. Michael Jordan won his second MVP award for the 1990–91 season, and deservedly so. And you can bet that David Robinson, the admiral, will win it before I do.

It's not a major deal. I'll still consider my career a success regardless of whether I ever win the MVP award, and regardless of whether the Sixers ever win the title. I've come from Leeds, Alabama, developed myself into a helluva basketball player, and I'll always be able to care for my family financially. Those accomplishments are more important to me than any award or championship.

It hasn't helped my image that a lot of NBA fans sit close enough to the court to smell my deodorant. Spectators who attend baseball and football games are usually too far away for the players to hear most of what fans are yelling during games. In basketball, they're right in our faces. Most NBA teams sell seats that are directly on the floor for as much as hundreds of dollars per game to sit next to Dyan Cannon, Arsenio Hall, or Jack Nicholson at The Great Western Forum, home of the Lakers. The price also includes the privilege of having a bunch of huge, sweating guys fall into your lap, or worse, *crash* into your lap.

One of the weirdest fans in Philadelphia is a season-ticket holder named Irv Block, who in 1989 bought one of the front-row season tickets on the floor and then proceeded to sit *on the floor!* He sat cross-legged directly on the court. His outrageously expensive seat, which cost $125 a game, was empty directly behind him while he rolled around on the hardwood floor like he was at home watching the game on television. The Sixers might have saved him from an ugly scene—imagine if his head had been squished by an ill-placed size 21½EEEEEEE Will Perdue foot—during the 1990–91 season when they placed those seats behind a table that was covered with advertising banners. Now Irv sits in his chair like a grown-up. He and the other fans with tickets in the front row weren't very happy about the table; they even talked about suing the team for breach of contract. My kind of people, standing up for what they believe, no matter how stupid. Before last season I thought I was going to step on his face—by mistake, of course. It still wouldn't have been pretty.

As far as I'm concerned, fans have the right to come to the games and express themselves any way they choose. They can say almost anything. Almost. I even think booing is a sign of respect, especially at home, because it shows me that the fans know we're capable of performing at a higher level, that some of us aren't giving our best effort. In those instances, we deserve to get booed.

But I draw the line at any fan who abuses my family or my teammates. That's when I get mad. That's when I attack. That's when any fan sitting at courtside wishes he had a place in the cheap seats.

I wish I could say that I've never gotten into it with a fan. I wish I could say that I'll never ever get into it with a fan again. Sorry, I can't—despite what happened in New Jersey.

That's because too many fans—not most fans, but too many—are out of control. They'll say things about your wife, about your mother, about your children, anything they feel will hurt you. They'll call you every name in the book, something they feel is their right simply because they bought a ticket. Well, that's bullshit and I won't stand for it. And I don't give a damn what the do-gooders in the league office say about how we should ignore fans who provoke us.

On November 17, 1990, the Sixers were getting our butts kicked by the Knicks at Madison Square Garden in New York, and a fan sitting at courtside was trying to get his money's worth by getting under my skin. Most of us were battling the flu. We were also playing without our two best point guards—Johnny Dawkins and Rickey Green, both of whom were injured. Needless to say, I wasn't in the mood to take any shit. It was enough that we were taking it from the Knicks, a team with a lot of talent but absolutely no idea what to do with it. The last thing I needed was a jerk in the stands. I didn't pay much attention to him for most of the game, but in the second half I reached my limit and I told him so. Basically, I told him to go fuck himself, or something to that effect. Whatever I said, he got the message. A few weeks later, so did I—from the league. Again they told me to cool it with the fans. I said I would. Right.

There have been a couple of other fans whom I've gotten to know all too well. On the night of December 20, 1987, I was cursing up a storm while sitting on the bench at Boston Garden. Again, we were getting our asses kicked and eventually lost the game by 37 points. Otherwise, I don't even remember why I was in such a rage. All I can recall is that I got so mad I smashed a chair in disgust. That's when a lady sitting nearby, a season-ticket holder named Linda Arons, criticized me about my language and my behavior.

"That's very, very nice," she said mockingly.

I hadn't said one word to her, or to anyone else in the stands. I was mad at myself and my teammates, nobody else. All of a sudden, here's this woman talking to me like I'm a child, like she wanted to slap my wrist for being a bad boy. Well, her timing was real, real bad. She shouldn't have said a word to me or any of my teammates. You could say I went off on her. Okay, I went nuts. I lost it.

"Shut up, you bitch," I said, adding a few other choice messages. That woman probably heard more abusive language in those ten seconds than she ever expected to hear in her life. She was shocked, stunned. But afterward, she was also quiet. I didn't hear another word from her for the rest of the night. She later complained to the league office. (Does Rod Thorn cringe every morning after Sixers games, or what?) She said she thought I should have been fined for fan abuse, or some other such criminal offense. She called me a disgrace. But for once, the NBA was on my side. Thorn hands down all of the league's fines, so he knows me *real* well. This time, he put the fan in her place.

"If fans come to the zoo and feed the animals, they should expect to get bitten," he said.

Hilarious.

I wasn't so lucky after an incident in Indianapolis later that same season. On the night of April 19, 1988, I crossed paths with a total jerk. One thing I'll always do is defend my teammates. We've got to stick together, especially when we're getting our asses kicked. Just like the Knicks and the Celtics, that's just what the Pacers were doing to us. The final score was 126–92, but we were losing by as many as 40 points late in the game when this guy started laying into G-Man (that's what we called our center, Mike Gminski) and Albert King. After a while, I screamed to the guy not to say another word to one of my teammates. I told him to shut up and leave us alone. So, being the jerk that he was, he started laying into me. I snapped.

I slapped him in the face—an act that eventually cost me $10,000 in an out-of-court settlement.

I actually felt bad, but he had earned it. NBA games are played in such an intense environment that players can't be expected to control their emotions all the time. That's why I get pissed when the league office tells us to bust our asses every night but never lose our tempers. That's ridiculous. Every human being in the world will lose his or her temper at some point in life, particularly if they're an intense conpetitor.

I want fans to enjoy the game. I'm an entertainer, and I know most fans don't want to pay their money to see someone who just comes out and plays. They want to feel like they know you, like they know your emotions and feelings. That's why I'm so animated during games, why I sometimes get carried away, smiling, hugging, chest-pounding, and head-butting with my teammates. Some people have accused me of being a court jester. That's bullshit. But I play basketball for a living, and I make a lot of money. Why the hell shouldn't I be happy all the time?

On the other hand, no one will ever accuse me of being a nice guy on the court. Once the game begins, my attitude is that it's either me or the other guy and only one of us will win. I'll try to physically and mentally intimidate anybody I play against. But no athlete is the same person in the shopping mall as he is in the heat of battle. It's not real life.

No one in the NBA goes into a game looking to fight in order to win. Even the guys who have reputations as the most fight-happy players in the league—Danny Ainge, James Edwards, Tree Rollins, Xavier McDaniel, and my good buddy Laimbeer—only get into one or two fights, maximum, during the 82-game season and the two months of the playoffs. It's a wonder that there aren't more fights, considering how much physical contact and mental pressure we experience every night. Believe me, if we wanted to fight, we'd always have a reason.

That there aren't more fights has nothing to do with the fines that are given after every incident. In fact, nobody gives a damn about the fines. With guys making so much money these days—an average salary of over $1 million in 1990–91—fines don't have much of an impact. To most guys they're parking tickets. The fines are just window dressing created by the do-gooders at the NBA who want a league filled with robots who are only allowed to smile, or maybe pump their fists and point into the stands after a big play.

If the league wants us to perform with intensity every night of the season—which, by the way, is humanly impossible—then they have to expect us to lose our tempers every now and then. Losing your temper is just a normal part of life. It's human. And it's gonna happen, but only rarely. It's a good thing, though, that I don't have to see Laimbeer more than six nights during the season. It might shoot my whole theory to hell.

I've been punished for fighting about a dozen times during my seven years, and I've paid the league more than a hundred thousand dollars in fines for various offenses. The league says it uses some of the money to purchase food for needy children. If that's true, then my contributions alone should assure that there aren't many more hungry kids left in the world.

Memo to the league: The only way to cut down on the number of fights is to add suspensions to the fines. When two guys are starting to square off, they're not thinking about the money. They're thinking about whether they're going to get thrown out of the game. More than anything else, everybody wants to play.

Make guys sit out a game or two and maybe they'll think about it before throwing a punch. Maybe.

I had no problem paying the guy in Indianapolis. It was a small price to pay in order for me to let everyone know that no one should ever come to a 76ers game and abuse my teammates without expecting to suffer some serious, sometimes painful, consequences.

PEOPLE CLOSE TO me ask me why I haven't compromised in some of the situations that have gotten me in trouble over the years. They seem to think that in the long run it would pay off for me, that it'll improve my image and popularity. Well, I don't worry about what people think of me anymore.

If someone asks for my opinion on any subject, I won't lie to make them feel better.

If someone doesn't like me for being honest, I really don't care. I'll always have to live with that, and I can.

Maybe we've all become so scared of reality that we force ourselves to like and respect only those people who say the things we want to hear, rather than those who try to speak the truth.

Sad, isn't it?

2

"LET ME TELL YOU SOMETHING, YOU FAT . . ."

IT ALL BEGAN when I reached into the mailbox that morning in the spring of 1984 and grabbed the telegram that had found its way down to Leeds, Alabama. I already knew what message was waiting for me inside the envelope: I was being invited to try out for the United States Olympic basketball team.

This wasn't going to be just any Olympic basketball team, either. It was going to be one of the best teams in the history of Olympic basketball—if not *the* best—better even than the 1960 team, which, with guys like Oscar Robertson and Jerry West, was so strong that John Havlicek, maybe the best reserve ever to play the game, was only an alternate. And better even than the 1976 team that rolled over the world with talents like Quinn Buckner, Walter Davis, Mitch Kupchak, Phil Ford, Scott May, and Adrian Dantley. Forget it. We were going to kick ass all over Los Angeles because of guys like Patrick Ewing of Georgetown, North Carolina's Michael Jordan, and Chris Mullin of St. John's, all three of whom were virtual locks to be on the squad. Hell, those three guys might've beaten the entire world by themselves.

Bobby Knight of Indiana was the team's head coach, and he was going to make certain that the good old U.S. of A. was going to romp—no matter which countries ignored the boycott by the Soviet Union and eventually showed up.

I should've been pretty excited about getting the chance to represent my country on such a team. It was undoubtedly going to be composed of some of the very best players from the very best programs in college basketball, guys I'd been watching on television and reading about during my three seasons at Auburn.

But I wasn't excited. Not one damn bit.

Rah-rah patriotism has never been my thing. I'm proud to be an American; it's the best country in the world. I'm going to represent the U.S. in Barcelona at the 1992 Games, the first Olympics in which NBA players will be allowed to compete. And I'll love it.

But given the choice in '84, I would much rather have spent the summer relaxing back home in Leeds, hanging out with my family—my mother, grandmother, and my brothers, Darryl Barkley and John Glenn—and my friends, people who didn't give a damn whether Charles Barkley ever grabbed another rebound in his entire life.

But I'm not stupid. I knew better than to tell anyone that I didn't want to spend my summer sweating for Old Glory because the Trials were really my big chance, my opportunity to prepare myself for a new challenge: professional basketball, for which I hoped I was going to get paid big money. I knew that if I was going to cash in on my basketball skills, I would have to go to the Trials and show people that I was ready for the NBA. I hadn't announced my intention to leave school, but in my mind I was gone. And the Trials were going to be my springboard.

Considering how far I'd come as a player from when I was riding the bench in high school just six years ago, I should've been honored to be invited to the Trials. Instead, I thought I was a shoo-in for the team, even though I was just a 6′4″ center from a school where nobody gave a shit about basketball until I arrived in 1981 and lit a fire under Coach Sonny Smith and the school's nonexistent program.

During my freshman season at Auburn, student basketball tickets sold for a dollar—probably the best entertainment deal in the entire country—and we still only averaged about 5,300 fans a game at the 13,000-seat Memorial Coliseum. That was about the same number of fans who showed up for basketball games the year before when Auburn won only seven of thirteen home games. We won eleven of thirteen games at home when I was a freshman, including an overtime victory over our arch-rival, Kentucky, that stunned basketball fans from Lexington to Auburn and everywhere in between. Yet attendance was still pitiful. Playing at Auburn was like playing in a morgue, or at the Meadowlands. But roll out a football on Saturday afternoon in the fall at Auburn and 85,000 people would just about damn near kill each other to watch a bunch of guys with big necks beat the living shit out of each other. Three years after I arrived on campus, though, by the spring of 1984, all of that had changed.

MY SPECIALTY WAS rebounding. It had always been my passion in basketball, my only passion. That was partly out of necessity; in high school, I was one of the two or three worst players on the team at Leeds High School. When I played, I was always the third option on the floor, so I never got to shoot. The only way I could shoot was to rebound. I soon began to enjoy re-bounding even more than scoring. Any nitwit can score, but rebounding is hard work. It's something a player can be proud of. Under the boards is where I learned the value of hard work, which would have helped me no matter what I might have done with my life.

As a junior at Auburn, I led the SEC in rebounding for the third straight year, something only one other person—Clyde Lee of Vanderbilt from 1963–64 to 1965–66—has ever done. I also carried the Tigers to their best record, 20–11, in nine years, and we qualified for the NCAA tournament for the first time in the school's history. Along the way, I had also gained some notoriety outside of Alabama, even though most people rarely talked about my game. They talked about something that didn't have anything to do with the way I played—or rather, the way I *outplayed* centers like Kentucky's 6'11" Mel Turpin and 7'1" Sam Bowie. Instead, everybody talked about my weight—all 280 pounds of it.

I began to become known by such insulting names as the Runaway Bread Truck, Amana, or Doughboy—all of which failed to acknowledge the fact that I was one of the best damn college basketball players on the planet. Reporters from around the country were more excited about how many chickens or pizzas I could eat in one sitting than how many rebounds I could snatch down during one game.

It made me sick, but I took most of it with a smile; I even posed for pictures while stuffing my face with food. I only did it because I knew the program at Auburn needed the publicity, and at the time I thought any publicity was better than none. Even degrading publicity.

I went to the Trials intending to change everyone's mind about Charles Barkley. I was going to, as Muhammad Ali used to say, "shock the world." That's what excited me most about the Olympic Trials—that, and the prospect of making money. I went to Bloomington with only one goal in mind: to play well enough to convince all the NBA scouts that I should be one of the first few players picked in the 1984 college draft. *U!S!A!*? Please. Give somebody else the gold medal; I just wanted the gold.

During the weeks before I left Leeds for the Indiana University campus, I began to have second thoughts. I worried if I would be able to make a favorable impression, given my image as an overweight curiosity. I didn't know if anyone would take me seriously, or if they would continue to focus on my weight rather than my game. There was only one thing I could do to ensure that my size wouldn't become an issue: lose weight.

I placed a call to Coach Knight about ten days before the Trials were to begin to ask him how much he wanted me to weigh at the Trials. If he had wanted me to lose ten pounds, I would have lost ten pounds. If he had wanted me to lose twenty pounds, I would have lost twenty pounds. Thirty pounds? I would have thought about it.

I left a message with Coach Knight's secretary, but he never returned my call. Fine. "Fuck him," I thought. I weighed in at the Trials at about 280 pounds, 284 to be exact. And I felt damn good about it, too. My weight didn't bother me nearly as much as it seemed to bother everyone else at the Trials, particularly Coach Knight. But I didn't give a damn what he, or anybody else, thought about it.

During the first week of Trials I finally asked Coach Knight why he didn't return my telephone call. "I would've wanted you to report at 215 pounds, but I didn't think you could make it so I didn't call you back," he said. Maybe he was right.

At the Trials, I was usually Knight's straight man, the butt of his sometimes-biting jokes to reporters, who lapped it all up like thirsty dogs. One day he said, "Asking Charles Barkley to get down to 215 would be like asking Raquel Welch to undergo plastic surgery." He wasn't talking about face-lifts or tummy-tucks, either. When someone told me later what he had said, they expected me to blow up and trash Knight. But actually, I thought it was a great line. I laughed.

Someone later asked Knight if he had ever coached a player as heavy as I was.

Knight smiled. "Not for long."

No matter. By then, I was used to hearing jokes about my weight, even though they still pissed me off. By then, hearing all those wiseass remarks about my size had become a source of motivation for me, especially when I was playing in opposing arenas all over the SEC, or when they came from asinine strangers in the street. The only nickname I could really stomach—sorry about the paunch-pun—was the Round Mound of Rebound. It had a royal ring, and it referred to the only thing about basketball that I truly cared about, other than winning: rebounding.

The Round Mound of Rebound is a proud name, and I've always had the greatest pride in my ability to rebound. Anybody can learn to shoot if they learn the right techniques: eye, arm, legs, and follow through. And anybody can learn to play defense if they're willing to sweat. But rebounding is a gift from God.

Nothing in the game gives me as much of a rush as the feeling I get when I grab an offensive rebound over two or three guys in the final three minutes of a game; it not only allows my team to get two chances to score to every one for our opponent, but it also pisses off the other coach and completely demoralizes the other team. I'm talking major orgasm. It's also something nobody really wants to do. Not at any price, especially when the price is an elbow in the face.

In high school, after I had established myself as a rebounder, crowds started cheering my rebounds louder than they cheered when we scored. That's when I began to feel the rush, which made me want to grab every rebound I could—every rebound there was. Rebounding became my calling card.

Being able to grab more rebounds than almost anybody else on the floor is something special, which is why I call it a gift from God. Just look at the statistics: in the NBA, very few players average 10 rebounds a game for an entire season. In fact, since the 1984–85 season, my first year in the league, just six players have averaged double-figure rebounds for the entire period: Moses Malone, Bill Laimbeer, Buck Williams, Hakeem Olajuwon, Robert Parish, and myself. In that time, my first seven seasons in the league, I averaged 11.7 rebounds a game. Subtract my rookie season, when I played fewer minutes and averaged just 8.6 boards a night, and my career average is 12.2 rebounds every night over the course of a nearly 600 regular-season and playoff games. With numbers like that, I know that Somebody is looking out for me.

I always laugh when people ask me about rebounding techniques. They want to know my secrets when it comes to rebounding. Most young players have been told that they should concentrate first on boxing out underneath the boards; find a man and put a body on him, is what most coaches say. Then the players are told to read the spin and trajectory of the basketball so they can anticipate in which direction it will come off the rim, and how far. Well, all that is garbage.

"Yeah, I've got a technique," I always say. "It's called, Just Go Get the Damn Ball!"

Rebounding is a battle for turf. In a sense, all sports are the same. In football, whoever controls the line of scrimmage wins the game. In baseball, it's whoever controls home plate. In basketball, the winner usually controls the lane. Rebounding is a territorial matter where the most essential element of victory is desire.

The most important thing in the game of basketball is the basketball itself. Without it, you can't do anything, so you spend most of your time trying to get it back. (That's the only reason we bust our butts on defense anyway, isn't it?) With the ball, the outcome of the game is in your hands. Without it, you're at the mercy of the other team. So just get it—no matter what it takes. A lot of NBA players spend so much of their energy boxing out that they don't get the rebound.

As for my personal rebounding secrets, I've got just a few: first, I always try to position myself on the opposite side of the basket from the shooter because nine out of ten missed shots bound to the opposite side of the basket. Secondly, and probably most importantly, I try to be the first player off the floor, even if I haven't established great position underneath. In most cases, the first player with his hand on the ball will have the advantage. He'll either get the ball or get the call, either one of which is a plus. Finally, I pursue the basketball. Jumping is one thing; pursuit is something else entirely. The bottom line is that the player who wants the ball more than anybody else on the floor will come down with it.

Early during my career at Auburn, I learned to make any player pay for it if he tried to take away any of my rebounds, pay for it with pain. More than anything else, I took that attitude with me to the Trials.

STEVE ALFORD: *He was definitely one of the top five guys there in terms of talent. He had a great Trials. He was stronger than everybody else. He banged everybody around. The best seventy-two collegiate players in the country were supposedly there, and if any of us hadn't heard about Charles before the Trials, we certainly heard of him during and after the Trials.*

The thing that shocked everybody was that a man weighing 284 pounds could get up and down and off the floor quicker than anybody. When he got the ball, you thought that at 284 pounds he wasn't going anywhere, but he was explosively quick. It was the most amazing thing that happened at the Trials. Nobody could believe that anyone that size could jump like that, nobody but Charles.

ALVIN ROBERTSON: *During the Trials, every time we heard the rim snap—boom!—everyone turned around to look and see who had done it, and it was either Charles Barkley or Antoine Carr.*

Every time. The coaches would get mad at him because he would dribble the ball, break the press, whatever it took to score. He and Sam Perkins were the best players there.

Coach Knight was always very vocal about the players being punctual for all of our meetings. Well, Knight was late for one of our nightly meetings; he kept us waiting about fifteen minutes. When he finally walked through the door, Charles jumped up out of his seat and started shouting, "Hey, where the hell have you been?"

Well, Knight just went off. "Let me tell you something, Charles, you fat son of a bitch! There's only one chief in this army, and that's me! Your fat ass won't be around here much longer!"

That's when I knew Charles didn't have a chance of being an Olympian, even though he had been a terror at the Trials. But you know how that goes; they choose whomever they want to be on the team. After that night I knew Coach Knight didn't want Charles Barkley.

MICHAEL JORDAN: *He was funny, same as he is now. He never held his tongue. I'd never seen him play. Only heard about him. I was frankly amazed. He was very creative, an unbelievable player. No one thought someone with that type of body could do the things he did. I can relate very well to him because I can relax around him. With Charles, I don't have to be anybody but Michael. In that sense, he's like a brother to me.*

At the Trials, he was guarding me a lot. I wasn't guarding him, but he was guarding me. Why wasn't I guarding him? Because I couldn't control him. The guy was twice as big as I was. Every time I would try to drive on him, he would basically knock me out of bounds. I thought it was funny because he was going to physically challenge me and I liked that. I like to be challenged.

I thought he was going to make the team; he should have made the team. Bob Knight must have had his reasons for not picking Charles. Maybe because Charles is a little bit more vocal than most. But if you look at his talents, he certainly should have been on the team.

PATRICK EWING: *I was shocked that he didn't make the team. The only player who came close to him was Antoine Carr, but he didn't make it either.*

The other hot topic in Bloomington, besides my weight, was my relationship with Coach Knight. It was billed as the most explosive and controversial coach in the country verus the most explosive and controversial player in the country. People thought we would be at each other's throat before the end of the first week. But Knight kept his distance, not just from me but from all of the players. He fed his hard-ass image by looming over us from atop a tower in the gym while the assistant coaches ran the seventy-two players who had been invited to the Trials through drills and scrimmages.

We called Knight "crazy man," but not to his face, because from the very beginning of the Trials he had every one of us completely intimidated. Even me.

Knight hardly said a word from up there on his throne, and even though you knew he couldn't watch every player at all times, you felt like he was watching *your* every move at all times. Now that's intimidation.

When he gathered us together in the middle of the gym and spoke to us before and after each of the sessions, everybody grew quiet. When he yelled during workouts, everything stopped. The sound of squeaking sneakers and balls bouncing on the court suddenly went silent and no one dared move. You could almost hear seventy-two hearts pounding in fear. I thought it was funny, but I wasn't crazy enough to make anything of it or even laugh anywhere within earshot of Coach Knight. Or at least, I usually had more sense than to upstage Knight.

During our huddle one day, I started making fun of his shoes. They were some of the ugliest things I'd ever seen—some old wing-tips—and I told him so. "Hey, Coach, where'd you get those granddaddy shoes?"

Everybody cracked up—except you know who.

"Listen, you fat pig!" he screamed. "The privates shouldn't make fun of the generals!"

I was somewhat luckier than a lot of the players at the Trials because my roommate turned out to be my best informant. He was Indiana guard Steve Alford, who had just finished his freshman season—I mean *survived* his freshman season—under Knight. When I first heard that we were rooming together, I thought it was someone's idea of a very sick joke, or at least a psychological experiment. Putting a little white kid from the Midwest together with a big black kid from the South, what could be more entertaining? What could be crazier? You never know how a kid will be after playing for somebody like Knight, and to be truthful, I expected the worst: a stuffy, uptight jerk who would be critical of everything I did because he was Mr. Perfect. I was ready to chew him up and have him for breakfast, lunch, dinner, and midnight snack. Instead, I was pleasantly surprised.

Steve and I were a perfect match. He was a great guy, a lot of fun, friendly, down-to-earth, everything nice that you can say about a person. He also had a great family; they made me feel welcomed and comfortable in Bloomington, which was no easy task, and he helped me get a better understanding of Coach Knight, which some people thought would be damn near impossible.

ALFORD: *The first time I met Charles I remember thinking that he truly was the Round Mound of Rebound. He was a very big guy. I came to Indiana as a freshman weighing 155 pounds and had gained ten to fifteen pounds, and here my roommate was almost double my size. I don't remember him ordering any big snacks, but it was still scary.*

"He's just intense," is how Steve described Coach Knight.

"Yeah, right," I said. "Thanks a lot. Is there anybody on earth who didn't know that already?"

"Okay," Steve said. "He's the hardest coach in America to play for."

Wonderful.

"Coach Knight," he concluded, "demands you to be perfect."

That was quickly apparent to every player at the Trials, which explains why probably the best group of college players ever assembled for an Olympic Trials remained so insecure. Some of the best players in the country looked like bumbling idiots during the drills and scrimmages because we all knew that at any time we could get our asses kicked by any of the other players on the floor. That's how much talent was there.

Coach Knight could not have picked a bad team. Besides Patrick, Michael, and Chris, three consensus all-Americas, there was Wayman Tisdale of Oklahoma, Ed Pinckney of Villanova, Mark Alarie and Johnny Dawkins (who would one day become my teammate on the Philadelphia 76ers) of Duke, Jon Koncak of SMU, Antoine Carr of Wichita State, Chuck Person (one of my teammates at Auburn), and Danny Manning, who had just gotten out of high school—all of whom would eventually have successful NBA careers.

We were a pretty tight-knit bunch. We spent a lot of nights talking about something we all had in common: pressure. Away from the court, away from basketball, and especially away from Coach Knight, very few of us took life too seriously because we all had experienced the stress of having to play for our lives every day for our respective teams, and every day at the Trials. So when the coaches put away the whistles, all we wanted to do was have fun.

ALFORD: *Fun? Try danger. Charles and Chuck [Person] would come in the room and have some of the most unbelievable wrestling matches you could ever see. I just cowered in the corner because I didn't want any part of it.*

For those of us who didn't come from any of the traditional basketball conferences, such as the Big East, ACC, and Big Ten, the Trials were a time for introductions. I'd seen a lot of the players at the Trials on television during the season, but in Bloomington, I saw a lot of them in a whole new light.

Michael Jordan became my biggest opponent at the Trials. Not on the floor; he was smart enough to keep his skinny body out of my way. But we went head-to-head every night in a card game called Tonk. To this day, I think Michael still owes me money. None of us knew much about Michael's game before he got to the Trials. He hadn't been an explosive player at North Carolina, thanks to Dean Smith's superstar-prevent offense, and like the rest of us, he wasn't in a class by himself at Bloomington. He was solid, competitive, and smart. But none of us said, "He'll be a superstar."

Ewing? *An intimidator*. End of discussion.

Next to the guys in our star-studded group, I was not a very confident player; I was something of a mystery man, even to myself when it came to competing against them. Auburn had never been on national television, so no one in Bloomington knew what to expect from the fat kid from Auburn—not even the fat kid from Auburn.

People found out soon enough; from the start of the first scrimmage I was killing people, playing as well as anybody there—if not better. I thought to myself: "Damn, I can play with any of these guys."

Deep inside I was excited to meet a lot of these players, but I wasn't in awe of anyone. Instead, most of the guys were in awe of me because I was stronger and quicker than anybody else in the gym. When I got out on the break during the scrimmages, I could feel the field house humming in anticipation. Would I pass it? Or would I jam? Either way, I didn't care who got in my way because they would pay with pain. I did spare one player, though. When 6'6", 210-pound Mark Halsel of Northeastern stepped in my path, I didn't run him down like I normally would have, by planting one knee into his ribs. Instead, when I saw him step in front of me like he was going to take a charge, I placed my left hand on his face, then boosted myself toward the basket and jammed with my right hand. The place went wild.

"After that," Halsel told reporters, "I just tried to be Charles's friend."

It didn't take long for most players to figure out that trying to impress Coach Knight by taking a charge against me wasn't worth the price: possible loss of life. I've always tried to kill guys who get in my way on a breakaway play. They'll sometimes get the call the first time they try it, like receiving a Purple Heart. But there's hardly ever a second time. It's called physical intimidation and it's one of the most important aspects of my game. A knee in the chest, right into the ribs, will do wonders for my opponent's self-esteem. He starts thinking of himself as a pretty smart guy, smart enough never even to think about stepping in my way again.

Joe Dumars was an exception.

Nobody knew much about Joe because he had played for a small school that most guys hadn't even heard of, a place called McNeese State. Six-three guards from tiny schools had to do something extraordinary to catch the eye of the coaches, so Joe decided he would make his mark by trying to take a Charles Barkley charge. Guess who made the mark—and where. I couldn't believe it! I was flying down the court, just about to take off and rock the house with a thunder dunk when this runt stepped right in front of me. I was shocked! So was everybody else in the gym; the place got real quiet when Joe went crumbling to the floor like a condemned building after I hit him like a wrecking ball.

"I couldn't believe you took a charge," I said as I helped Joe off the floor. He was still shaken, and shaking. He could hardly catch his breath, or talk. But he looked at me and said, "I couldn't either."

JOE DUMARS: *That was the first time I'd ever been around anybody that big who could be that explosive. I was just amazed when I first saw Charles, how cat-quick and how agile he was. I'd heard about how big he was, but seeing was believing. That was Charles's national debut. Don't let him tell you that none of us stood out at the Trials; he did. He was much different from anybody else there. As for taking that charge, I was young and silly. That was the last time I took a charge on him. Ever. At the time I thought it was admirable; now that I look back on it, it was pure foolishness. Pure, pure foolishness.*

I was spared much of Knight's wrath during the Trials, but only because I was kickin' everybody's ass. I was rolling. I played as well as anyone there, better than most. I was running the floor like a guard. I was jammin' like a monster, and I was making Magic-like passes to Michael on the break. I was the hit of the Trials. Reporters, NBA scouts, and the fans in the stands at the scrimmages were speculating about the damage I was going to do to the foreign teams under international rules, which allow more contact than American rules. It's practically mugging.

Yeah, it would've been my kind of game, but every moment of the Trials I had just one thing on my mind: money. I wanted to take care of my family, to buy my mother and grandmother a house and cars and take care of my two brothers. I owed them that, and as the Trials ended at the end of April, my only thought was that I wanted to give it to them as soon as possible.

After watching a couple of scrimmages at the Trials, Mark Heisler of the *Los Angeles Times* wrote that my "worth in the draft must be going up $250,000 a day." But there was actually more than money to consider.

To be honest, I had become bored with school. If I had the chance to do anything differently in my life, I would have had a better attitude toward academics. I would've placed more of an emphasis on my education because I know now that among everyone I knew who thought they could play basketball, I was the lucky one. I was the one-in-a-million guy that young players hear about when someone reminds them that the odds of their becoming a professional athlete are against them. A lot of guys I went to school with took the same attitude about education that I did; they hardly gave it a thought. All we thought about were three things: basketball, basketball, and basketball. (Well, four: women.) We didn't get the kind of grades that we could have gotten, not to mention the kind of grades we *should* have gotten. The only difference between me and my friends was that a lot of them never recovered.

In '84, I considered the impact of leaving college without a degree. I was smart enough to know that almost everyone in America has to have a degree in order to have a chance to become a successful professional. But I also realized the reason I went to college was to get an education so that I could get a job. Once I came to grips with that reality, I simply told myself, "I'm ready." One of my coaches at Auburn, Roger Banks, agreed with my assessment, even though my leaving the school would affect his own livelihood. He told me, "You go to college so you can make money, and you'll never make more than you could make next year. I advise you to leave."

I announced that I was leaving Auburn on April 28, 1984, less than two weeks before the best twenty players from the Trials returned to Bloomington for a four-day minicamp. I was there, of course, having survived cuts to fifty-four players, thirty-six, twenty-four, then finally the lucky twenty. But I was there in body only.

Reporters weren't allowed at the minicamp. If they had been, they would have known that I wasn't even close to the same player that I had been at the Trials. I was just hanging out and having fun, secure that I had accomplished what I wanted to do: shock the world and move up in draft. That had been my major objective. Mission accomplished.

By the time the day arrived when Knight was going to make his cut down to sixteen players, I already knew my fate. I was actually happy to get out of there because for several days Knight had been criticizing my skills, almost like he was trying to devalue me for the draft. Obviously, I didn't appreciate it. He said all I wanted to do was post up, and that I didn't have good ball-handling and shooting skills. He said he didn't want a 6'4" guy on his team who would do nothing but post up all the time. He wanted me to score from the outside, but said that I couldn't.

"You've got to be versatile," he told me.

"That's not my game," I said. "I'm an inside player."

When he called me into his office to tell me that I had been cut—along with three other players: John Stockton of Gonzaga, Maurice Martin, who played at St. Joseph's University in Philadelphia, and Terry Porter of tiny Wisconsin–Stevens Point, all future NBA players—I was stunned by what happened: I saw genuine hurt in Knight's face. Suddenly, the hard-ass became a softie. I thought he'd be glad to get rid of me, but he was truly upset. I think it hurt him to cut all of us, and it was an emotional moment for him. It really affected him. I believe Bobby Knight is more compassionate than he would like anyone to believe.

That's when I finally gained respect for Knight because I realized that we were very much alike. We both do crazy things and say things that we sometimes later regret. But neither one of us will ever bullshit anyone either, and that's the only kind of person I can respect.

Coach Knight wished me luck, but I knew that luck had nothing to do with the NBA draft. I came to the Olympic Trials to make my own luck, and I was convinced that I wasn't going to be drafted any later than fifth, maybe sixth. One way or another, I was gone from the college scene, and I haven't regretted it for one single moment.

3

I ALWAYS THOUGHT I'D LIVE AND DIE IN LEEDS

I ALWAYS THOUGHT I'd live and die in Leeds. It's a friendly, small Southern town where the people are down-to-earth. There's nothing resembling what most people would consider to be a downtown, only a lot of little stores like the local five-and-dime and a hardware store. There are no major department stores, nothing like that. There's a Wal-Mart and a Winn Dixie grocer. That's about it. And a couple of local bars. A nightclub? Forget it.

In Leeds, everyone knows everyone else, and the people, blacks and whites, generally look out for one another despite their differences. That's where I got my friendly outlook on life. People in Leeds were good down-home people. They relate to you, for the most part, as they would want people to relate to them in return. Of course, like anyplace else, it's got its problems. It's Alabama, not Mars, so it can't escape the kinds of problems that affect a lot of larger places, problems like drugs, homelessness, and poverty. But all in all, it's a great place to raise a family.

Like in a lot of places, life in Leeds is hard these days. Kids who were once known only as being mischievous are now getting into more serious trouble, trouble involving drugs.

When I was growing up, I never heard the word *cocaine*. Pot was the "in" thing, the drug of choice among the kids who wanted to get high. There were a lot of kids who smoked pot, but no one had ever even heard of cocaine. Not anymore. Even Leeds, a small town, is really deteriorating because more kids are getting involved with cocaine.

Still, much of what I am now came from Leeds. To this day, it's where I find my peace.

CHARCEY MAE GLENN: *Frank Barkley and I were still pretty much children when our first child, Charles, was born at Leeds Hospital on a cold February morning. We had graduated from Moton High School in Leeds in May 1962 and were married the following month. A few months later, I was pregnant with Frank's baby, and Charles Wade Barkley was on the way. I was so happy that I was going to be a mother, but in a lot of ways I was only a baby having a baby. But Frank and I didn't think about that at all. We were just real excited and anxious to be beginning a life on our own, in Leeds.*

I'm a native of Leeds; I've never lived anywhere else. I was myself an only child, of Charles and Johnnie Mae Gaither, so I was spoiled rotten. But Johnnie Mae always preached to me about maintaining my sense of independence, and to be beholden to no one. "Not even your husband," she told me.

Good thing for that, because Frank didn't stay around very long. Like me, he was young and untrained, not for skilled work nor for marriage, and he simply couldn't cope with the responsibilities of fatherhood. Just thirteen months after Charles was born, Frank was gone. We separated for two years before we divorced. Without any income, I couldn't afford to live alone, so Charles and I moved in with my mother and her second husband, Adolphus Edwards. Soon, Charles started calling Adolphus "Little Daddy." He knew that Adolphus was married to his grandmother, and he just couldn't understand why his own father was not around, even though I tried to explain it to him at an early age because I didn't want him to hear rumors and whispers from the other kids in the neighborhood.

In time, Adolphus became the most important man in Charles's life, a father figure for a boy who had been abandoned by his own flesh and blood.

It would be eight more years before Charles saw his father again. By then, Frank was remarried and living in Southern California. His wife had four children of her own, which Frank easily accepted as his new family. Meanwhile, his old family— his real family—was forgotten. Frank Barkley was one of the few mistakes I've ever made in my life. The only good thing that came out of it was Charles.

For much of my life, I had no image of my father. He left us when I was only a year old, and until I saw him again when I was nine, I had no real idea of who he was, what type of person he was, nothing. I only knew that he was living with another woman in Southern California, a woman he would eventually marry. That alone was enough to make me hate him. I hated the fact that he left my mother alone to fend for herself. In those few years before I saw him again, I came to think of him only as an evil man because only an evil man would leave his wife and son.

CHARCEY MAE: *I needed a job, badly. So I took a job as a domestic, a maid, supporting myself and Charles by cleaning the homes in the white neighborhoods in Leeds. My employers were nice families who treated me well. It wasn't the gettin'-on-your-hands-and-knees kind of cleaning, scrubbing floors. Nothing that straining, or demeaning. I brought home $15 for a day's work, good money at that time. And good work. I was my own boss and they never cut me a hard time. I cleaned white people's homes and worked in the high school cafeteria until 1989 when, finally, I quit, something Charles had been trying to get me to do since his first year in the NBA. He'd say, "Come on, Mom. Quit. I'll take care of you." But I remembered about what my own mom had told me about not being beholden to anybody. Besides, I had worked all my life and it was all I knew. And I enjoyed it. It wasn't easy to quit.*

I owe everything I have to Mother and Grandmother, Charcey Mae Glenn and Johnnie Mae Edwards. They were my mother and father, my support and my security. They were everything I needed.

By anyone's measure, our family was poor. We lived in the projects until I was thirteen years old and in junior high school, although they were not the sort of projects that most people envision when they think of government housing. They were clean and relatively safe, not like now when housing projects are being overrun with drugs, gangs, and violence. It was a warm place, a good place to be born and raised. In fact, the community feeling in the projects probably kept me from hanging with the wrong crowd. Everybody knew everybody else's kids, and they all looked after one another when someone had to work or be away from home.

But make no mistake: the projects were also someplace you wanted to leave.

My mom and Granny did a tremendous job of making it seem as if we weren't poor. We couldn't go out for dinner, and we didn't eat extravagantly. We didn't have a lot of furniture. But we had clothes on our backs—my brothers and I shared clothes— and food on the table. And we were never hungry. I knew we were poor, but in that there was no shame. You could never have told me that our family was in need of anything. Not one thing.

CHARCEY MAE: *There weren't many men in Charles's life. The most important was "Little Daddy," my stepfather. He had a real influence on Charles, primarily because he was there when Charles needed a male influence. They had some good times, even though Little Daddy and my mother separated a few years after Charles and I moved in, and they eventually divorced after fifteen years of marriage. After the divorce he was still good to me and all of my children, but Charles was his heart. Me, Momma, and Charles moved into a one-bedroom apartment in the projects. Little Daddy would come get Charles on weekends, and Charles would stay with him all night. Charles was just seven or eight years old at the time, so Little Daddy wouldn't let his girlfriends stay over when Charles was there. That really made them mad. Some of those women used to tell Little Daddy, "You think more of that little kid than you do about me."*

Little Daddy used to joke about Charles being such a big eater. In the morning, he'd ask Charles, "How many eggs you want for breakfast? One?"

Charles would say, "Uh-huh."

The next day, Little Daddy would ask Charles, "How many eggs you want for breakfast? Two?"

Charles would say, "Uh-huh."

Next day: "How many eggs you want, Charles? Three?"

"Uh-huh."

Finally, Little Daddy figured out that whatever he asked Charles about the eggs, Charles would say yes. After a while, he said. "I'd better not go any higher because Charles'll eat every egg in the house."

Charles wasn't like his brothers or most boys his age. He was always more serious. When something would happen that needed to be discussed, I could always sit down and talk to him like a man. That's what he always was, a little man. And when it came to our financial condition, he was always very understanding. He never wanted the kind of material things every other kid had. If I told him we didn't have money for something he asked for, he didn't get upset. He would just say, "Okay, Momma."

He and I always had a certain closeness. A lot of people call him a momma's boy. That's not so, but from the time he was a child he always liked to stick up under me. Most of the time he would lay across my bed and watch TV.

Every morning since he was old enough to know what he was saying, he'd tell me, "Momma, I love you." Just like it was part of his vocabulary. He was always very passionate: whenever he was with me or his granny, he'd always give us a hug no matter who was around. That's why the toughness he started to show in the NBA took me totally by surprise. The cursing, the fights, the runnin' off at the mouth, I was not used to that kind of behavior by my Charles.

Not that he didn't have his moments. One afternoon when he was about seven or eight years old, Charles thought he was Superman. So, cape and all, he jumped off the roof of the projects. The building was two stories high. Charles landed on his face and knocked himself out. I heard the commotion outside, and when I got there, I thought he was dead. He was bleeding from what seemed like everywhere. When I found out he was all right—he suffered a slight concussion—I could have killed him myself.

Hey, I was a wild child. When you're a poor kid in the projects, you'll do anything for excitement.

CHARCEY MAE: *After Charles joined the NBA, I sometimes looked at the television when Charles was playing—beating on people like a madman and cursing people every which way—and I said, "That's not my son, is it?" In college he wouldn't even say "damn" in front of me and his granny. But Lord, when that child got to the NBA, I just couldn't believe it!*

Now, Charles's granny will swear, so if you want to know the truth, I was actually surprised that I didn't hear him talk like that sooner. With her, what comes up from the gut just about comes out of her mouth. So I guess Charles got that from his granny, too. I tell you, they've got ways so much alike that it's just unreal. I used to say to Granny, "Momma, I know I had Charles, but sometimes I don't know whether he's your child or mine."

When Charles was growing up, a lot of people used to call him Big Head. And believe it or not, a lot of people called him a wimp! He was always shy. He didn't talk to girls too much. Even when he was old enough to date, he didn't. He took Amy Shorter to the high school prom, but by that time he was so popular because of his basketball skills, it was unreal. The girls were on him like white on rice. But Charles was not into girls. He was into basketball.

Granny worked at a local meat-packing house, a huge plant in Leeds called Lumber Jacks. She packed frozen meats on an assembly line until the plant closed in 1962. By then, she was in her fifties and still active, so she went into nursing.

Granny and I are like twins. We're both determined, stubborn, and very aggressive at whatever we set out to do. We both believe in hard work and in getting out of life exactly what we put into it, nothing more, nothing less. We've always known what we wanted to achieve, and we've gone after it rather than depending on anyone to get it for us. That's what kept her going to that meat-packing plant every day, on time, no matter how bad she might have felt that day, or how tired she was.

Even now, when I see professional athletes who want to sit

out a game because of a headache or some other minor injury, it makes me sick. When people mention the fact that I've only missed thirty-nine games during my career because of injuries, I don't take the credit. That's Granny. During the 1990–91 season when I suffered a sore shoulder, a stress fracture in my ankle, and torn knee ligaments, but missed just fifteen games, that was Granny, too. After seeing her work so hard for so much of her life—and for so little money—I couldn't even consider sitting out more games as long as I could still walk.

Both Granny and I have also always believed in the philosophy of giving an eye for those who take an eye. In other words, neither one of us ever took any shit off anyone, not Granny on the assembly line and not me on the basketball court. Whenever I've gotten in trouble with the NBA, there's always been one person who understood: Granny.

"Charles, I wish you wouldn't do those things," she tells me. Then she smiles. "But dammit, I would've done the same thing."

Mom wasn't as mentally tough as Granny. If you slapped my mom, she'd just stand there and ask you why you slapped her. But if you slapped Granny, she'd just slap the shit out of you, *then* ask why you slapped her. To be quite honest, the way I play basketball is the way Granny would have played.

CHARCEY MAE: *I went through some trying times when Charles was young, yes, I did. I was used to working, but I was really, really struggling at the time—working two jobs, leaving one and going right to the other. Charles was the son who took over while I was gone; he became the head of the house. He was always a clean person, especially for a boy. I never had to tell him to pick up his room. He kept it spotless, even changed the linen twice a week. Sometimes, I would come home dead tired, and he would have the house superclean. He could clean up the kitchen as good as I could but he hated to wash dishes. He would wash the floors, the cabinets and sink, but then he would stack all the dirty dishes very neatly in the sink and put a clean towel over them. When it came to his two younger brothers, Darryl and John, he became their father figure. When I'd come home dead tired, he always told them, "Leave Mom alone, she's tired." But when I would* *get on them or punish them, he would always tell me to give them another chance.*

One of the jobs I took on was taking care of my brothers. I became the person they looked to for advice and protection. They were typical brothers. Darryl, who's three years younger than me and four years older than John, was the bossier of the two, and they fought almost all the time. I was never into sibling-rivalry stuff because for as long as I can remember, I had other things on my mind: I just wanted to do whatever I could to help my mom and Granny. So while I tried to keep my brothers from killing themselves, I also made it my job to keep our home clean—whether it was in one of the two housing projects we lived in, or one of the houses we moved into after I was thirteen.

CHARCEY MAE: *Charles was nine years old the first time he ever saw his father. Frank came back to Leeds one summer and asked me if Charles could come back to California with him for a visit. I agreed because I always thought it was important for Charles to get to know his father, no matter what the man might have done to his son. Charles said he wanted to go, that he wanted to get to know his father. And I figured that maybe Frank could help financially. It wasn't long before Charles and I both realized that it was a wasted visit. Charles took his first plane ride for the visit, but he didn't enjoy himself one bit. He stayed in California for two months. Over the next few years, his dad sent me ten to twelve dollars on a couple of occasions.*

Once he came back to Leeds with the woman he married, the one with four kids from a previous marriage. I once asked her, "Why can't ya'll do anything for Charles? Why can't you try to make Frank do something for his son? I'm sure you get your hands on some cash, so why don't you take it upon yourself to make sure Charles gets a little something?" It didn't work.

When Charles was in the tenth grade, Frank called him and said he'd send Charles something for Christmas. He said he'd send it with Charles's aunt, who lived in California but was coming home for the holidays. Well, she had been home two or three days already, it was Christmas Eve, and Charles still hadn't

heard from her. Finally he said, "Momma, I can't wait any
longer. Can I go get the stuff my daddy sent me?"

I said, "Sure."

The house where his aunt was staying was right down the
street. Charles went down there and found out that his father
hadn't sent him anything. In fact, his aunt didn't even know
Frank was supposed to send anything. She was so hurt and upset
when Charles told her what Frank had said that she gave him
ten dollars.

When Charles got home, he was more hurt and upset than I
had ever seen him in his life. Lord forgive me, but I think if
I could have gotten my hands on Frank that night, I think I
could've killed him. Charles said he would never ask his father
for anything else as long as he lived. He never did.

Thoughts of my father bugged me throughout my life. When
I was young, I would see other kids with their fathers and felt
empty, like I was being cheated. I missed his companionship. I
missed having an older friend. For a while when I was still young,
I talked to him quite a bit, even though it wasn't easy. He would
call from California, and I was excited to talk to him. As long as
I was talking to him I was content. On the phone he was my
father. He was what he was supposed to be. But as soon as we
hung up, it was like everything went quiet, like I was suddenly
alone. After a while, he didn't call very often. I didn't have
anything to say to him anyway.

It burns me up when I read these days about all of the teenage
boys who are becoming fathers with teenage girls, then leaving
the mothers alone to raise the babies by themselves. A lot of the
kids are being born in black communities across the country, but
don't be fooled: white teenagers are having kids, too. It's not
one group's problem; it's everybody's problem.

A generation of kids is going to grow up hating their fathers,
and unfortunately it's the kids who'll end up getting screwed.
They'll feel abandoned, alone, and hated—all while the men
who should be responsible for them are off having a good time,
probably making more babies.

Some of these guys, these low-life fathers, should be put in jail until they agree to live up to their responsibilities. And these guys who have three or four babies by different women should have their balls cut off. They should just be castrated. Anyone can be a daddy, but it takes a man to be a father.

A father—a real father—has to make sacrifices to spend time with his kids. Every day from the day they're born, kids learn something from the people who take care of them and the other people around them. A father has to be there to do his part, to be a real man; otherwise there's a gap that the kid has to struggle to replace.

When the father's gone, it puts too much stress on one parent. The mother has to be the mother and the father. She has to be a strict disciplinarian as well as a loving parent.

When the father is gone, a lot of kids blame themselves.

At times, I know I did.

That said, listen to this: being an abandoned child is no excuse for becoming a failure in life. A lot of kids being raised by one parent blame their long-lost parent for everything from bad grades to bad behavior. *I can't do my schoolwork because my father left me.* Or, *I take drugs because my father left me and I've got no hope.* Well, that's garbage.

It's a cop-out.

Just as poverty is a cop-out.

Racism, too. Cop-out.

Anyone can raise themselves out of their condition if they concentrate on getting an education, working hard, and understanding what it takes to be successful.

I lived in two projects, had no father, and my mother had to clean other people's homes so her three kids could have nice clothes to wear and enough food to eat. I was mad. Boy, was I mad at my father for leaving us. But I never felt sorry for myself or my family. In some sense, it might have made me stronger because I focused my anger toward helping my family.

We got through our pain and poverty and survived the absence of my father because we always knew that we had each other. My mother and grandmother made sure that we learned the lessons about life that we should have been learning from my father. They didn't sugarcoat anything. They told us the truth—

about my father, about the importance of hard work, and about why we didn't have enough money to buy some of the things that other kids had.

With their help and support, I vowed that I wasn't going to let anything stop me from being successful. I'm not saying I thought I was going to be in the NBA, and I'm not saying that everyone should go to college. But there is no excuse for any-one—no matter their circumstances—not becoming a hard work-ing, useful, and productive person in society. No excuse.

And that includes racism. My attitude has always been this: the white man cannot stop me if I *want* to be successful. He might slow me down, but he can't stop me. I can only stop myself, and that was never, *never* an option.

If you've got the truth, then you can deal with reality. Without it, as long as kids ignore reality by blaming their lack of success on someone who's not even at home, or anything else that lies outside their control, then they'll never overcome the obstacles in front of them.

CHARCEY MAE: *Charles was always so bitter when it came to his daddy. Even during his rookie season in the NBA, he didn't want to involve his daddy in any way. He never even mentioned his father in any story that was done about him. After a while, Frank called and asked me why Charles was treating him that way, why he was pretending like his daddy didn't exist. Can you believe that? Frank acting like he didn't know! I wanted to tell him. I truly wanted to tell him. But instead, I said, "Frank, you'll have to ask Charles yourself. But I think you know the answer already. We were both young, and maybe we made some mis-takes. But there was no excuse for you not taking care of your son. I didn't see my own father till I was fourteen years old, so I can relate to how Charles felt all those years. Every kid wants a father. I used to just wish to see my daddy.*

"You could have picked up the phone, Frank, and said you were thinking about him."

Frank then tried to get in touch with Charles. He wrote let-ters and called numerous times. He said he was sorry about what he had done and tried to explain to Charles just why he had been such a bad father. But Charles wouldn't answer the letters. He wouldn't take the calls. He wouldn't even read the letters.

Charles and I sat down right before the Sixers played in Los Angeles for the first time. He knew Frank was there, and that he wouldn't be able to avoid him forever.

"Mommy," he asked, "do you think I ought to see Frank while I'm in California?"

"Baby, it's entirely up to you. I can't tell you not to see your father. He'll be your father for the rest of your life."

"Should I leave him tickets?"

"If you want to."

Charles left Frank tickets, and Frank went to the game. But the night was very strained. To say Charles hated his father is not an exaggeration. He called his father "scum."

I told him, "Charles, I know how you feel, but you can't pay him back for what he did to you. Only God can. Try to get past your bitterness and have some sort of relationship with Frank. Maybe you can be friends or buddies, even if you can't be father and son."

Charles had an uncle at the time who was dying. He had terminal cancer. Somewhere in there, his uncle said something to Charles. I don't know what his uncle said, but Charles changed. It was slow, but he changed. Charles told me that he would never call Frank, but he said that if Frank called and asked for his telephone number, I could give it to him.

Uncle Simon had cancer. It runs in my father's family. When I last saw him, he told me that he wanted me to be at peace, and he knew that wouldn't happen until I started to form some kind of relationship with my father. My father had also confided in him that he was troubled by what he had done, that he was truly sorry but didn't know how he could make up for the past. Uncle Simon told me that it was time for me to start trying to forget the past because you never know what turns life takes. Two weeks later, he died.

I always listened to Uncle Simon, but I didn't really need him to tell me to seek out my father. It was something I wanted to do for myself. I wanted to have a relationship with my father. But neither one of us knew where to start.

All I can say about my father now is that I'm cautious, extremely cautious. You just can't not see someone for more than ten years and pretend that nothing's changed. It's impossible.

Now that I have my own child, my daughter, Christiana, I realize even more the importance of a father's care and love. I want Christiana to know her grandfather, but I can't get rid of the images and emotions in the back of my mind. I can't forget that he left, and I can't forget that he didn't communicate with his children, his sons.

I'd like nothing more than for Frank and Charles Barkley to someday be a true father and son. I'd like to rebuild that trust. But only time can do that. He still lives in Los Angeles and we talk on a regular basis. There's no more pain. Bygones are bygones. I'm not holding a grudge. A father is something I want, but I don't want to jump into it wholeheartedly.

After all these years, I just can't. Not yet.

CHARCEY MAE: *They seem to have gotten closer over the last few years. I can hear a different tone in Charles's voice when he talks about Frank. Some of the meanness is gone out of his voice.*

For a long time, Charles would never go to our family reunions because he didn't want to risk seeing his father. In 1990, we had our family reunion in Leeds and Charles came.

It's good to see them together again. It makes me very happy.

.   .   .

There were still racial tensions in the South by the time I was old enough to know the difference between black and white. In Leeds, you couldn't really forget about race because the town, like most cities, was extremely segregated. And when it came to mixing the blacks and whites, well, everyone was very leery of each other. When they integrated the all-white Leeds Elementary School when I was young, very few black families had the guts to send their kids there rather than to the all-black school that all of us had been attending—even though everyone knew that the kids at Leeds Elementary were getting a better education.

It was an old story: the all-black school didn't have the money to purchase the kinds of equipment and books that they had at the all-white school. That's why my mother had no problem in shipping me off to Leeds Elementary. She was doing what would be best for me in the long run, not the short run.

CHARCEY MAE: *We were determined to see to it that Charles got the best education he could get, and like most places around the country, the white schools had been getting a lot more than the black schools. Once we had a choice, we sent Charles to Leeds Elementary. It was one of the best things that ever happened to him and our family.*

I was joined at the school by only a couple of other black kids, and during the first few weeks of classes, there was obvious tension. The school was located in downtown Leeds, which meant that the black kids had to be driven to the school. The black school was only about the length of a football field from my house, in the opposite direction from downtown. It wasn't easy for us. We took heat from some of the white kids at school, then caught more shit from the black kids back home in the neighborhood who said we must have thought we were too good to attend the black school.

But the majority of white kids at school made us feel good about being there. All of us were under a lot of stress at the time, more than we probably realized, being kids and all. There were obviously some white kids who were like poison, trying to turn the rest against us. They challenged us in the halls, tried to pick fights, and most of all called us names, names they probably heard from their asshole parents. Kids just don't think like that by themselves. They need help, and there were plenty of redneck parents in Leeds who were more than willing to try and make their kids think like them.

Fortunately, it didn't always work.

AS LONG AS I can remember, my mother was a maid.

She and Granny worked all day and well into the night. For a long time, I resented the fact that my brothers and I had to spend so much time without them, especially when I was a teenager. But they were just trying to survive, to make our lives better. Understanding that, how could I and my brothers not be grateful—grateful for the rest of our lives?

As a kid, I didn't understand what a maid's duties were. I didn't know that they cleaned up after other people—white people. I didn't understand how hard my mom worked, how much time and effort was involved in her job. I only knew that when she got home, she was too tired to do for the rest of us what she had done all day long for white people. So, as I grew older, I became concerned with trying to help her any way I could.

Working around the house—cleaning all of the rooms and looking after my brothers—was the least I could do for the two people who spent most of their waking hours doing anything they could to feed, clothe, and house their children. Watching them work for years and years only drove me more to become successful at whatever job I chose to pursue.

That's why I always felt that I had to go to college. I thought that if I could just learn enough in order to get a good damn job at anything, then my mother and Granny could finally quit working. That was all I wanted to do with my life, to be able to take care of them when I was an adult, and achieving that goal is what motivated me to graduate from high school and attend college rather than drop out and get some dead-end job in Leeds.

Sometimes, I went with my mother to work and played inside some of the homes on the other side of town. The other side of town in Leeds wasn't very far away in actual distance, but it might as well have been a fantasy island in the middle of the Pacific, for it was about as far from the projects as a child could get. Most of the homes had several rooms and large backyards that didn't have to be shared with every other kid in the area like the public areas in the projects. But while the people who lived in the homes lived a very different life from my family's, I wasn't ever jealous of them.

I never despised these families for the way they lived because they never made my family feel as if we were anything less than they were. They were all nice people, and they treated my mother well. No hassles. No condescending remarks. Most importantly, no disrespect.

Over the years, the families my mother worked for have stayed close to our family. They've invited her to their children's weddings, and some of them attended the weddings in my family, including mine. I always respected them for the way they treated my family, almost like members of their own. And it truly taught me something: to treat anyone who ever worked for me as well as those families treated my mother.

That's how I ultimately learned that you shouldn't judge people by their color or race. Even when some of the white kids were trying to pick fights with me, there were a lot of whites who treated me like a friend. And we were sometimes treated worse by some of the black kids who resented the fact that we were going to the white school.

CHARCEY MAE: *Leeds Elementary was where Charles got his start in basketball. He was one of the first black kids to get a membership at the Leeds Civic Center, where most of his new friends—his white friends—played on the weekends. He played on a team with only two black kids and all the rest whites. The membership cost $30. It was a big sacrifice for me, but Charles was eight years old and he was a good kid.*

The main reason I started playing basketball was that it was a better lifestyle than the alternative: stealing.

By the time I reached junior high school, I was a petty thief. Basically, I was bored. In such a small town, kids had to create things to do, so my friends from the neighborhood and I would go to the stores downtown and steal pens and other pretty insignificant things from the shelves.

Later, we started stealing cakes. Every Sunday night the grocery stores would get their shipment of cakes for the week. At around ten or eleven o'clock in the evening, the delivery truck would drop tons of boxed cakes directly in front of the stores. Once we found out about the pattern, we got together every Sunday night and waited. When the truck dropped off the cakes, we'd go through the boxes and get whatever we wanted. I'd eat a couple of cakes myself, then take some home.

One night while we were at the store trashing the cakes, the police showed up. They just cruised by at first, pretending they didn't see us. But before we knew it, they were on us in a high-speed chase that lasted for several blocks until we ran into the woods near downtown. The trail we took was just large enough for a car to get through, but we didn't think the cops had the balls to drive in. They did.

We were running for our lives. I was almost killed because it was so dark we couldn't see anything in front of us—not even our feet—and we were running full speed. I was in high gear when I ran into a tree, face first. When I hit the ground, I thought I was dead.

The funny thing about that night was that we didn't steal any of the cakes in that particular shipment because they didn't have anything we liked. So instead of taking the cakes we started throwing them at each other. Cakes were flying everywhere. Then we started running the grocery carts at each other like bumper cars. I think what brought the cops was that one of the guys in our group accidentally ran the cart into one of the store windows. We thought he'd broken it, but he didn't; he must have set off the alarm instead.

The cops never caught us, but that's when I became scared straight. I was more scared that night than I had ever been in my life. When I thought about the prospect of being arrested, of the embarrassment my mother and Granny would feel, I knew right then that it had to stop.

Some of my friends were doing things that were a lot worse than the little stuff I did. They were committing more serious crimes, getting involved in the drug business, robberies. Being around them made me understand that it was only a matter of time before my petty thievery turned into something more serious.

From that point on I said, "I've got to find something else to do."

It was basketball.

Without basketball, I'd probably have ended up in jail. Probably not for anything major, but I would certainly have been caught eventually for some of the petty thefts I was committing. But when you're in jail, nothing's petty.

A lot of kids today tell me that I don't know the kind of peer pressure they're under. That's a bunch of crap. Kids today are lucky enough to hear more antidrug messages from everywhere than there were when I was a kid. The only antidrug message I got was at home, where my mother and grandmother made it clear that there weren't going to be any drugs in the house, period.

But on the other hand, kids today are up shit creek without a paddle. Already, we've lost one generation to drugs and crime. And we're about to lose another one.

Sometimes, I wonder if I'm partly to blame. I've never gotten involved in drugs, but I've seen money and materialism become too prominent a part of most kids' thinking. And I feel somewhat responsible. My lifestyle, along with that of other athletes and entertainers, is glamorized every day in the media, and that's what kids today are trying to achieve. When they sell drugs, steal, or kill, they're usually doing it for money, nothing else. They don't understand that there's a dignity to working and living an honest life, like my mother and Granny have.

We all have to try to convince kids that there are other ways to achieve their goals. That's why I speak out more than other athletes, and why I've tried to get some of the prominent black businesspeople in Philadelphia to join me when I speak to kids.

It's unfortunate that some of the other people in society who've achieved as much material success as I have aren't as well known. No one writes about them or puts them on television. In fact, unless you're a famous athlete or entertainer, about the only way to get on television is to do something wrong. The media doesn't provide a balanced picture of life and it's killing our kids.

Maybe I was luckier, after all, because the message I got was from the people who loved me, people I respected—not from someone on television who didn't really give a damn whether Charles Barkley lived or died. What my mother and Granny said to me meant more to me than a hundred Just Say No commercials. What they said to me was real.

Mom and Granny were very, very strict with their kids. I had to be home before dark or get my butt whipped. They were smart. They knew what was out there in the streets, so I never got to hang out too late, like after midnight.

"There ain't much you can do out there after dark anyway," Granny would say. "Besides, whatever you're doing out there, if you don't have it done by midnight, it just won't get done."

I was also criticized a lot for not doing drugs. I was pressured to use drugs, but I made a choice, just as kids today have a choice. That's why I often get upset when I hear people say that using drugs is a disease. Bullshit. Cancer is a disease because you've got no control over whether you contract it or not. Sickle-cell and leukemia are diseases because you have no control over whether or not you get them. Drugs are not a disease: drugs are a choice. Addiction might be a disease, but using drugs initially is a choice. No one can make anyone smoke crack or stick a needle in their arm. That's their choice.

I also received a lot of criticism around the neighborhood for not going out with girls. I didn't start dating until I got out of high school, and then it was never a big deal to me. By then, I was possessed with basketball.

CHARCEY MAE: *Unlike Leeds Elementary School, Leeds Junior High School was more completely integrated. It had to be because it was the only junior high in town. The basketball coach was black, which I thought would be good for Charles after being at a predominantly white elementary school. But when Charles went to practice, the coach told him that he didn't want him on the team because he had only been playing with the white boys. He wouldn't put Charles on the team during his first year at the school, and even when he finally made the team, the coach would never move Charles to the varsity.*

Charles was an average player when he got to high school, not nearly as good as the other kids. He enjoyed playing, even though he didn't make the varsity as a freshman. He was really too short for the team, but he had so much determination.

He would come home after school and talk to his grandma. "They just won't give me a chance," he said. "I know I can play."

"Baby, just keep on working," is what his granny said. "If it's meant to be, you'll get your chance."

It was during the summer before the eleventh grade when Charles did a lot of his growing—but not quite to six feet. But more importantly, he practiced basketball for the whole summer. There was a court right down the street from our house, but he never liked to go down there during the day when all of the other kids were there and people were standing around watching. He waited until night, after everybody had gone home, and he would play by himself for hours.

He also asked me to buy him a jump rope. When I did, I thought he was going to jump that rope to death. He would jump and jump, jump, jump, jump, jump, jump. Again he did it for hours at a time. While every other kid in the neighborhood was going to movies or out dancing, Charles was either jumping our fences, jumping rope, or doing something to improve himself physically.

If I was going to play basketball for Leeds Junior High, I was going to have to force myself onto the team. I knew I had to be stronger than the guys already on the team, and I knew that I got my strength from my legs. I knew I had to be able to jump high and go until they all dropped from exhaustion. No matter how tired I got, I knew if my legs kept working, I could keep working.

Jumping rope was good for my legs, but it wasn't enough, so one day I decided to try and jump over the chain-link fence around our house from a standing start, back and forth, like a jumpin' jack. To be able to do it looked impressive. But once I did it, I realized that it felt good, too. Just being able to clear a three-and-a-half-foot fence was like a high, a rush.

"Man, this'll work," I thought.

So, I did it again. And again.

I didn't care how dangerous it was, but my fence-jumping used to drive Granny crazy. She tried to warn me that if I made a mistake and missed, I could mess myself up for life, "as for having children, you know," she used to say. So she'd sit on the porch and watch me, like sitting there was going to make a difference if I fell. She sat there watching me for two or three hours, back and forth. I don't know how I did it, but I truly believe that those fence-jumping afternoons are what gave my legs their strength. And fortunately, I never hurt myself. I was very lucky.

A warning: This exercise could be hazardous to your health—or your future children's lives.

CHARCEY MAE: *That next season, his grandma and I sat in the stands one night and were stunned at how, all of a sudden,*

everybody was cheering Charles like he was some kind of hero.
It was pretty unbelievable how much he had learned about bas-
ketball, and how good he'd gotten. We looked at each other and
I said, "How come they're yelling for Charles?"

I was never really any good at basketball until late in my junior
season. That was the first time I really got to play. Until then,
I was strictly JV, a 5'7" kid who could do one thing well: jump.
I was shorter than everyone else and pudgier than everyone else.
I also played mostly guard all those years, which explains my
ability to handle the basketball. But I was also the last player
picked whenever sides were chosen for scrimmages, always. If
it wasn't my up, I didn't get picked. Part of that might also have
been because I was a gunner—a halfcourt gunner, no less. That
was my "rep" among the players. I'd come across halfcourt and
just throw it up. That's not the best way to help your popularity.

Going into my junior year, I was still only 5'10", but I had
improved my skills to the point that I was at least promoted to
the varsity, which for me was something to celebrate. In truth,
I was just another guy on a pretty good basketball team, a typical
sub. No high school athlete is ever completely confident in his
skills. Maybe there were some exceptions among the starters,
but the rest of us were scared shitless every time we got into a
game.

Late during the season, I finally got my break, thanks to a guy
whose name I'll never forget: Austin Sanders.

Austin was an awesome player. Not our best player; that honor
was reserved for my cousin Travis Abernathy. But he was a
legitimate Division I college prospect, until one night when he
and our coach, Billy Coupland, got into an argument during
halftime of a game. He and the coach yelled at each other until
Austin got up and acted like he was going to the bathroom. But
he came out with his clothes on and announced that he was
quitting the team—in the middle of the game! Just like that, he
was gone. Everyone sat there stunned, including the coach. After
a few moments, Coach Coupland turned to me and said,
"Charles, you're starting."

Suddenly, *I* needed to go to the bathroom.

I don't remember much about that particular game. But for

the rest of the season, I was respectable, and I finished the year averaging 13 points and 11 rebounds. By then, I was up to 6'1" and I was starting to get some attention from some of the small-college recruiters who were always coming to our games.

As for Austin, when he walked out of that gym, he might as well have walked out of life. Several years later, he ended up in prison. Killed somebody.

LEEDS HIGH MAY have been a small-town team, but we were damn good. It was a mixed team. Our center and point guard were white, the other starters were black. None of that mattered because everyone could flat-out play. My junior season we were rolling along with a 26–3 record before losing in the finals of the state championship. Then when I was a senior, we got a little too cocky and got beat in the semifinals.

Our coach was not a strict disciplinarian. He was just a good man who let his players perform up to their capabilities without a lot of restrictions and complications. He didn't go overboard with running fancy plays or defenses, and he didn't try to change guys' games to the way he wanted them to play. Coach Coupland just gave us the ball, drew up a few plays, and said, "Fellas, it's yours."

That's the way all high school coaches should coach, if they have talent. Just throw the ball out there and let basketball be fun. For me, my years at Leeds High School were the very last time I played basketball strictly for fun.

Late in the year I lost my basketball virginity: I made my first dunk. It came during a tournament late in the season. It was the only dunk I had all year, and it was pretty much of an accident. We had been having dunk contests during practices since I was in junior high school, but I could never get the ball over the rim. That's why when I got up there and jammed it through, I stunned myself. To me, that dunk was the moment when I reached manhood. Remember, I wasn't much of a Don Juan at the time.

That's also when I started looking at basketball as a way to get to college. I knew my family would never be able to afford it, but it wasn't until I made that dunk that I thought I would have an opportunity to win a college scholarship. All I wanted at the time was to get into a small Alabama college where I could get a degree, then get a good, decent job somewhere near my home.

I wasn't thinking about the NBA. I just wanted to get a job, live and die in Leeds.

I'VE GOT A confession to make, about something that nearly cost me even that small opportunity. As a student, I was a loser, and it's probably the most disappointing thing about my life. In high school, I did just enough to get by in the classroom. I never pushed myself academically. To stay eligible, students had to maintain a C average every six weeks. I did just about enough to get my C, then joked around for the rest of the six weeks. I kept track of my points and would always add them up so that I knew exactly what I needed to get that grade. I could have done so much better in school because the work wasn't hard. In fact, I was damn near a math whiz. Numbers always came easy to me. I even tutored some of my classmates in math. But I took my education for granted, and I'll always regret it because I was cheating myself.

If I hadn't made it in basketball . . . I don't know.

Because of my poor academics, I probably couldn't have gone to college outside of Alabama even if I'd been recruited by every major college in the country. What saved me was that a lot of the schools in the state allowed students to attend even if they hadn't taken one of the standardized tests, the ACT or SATs. I took the ACT anyway, just because it was what everybody else was doing on that Saturday afternoon. I scored a 13. That's well below the national average of 18, but I wasn't a complete idiot or anything, either. I was just lazy.

Thank God I never had to take the SAT. It was something altogether different from the ACT. I think I would have been guessing on almost every question. The ACT was traumatic enough. When I left the room that afternoon, I really thought I had missed almost every question. That's how hard it was.

"There's no way in hell I got any of those right," I said to some of my friends after we finished the test. When the results came back and one of the teachers told me my score, I thought I'd died and gone to heaven. I couldn't believe it. I felt even better when I found out that the class valedictorian only managed to score an 11 on the test. That shit was hard!

But it wasn't too hard. I should've been a better student, and I would have if my teachers hadn't always allowed me to get away with whatever I could when it came to my classes. My teachers and coaches, my mother and grandmother, none of them expected me to do anything academically but get by, so that's what I did. I should have expected more of myself, but it would have been nice if someone had told me that *they* expected more of me, too.

I'm just lucky that my attitude didn't cost me the chance of going to a major college. A lot of it has to do with timing. In 1986, five years after I left Leeds High, Proposition 48 went into effect. If it had been in existence when I was a high school senior, I don't think I would have qualified to play college basketball.

High school seniors now have to score at least 700 on the SAT or a 18 on the ACT and have a grade point average of at least 2.0, a C average. My GPA was above 2.0, but I don't know how I would've done on the test. I'll never know. Prop 48 would probably have kept me out of Auburn, but I still think it's a good rule.

When Prop 48 was announced, the NCAA waited three years before placing it into effect. That should have allowed athletes, those who were then in the ninth grade, enough time to understand that when it came to academics, it was going to be a different game when they were seniors. The NCAA was smart. If it had suddenly thrown Prop 48 at the kids and required 2.0 GPAs and 700 SAT scores across the board during the first year, it would have been a disaster. Only a few athletes would have passed the SAT requirement, and colleges would've been slapped in the face with hundreds of black athletes sitting on the sidelines, playing at smaller schools rather than at major colleges. Many of the athletes would have been left without college altogether. That would have been a tragedy. Everybody deserves at least a chance to get a college education, even if athletics is the main reason they're able to get into college at all.

Unfortunately, too many young athletes didn't pay attention. Maybe they thought Prop 48 would just go away quietly. Or that it didn't really exist. Or that maybe somehow, someway, some-body would simply "fix" everything—starting with their grades—so they would be able to play for any college in the country. Athletes are used to getting their way. They expect their grades to be fixed. They expect their coaches and parents to allow them to do anything they want to do. And they expect everyone to look the other way when they cheat or are too lazy to complete their assignment. That's why too many athletes thought that, in the end, everything would turn out their way—Prop 48 or no Prop 48. They were wrong.

People who complain that Prop 48 is unfair to young athletes should give it a rest. Sure the SAT's a bitch! Some of the questions are impossible for anybody who didn't grow up in a middle-class environment. But as a whole, Prop 48 sets fair standards and it's long overdue. I've said before that I wished someone had set higher academic standards for me when I was younger. Prop 48 tells kids that if they don't reach these standards, then they can't play major-college basketball until they get their act together.

The reason Prop 48 has become necessary is that too many high schools and colleges have forgotten that their first obligation is to prepare students for survival in the real world where they have to read a job application and be able to function as a pro-ductive person. It's not to fill football stadiums and basketball arenas. So it's about time that schools at all levels were forced to start stressing education and academics as much as sports.

Prop 48 also isn't racist, no matter what a lot of critics try to make us believe. If you listened to some people, you'd think the NCAA sat around and said, "Let's see how we can get all these black kids out of sports." Right. These men are not stupid. Why would they try to get rid of cheap labor when sports revenues have multiplied into billions since the major colleges began al-lowing black and white athletes to compete together in the 1960s? No, the NCAA needs black athletes more than black athletes need the NCAA. Losing them would be financial suicide.

Yes, Prop 48 affects more black athletes than white athletes. But for one reason only: because blacks are, in general, better athletes than whites, particularly in football and basketball. That means there are more blacks among the group of athletes trying to pass the academic requirements of Prop 48, and thus more blacks who might not pass. The reason Prop 48 affects more black athletes than white athletes is *not* because blacks are worse students than whites. Get it right next time.

Eventually, Prop 48 will force young athletes, those who want to attend college and maybe turn pro, to study with more dedication and maybe even get a legitimate education. Not just a piece of paper that doesn't mean a damn thing because they can't even read it. And I don't believe that kids from poor areas are automatically doomed to receive a poor education, no matter how poor their school districts. Maybe their schools don't have the latest books or the newest lab equipment, and maybe their parents, teachers, and coaches aren't pushing them enough because of their athletic skills—which is also wrong. But the bottom line is that education is an individual's choice, and whether or not you get an education is up to you, not anyone else. My choice was to be lazy, but I was lucky. Basketball saved me from my own stupidity.

And yet I've always had to work really hard to be successful at the game. I've also had to be aggressive and mentally strong. That's because from the time I started playing, I was always at a physical disadvantage against everybody I played against. And I was always being told that I was too fat or too short. That was always the knock on me, that I was too short to go to a major college, too short to play center in Division I. Not one person ever said that I could be one hell of a player. No one. So, if anyone—*anyone!*—ever tells you they always knew that I'd become an NBA All-Star, they're telling you a damn lie.

Hell, not even Auburn thought I would be much of a player.

4

I WASN'T EVEN WORTH A USED CHEVY

NOT ONE MEMBER of the Auburn coaching staff really wanted me to come play at the school. Not in the beginning, at least.

The very first time one of the assistants traveled the one hundred miles between Auburn and Leeds while I was a member of the team, he was coming to scout my cousin Travis Abernathy. Travis was my basketball hero, more than anyone in college or the NBA. By the time he reached ninth grade he already had letters of interest from every major college in the state, as well as such legendary places as Kentucky. Some of the neighborhood kids would come by his house just to gawk at the stacks of envelopes that arrived on an almost daily basis. That's all it took to impress some people in Leeds.

I also received a few recruiting letters, but not until after my junior season at Leeds, and most of them came from small schools like Snead State Junior College in Boaz, Alabama, and Birmingham-Southern, places generally considered to be basketball wastelands. A lot of former Leeds players had attended these schools, not because Leeds had never produced any real talent, but because most players at Leeds didn't believe they were good enough to play for the most prestigious programs in Division I. Maybe the best player ever to come through Leeds was Ronald

Radford, a 6'8" center who was on everyone's wish list. But he didn't have the confidence to attend a big school, so he went to Sanford University and was never heard from again—as a player.

Even my friends tried to convince me to attend a small college because they thought I wouldn't make it in Division I. For a time, I believed them and I was all set to go to Gadsden State in Gadsden, Alabama, when my mom told me otherwise. She said, "You can't go to a junior college and we won't even discuss it." If nothing else, she wanted me to get a four-year education, to become the first member of our family to graduate from college.

I have no doubt that some of the letters I received from small colleges were sent to me out of habit, not because the coaches at these schools knew anything about me. And only a few major colleges thought it was worth the price of a stamp on the outside chance that I might be good enough to play for them.

In the months before my senior season, I received a couple of very bland introductory letters from Alabama, Auburn, Alabama-Birmingham, and Tennessee. But those schools wrote to practically every kid in the state who had ever *touched* a basketball—if for no other reason than to cover their asses in case someone was a late bloomer. No major-college program wants to have an all-American who had grown up in their area say, "(Fill in the blank) never even wrote me a letter." So I gave these letters about as much credibility as they were worth: none. Besides, there were no follow-up telephone calls. No invitations to faraway campuses. If the school wasn't within rock-throwing distance of Leeds, it didn't want to have anything to do with me.

Then in the middle of a game one night during my junior season, I looked up in the stands and spotted someone I recognized: Herbert Green, an Auburn assistant coach. I knew he was there to see Travis, but I was going to make damn sure I got noticed, too.

When it came to the in-state rivalry among the University of Alabama, Auburn, and Alabama-Birmingham, I was always partial to Auburn because at that time no matter who they played in football or basketball, they were nearly always the underdogs. When I was in junior high school, Auburn was getting its ass kicked in football by Alabama every year. The Tide, coached by Paul (Bear) Bryant, beat the Tigers to death every season, then laughed about it until they stomped them again. Alabama fans were always a pain in the ass, gloating about their supremacy over Auburn. They were even worse when talking about basketball, a sport in which Auburn was truly sorry. Those guys were pitiful, and they got their butts kicked all over the Southeastern Conference. Teams like Kentucky, Florida, and Alabama didn't have any respect for them at all. Across the state, Alabama was so huge and popular that when it came to sports, most Auburn students were too embarrassed to admit they even attended the school.

So what. I was a masochist.

When I was a junior at Leeds, Travis was our leading scorer, our Mr. Everything. He had been a monster since his freshman season when he went straight to the varsity, leaving the rest of us far behind. He was only the second player in the history of our school ever to skip JV ball. And he kicked butt on the varsity. He was a 6'4" guard when everyone else at that position was 5'10" or smaller.

But Travis's presence didn't mean I couldn't get every rebound that came off the rim, every free ball that hung above the basket. So that was my mission. On that night when Coach Green was in the stands, I must have finished with about 25 rebounds. A few days later, I saw him at one of our practices. I hadn't been sure whether he had really been watching me during the games, so I just walked up to him and introduced myself.

"Coach Green? I'm Charles Barkley." I grabbed his hand and shook it firmly. "You know, we've got another pretty good guy on this team: me. I like Auburn. I wouldn't mind going to school there."

He smiled, shook my hand, and said he'd pass my message on to the other coaches, but I think he was just being nice.

Every kid who plays high school sports loves the initial attention and glamour of being recruited by major colleges. But the enjoyment doesn't last long. The letters that arrive in batches every day and the constant telephone calls from famous coaches are nice, but not when the phone rings at three A.M., or when the recruiters—not just coaches, but the sleazy locals who are hired by the schools to baby-sit their prize recruits and shield them from other schools that are doing the same thing—are camping out in front of your house. In a sense, I was pretty lucky. I loved the recruiting process, but only because I wasn't heavily recruited. When I was a junior, I was still pretty short for a major-college postup player, just 6'1", a center in a guard's body. And most recruiters from Division I colleges were concerned about my weight, thinking that at my size I wouldn't be able to defend against taller, stronger players or keep pace with quick, smaller players, particularly if I didn't have the shooting range to play guard. (I didn't.)

Also, I wasn't a scorer. I didn't rack up fat numbers like most big-time recruits. I averaged only 13.0 points during my junior season, but I grabbed 11 rebounds a game. I truly didn't give a damn about points unless I scored after snatching down an offensive rebound. Still, a short, overweight postup player wasn't high on most recruiters' lists.

That didn't bother me, though, because I knew I could play major-college basketball even if the major colleges didn't agree. Still, there was one aspect of recruiting I actually missed: because I wasn't at the top of anybody's wish list, I didn't receive any of the—how can I say it?—incentives that were being spread around like lollipops in the doctor's office amid the recruiting wars over the top players in the state. Trips, meals, women— and sometimes even cash—were usually the order of the day for the recruits who were most in demand, and it sometimes seemed like an all-you-can-eat smorgasbord when you visited a new campus.

Going into my senior season, I had grown to 6'2" and was still a monster rebounder, but the high school scouts in Alabama ranked four guys ahead of me on the recruiting ladder: Bobby Lee Hurt, a 6'9" center from Butler High School in Huntsville; Ennis Whatley, a 6'3" guard at Phillips High School in Birmingham; 6'5" center Vern Strickland of Emma Sansom High School in Gadsden; and a 6'7" center named Myron Hughes, who played for Colbert County School in Leighton. They were considered the four best players in Alabama, so every college in the state with a gym went after them hard. Everybody took their best shot—their most generous shot—at them, so goodies were flying around Alabama like confetti at a ticker-tape parade, every place except where I was standing. Nobody offered me shit. By the time any school wanted to talk to me, late in my senior season, the vaults were empty and there were no leftovers.

I might never have received a single nibble from a major college—Auburn included—had it not been for my performance against Bobby Lee during a Christmas tournament game in Birmingham when I was a senior. I was really pumped for the game for two reasons: (1) Bobby Lee was ranked as the No. 1 big man in the state, if not the nation; and (2) Butler was ranked No. 1 in Class 4A. Leeds was ranked No. 1 in Class 3A, so our showdown was anticipated by basketball fans throughout the state.

During warm-ups my teammates and I spent most of the time searching the stands for famous coaches. Wimp was there. So were Gene Bartow of UAB and Norm Sloan of Florida. We acted like little kids, pointing toward the bleachers and saying, "He's here, he's here. Wow. He's here, too." We were in total shock.

We also knew why they were there—to see Bobby Lee Hurt.

Actually, just before the start of the game, I was struck by a sick feeling in my stomach. It was fear. I was scared, intimidated by the prospect of playing Bobby Lee. If I was ever going to have an opportunity to earn a college scholarship, this was it. The realization of the magnitude of the encounter was almost too much to bear. I damn near threw up. Once the game began, though, I stopped thinking about it. Our coach, Billy Coupland, didn't assign me to cover Bobby Lee because he didn't want me to get into foul trouble. Butler defended me with a guy named Norris Gerley, a physical specimen who was actually a pretty good player; he later received a scholarship to play at Virginia Tech. But he made a major mistake in guarding me: he tried to get physical. It didn't work. Gerley was on the bench in foul trouble about the time the singer reached "and the home of the brave." That left the opposing coach only one option: guard me with Bobby Lee.

From there, the contest was pretty simple. I kicked Bobby Lee's tail. I finished with 25 points and 20 rebounds, mostly against the Great Bobby Lee Hurt. Auburn assistant Herb Green was in the stands that night, too. But by the end of the game he thought he had blown it by not showing more interest in me earlier. Suddenly, I was no longer his little secret.

Word sure travels fast when it comes to recruiting. Based on that single performance, I started receiving letters from everywhere, schools outside the state of Alabama, even schools whose programs had already decided which recruits they wanted and more importantly, how much it was going to cost to get them.

My performance against Bobby Lee doused a rumor that had also turned a lot of coaches away from my direction. A lot them thought I had padded my stats my senior year against inferior competition. It all started when Ennis Whatley, who had long been a very good friend of mine, asked San Diego State head coach Smokey Gaines to come watch me play during a break in his recruiting trips. Gaines had come to Alabama to watch Ennis play at Phillips High in Birmingham, but Ennis made it clear to him that he should take a drive to Leeds. Well, Coach Gaines saw us against one of the weaker teams on our schedule, a team that didn't have a single player over six feet tall. Hell, they didn't have a single player who could even play. Needless to say, I got off, scoring and rebounding like I was playing against my mom, and we won by about 50 points.

Gaines went home disappointed. "I can't judge the kid by this team," he told Ennis. Those words got around, and my stock didn't change until the Christmas tournament. Smokey Gaines is a good coach, but he's obviously not the best judge of talent.

A word to future scouts: If you dismiss a player because of the level of competition he plays against, you're crazy. I averaged more than 19 points and 18 rebounds as a senior, and Leeds won 26 of 29 games. I don't give a damn if you're playing against girls! If you average 19.1 points and 18 rebounds in a season, you can sure as hell play basketball, particularly if your team is winning every night. The bottom line was this: with those numbers, I could play against anybody, anywhere, and at any level. But to some schools, I was the bottom man on the totem pole. I wasn't even worth a used Chevy.

While the major-college recruiters were finally making the trek to Leeds to watch me play, I knew in my heart that I would attend a school close to my home and family in Leeds. That's the reason why I originally committed to Alabama-Birmingham, just seventeen miles from Leeds. Right after the Christmas tournament, I gave Gene Bartow a verbal commitment, but a few weeks later I changed my mind. It happened after UAB reached the Sweet 16 in the 1981 NCAA tournament, where they lost to Indiana, which was led by a sophomore guard named Isiah Thomas. The Hoosiers went on to win the national title at the Spectrum in Philadelphia on the day John Hinckley, Jr., tried to kill President Reagan.

After the NCAAs, a lot of players in Alabama were suddenly jumping at the chance to play at UAB. Bartow had already earned a prominent national reputation after coaching at Memphis State, Illinois, and UCLA before arriving at UAB in 1978. But four of his starters from the 1980–81 team were returning for what would've been my freshman year. More than anything, I wanted to play, no matter which school I attended. So just like that, UAB was out of the picture. Why would I go to a team that had every starter back?

Most teams use the kind of success UAB enjoyed in the 1981 NCAA tournament to *attract* recruits, but that year's success *cost* UAB. It cost them Charles Barkley.

AUBURN IS LOCATED 110 miles southeast of Birmingham, 100 miles from Leeds. I didn't tell UAB that I had changed my mind until just a few weeks before I was supposed to report to classes. Bartow was pissed, and he had every right to be. But I didn't really give a damn. I wasn't going anyplace where I wasn't going to play. They quickly got over it; in fact, the team was even better the following season. UAB reached the regional finals in the 1982 NCAA tournament before losing to a great Louisville team that had seven players who would later play in the NBA. UAB was so good that it beat Ralph Sampson's Virginia team during the NCAA Regionals in Birmingham. They didn't need me at all.

And I sure as hell didn't need them.

Thank God for Herb Green. When Auburn finally began recruiting me after the Christmas tournament, Herb had to convince head coach Sonny Smith and the other members of the coaching staff that I was worth pursuing. They didn't act as if they were thrilled when I signed a letter of intent to come to Auburn. There was no celebration; instead of cheering—"Oh, we got Charles Barkley!"—they seemed to yawn, "Well, he's the only thing left. It still looks good that we got the fifth-best player in the state. That's better than nothing."

Better than nothing? Sonny Smith and the Auburn coaching staff got Christmas and all of their birthdays all rolled into one. They just didn't realize it. Not yet.

SONNY SMITH: *No matter what anybody tells you, Herbert Green discovered Charles Barkley. He called me one day and said there was this big fat kid in Leeds who we should maybe keep our eye on. He said the kid was lazy, but he kept talking about what great hands the kid had, that he was a quick jumper who had a great feel for the game. That Christmas tournament was Charles's coming-out party. After that he became a recruitable item by the majors. Wimp jumped after him, then Gene, but we had been there first. Herb was so persistent that he convinced Charles's mom and grandmother that Leeds was closer to Auburn than it was to Tuscaloosa—if you went the back way. It wasn't. Later, Wimp came into their home and started talking about how Alabama was the closest school to Leeds when Charles's mom jumped in. "Wait a minute. Auburn's closer if you go across the mountain." Problem was that they hadn't put the road in yet.*

When I finally saw Charles, he was everything Herb said he was: he had great hands and an unbelievable passing touch. But he wouldn't change ends of the court; he just did not want to play hard and wouldn't play hard. He'd do just enough to win. But I'll tell you this: Leeds needed a great pass to win, so Charles made an unbelievable full-court pass to an open teammate that won the game. I told Herb, "If we can ever get rid of that baby fat, then we'll have something special."

Another thing: When Charles came to Auburn for his official visit, he never left my home. That's when I knew there was something different about him. Most guys go on their official visits to have fun, but Charles said all he wanted to do was get to know me, to make sure he knew everything about me. My wife, Jan, remembers that while Charles was here, he ate two jars of green olives. All he wanted to do was watch television, talk to me, and eat green olives. I'd never had a recruit do that before.

Bobby Lee and Ennis were considered "program" players. Everyone knew that whichever schools got one of these two guys would be set for the next four years—as long as the players didn't jump to the NBA. So when they both decided to attend Alabama, it touched off a celebration across the state. Tide fans went nuts. They were talking about the Final Four and national titles. Basically, they lost their minds. All you heard was Bobby Lee and Ennis, Ennis and Bobby Lee. With 'Bamamania sweeping the area, I wasn't all that surprised when I arrived on the Auburn campus in the fall and discovered that nobody was talking basketball. But I was stunned to discover that most of the students hadn't even heard of me. Not even the basketball fans!

"Charles Barkley?" one student said to me during the first week of classes. "It must be great to be a football player."

In my first few days at Auburn, it quickly became clear to me that my basketball credentials didn't matter one damn bit to anyone on campus. In that sense, I was no different from any other college freshman in America. What we'd done in high school didn't mean a thing. It was history. Gone. If we were to make names for ourselves, we were going to have to start from the moment we found our niches in college life.

For me, that moment came on the day I first walked into the Memorial Coliseum on the Auburn University campus.

Basketball at Auburn was a rude awakening. In high school, I cried after every loss, which didn't happen very often. During my two years on the varsity at Leeds, we lost only ten games. By February of my freshman season at Auburn, we had *already* lost ten games, including losses to Tennessee, William and Mary, Duke, Vanderbilt, and Kentucky, the school everybody wanted to beat—real badly. Following the Tennessee loss, our first of the season, I sat in the locker room and cried like a baby. One of my teammates saw me and came over to where I was sitting.

"Why are you crying?" he asked.

"Man, I'm not used to losing. I hate the feeling."

He started laughing. "Man, you'd better not be crying around here after every loss. You'll flood us out of here."

By then I was beginning to wonder if I had made a big mistake, a real big mistake. And it had nothing to do with our regular contributions to the loss column. The mistake was Sonny Smith.

My problems with Coach Smith began because of—guess what?—my weight. I had played my senior year at Leeds weighing 225 pounds, heavy but not out of control. But I hardly played any basketball during the summer. Even now, I don't play at all during the off-season because my body needs to heal and rejuvenate itself from the pounding I take during the season. Naturally, I tend to gain weight during that period of inactivity. But I've always managed to lose much of it prior to the start of the following season, or soon thereafter.

When I arrived at Auburn, though, and stepped on a scale, I weighed 250 pounds. Two hundred and fifty! That was even heavy for me. But I wasn't concerned. I even managed to convince Coach Smith and his assistants that they shouldn't be concerned; I told them that I would lose all of the weight when I started playing regularly, which would be well before the start of the season. They didn't believe me, but there wasn't much they could do about it, either. Besides, I was killing guys in practice, even at two five oh. Seniors, starters, anybody. As a freshman, I was supposed to suffer an adjustment period to the higher caliber of talent I would encounter at the college level, especially at Division I. Wrong. Long before I played my first game at Auburn, I already knew one thing: I was clearly, obviously, and absolutely the best player on the team.

SONNY SMITH: *No question, Charles thought he should be starting from the day he arrived in the gym. To prove it, he tried to kill everybody during practice. Charles was unbelievable at accepting a challenge. If the guy he was playing against couldn't play, Charles wouldn't play. But if the guy was any kind of player, Charles would destroy him. He would do it verbally, physically, any way he could. My best returning player was a* *junior forward named Darrell Lockhart, who would later get picked in the second round of the NBA draft by the San Antonio Spurs. Well, Charles intimidated Darrell so bad that I ended up with a vegetable. Finally I had to stop Charles from guarding him.*

But I still wouldn't start Charles because I didn't want to throw him to the wolves. I also didn't want to just give him the starting job based on his ability. Charles came to practice with different moods. He never missed practice, but some days he was there physically but not mentally. Or he'd be there mentally, but not physically. When he was there both ways, he was unbelievable. But for the most part, Charles would only practice hard to beat the hell out of Darrell Lockhart, not for Auburn. I tried to tell him that he had to work hard every day and show me that he wanted to make Auburn win. But that didn't make any sense to him. So right off, we had a conflict.

I hated practice. I always have, and I always will. Drills are hell. Some guys are great in practice, but then can't play dead in the game. At Auburn, I refused to bust my ass in practice and *again* in the games. The only time I played hard during practice was during the scrimmages, which I dominated, usually at Darrell Lockhart's expense. It was nothing personal against Darrell, but he represented the best player at my position, so in order to become a starter I thought I had to prove that he was no match for me.

Prior to the start of the season the team toured through rural Alabama and held open scrimmages free of charge in an effort to generate interest in areas where fans and alumni don't often get to see us play. In each of those exhibitions, I led the team in scoring, rebounding, and butt whippings. It wasn't even a contest. When you see Darrell Lockhart, just ask him.

Still, Coach Smith never gave me a break. All he ever talked about was my weight. Wherever we played, he would make me run to the top of the arena and back several times. Or he would make me run baseline to baseline, six trips in a minute. Or he would make me run sideline to sideline, sixteen times in sixty seconds. Then, if we were at our home arena, he'd send me up to the mezzanine for laps.

SONNY SMITH: *I was extremely hard on him. If I had it to do over, I don't know if I would do it that way. I just don't think I would.*

One day after I had finished another set of running drills, Coach Smith walked over to where I was standing. "You're not gonna start, you know, unless you practice hard," he said.

I was pissed. "Fine," I told him. "Fuck it. I'm gone."

Before Coach Smith knew what hit him, I *was* gone. Not just from the gym, or even from campus. I was sitting in my living room back home in Leeds, bullheaded and determined not to play for Sonny Smith or Auburn ever again. If he wasn't going to start me, I wasn't gonna play. Period.

My mother and grandmother were stunned. My mother cried. My grandmother didn't say much because, like I've said before, she's so much like me that I think she understood exactly where I was coming from. If she had been in my place, she would have done the same thing. She might've even punched Coach Smith. But Mom was different. She had wanted me to go to college more than anything else in life. No one else in our family had ever gone to college, and she hoped that by getting an education I would have a chance to overcome our family's economic condition. She knew that I'd only get that chance if I had a college education. That's why she went to work in white people's homes every day, and why she never complained no matter how tired she was when she came home, sometimes late into the night. She also wanted me to learn something else, that I just wasn't going to get my way in life by running away from setbacks and challenges. As she sat there and cried, she must have wondered if I would ever learn.

"You've got to stay at least one year," she said, almost pleading. "I don't care what you do after that, but you've got to go back to Auburn and finish the first year. At least. You've got to stay. You've just got to stay."

Unmistakably, my mother's advice at that important crossroad in my life was the best thing that happened to me during my first year at Auburn. I might never have learned how to cope with adversity if she hadn't pushed me when I ran away from a challenge called Sonny Smith. If I hadn't returned to Auburn that fall, I wouldn't have been able to play basketball for an entire year. And without basketball, I would probably have gotten bored with school entirely and flunked out. That would have forced me to attend a small college where I might have struggled with frustration and perhaps never been drafted. Then I would have been back in Leeds, doing nothing but regretting one very stupid decision. Instead, my mother stopped that scenario before it began. She wasn't going to let me quit Auburn, not as a freshman at least. And because she wouldn't, I returned to school bound and determined to prove that Sonny Smith had been a fool.

Finally, six games into the season, Coach Smith promoted me to the starting lineup, just after I had kicked ass in our first important game of the year, against Tennessee. He wasn't stupid.

SONNY SMITH: *I think Tennessee's center was Howard Wood. Well, Charles kicked his tail somethin' bad that night. That's when it all started for Charles. From that point on, he was quite a legend in the SEC.*

By then, the Auburn basketball team was mine. Whether or not I was our best player was a dead issue. Hell, I was the second-best athlete on the entire campus. There was another guy at Auburn who could also play a bit. Play what? Anything he wanted. He played running back for the football team and was an outfielder in baseball. I once told him, "Man, one day you'd better pick one sport or the other. You'll never make it in the pros if you try to play both."

But Bo wouldn't listen.

Bo Jackson was one of the primary reasons why, during the early weeks of my freshman season, basketball was still an afterthought at Auburn. That's if anybody thought about it at all. He was one of the few football players who didn't treat basketball players like we were scum. The first time I ever saw him perform was in a high school football game when his team, McAdory High School from McCalla, Alabama, faced Leeds at Legion Field in Birmingham. Bo just ran over our guys. Pulverized us.

At Auburn, he was a quiet, down-to-earth guy who treated

everyone well. I can honestly say that I'm happy for everything he's achieved.

Before I came to Auburn, the basketball team hadn't helped its image by being a bunch of losers. Nobody cared about losers in Alabama, so on campus we were second-class citizens. First class was filled by the football team.

As athletes, we all enjoyed our share of perks. An occasional free meal. Discounts at local stores. All things that athletes at every major campus in America were also enjoying. But the football players at Auburn were treated like royalty, like gods in shoulder pads. Just about all of them had cars, though almost none of them could afford the payments. The cars were a given. I don't know where they came from, who paid for them—most of those guys claimed they didn't have enough cash to buy a round of beers—or how they managed to keep up the mainte-nance. But they managed. And they rubbed it in our faces every chance they got, which was plenty.

There were times when the basketball team would be enjoying dinner at a restaurant near campus—nothing fancy, cold cuts, fried chicken, dishes like that—when the football players would arrive. Suddenly, steaks and lobsters were everywhere. It was sickening. It wasn't sickening enough, however, to make me *play* football, though some of the assistant football coaches asked me more than once if I would come out for the team, if I would consider playing tight end. But I never gave it a serious thought. I may have been crazy for turning down daily steak and lobster, but I wasn't crazy.

Football was dangerous.

In basketball, *I* was dangerous.

ONE OF MY goals was to change the status of basketball at Auburn. I wanted the team to be the talk of the campus. I wanted the arena to be filled for all of our games. And I wanted us to win. I wanted to do everything I could to make that happen. In short, I wanted to do for Auburn basketball what Bo was doing for Auburn football.

Funny thing, the war between Coach Smith and myself be-came the spark that fueled interest in the team. Around campus, people started whispering about my status: Was Charles going to remain at school? Was Charles going to start every game? Was Charles going to punch Sonny Smith?

After I won round one of the conflict and became a starter, I started to gain weight again. I peaked at just over 270 pounds that year, the heaviest I'd ever been in my entire life. That's when Coach Smith lost control and our problems escalated to all-out head-butting on a daily basis.

SONNY SMITH: *Charles was very stubborn, but I also treated him like a dog. I dog-cussed him, is what we would've called it where I come from. I belittled him. I got right in his face and screamed. You know what? He coulda killed me with one blow, but he never did anything. I look back on that and realize just what kind of guy he was. All I wanted was to get him to play hard because it was evident that I had something special. What I always tried to do with good players was to break them down and mold them into what I wanted them to be. I did it to Chris Morris and Chuck Person, but Charles was different. For instance, we were working on defending the backdoor cut one day, but instead of stepping over to stop the little guy—a kid named Alvin Mumphord—Charles would just stick out his arm and knock the kid into the bleachers. I said, "Charles, stop knocking him into the bleachers. Get over there and cut off the drive." The next time we ran the play, Charles knocked Alvin into the bleachers again. I yelled to him, "If you hit Alvin again, Charles, I'll hit you." Well, here goes Alvin and I'm saying to myself, "Please, God, let Charles step over there instead of knocking the kid into the bleachers." Well, here goes Alvin backdoor again and—boom!—right up into the cheap seats. I ran over to Charles and I hit him in the chest. I reared back and hit him again.*

"What are you gonna do?" Coach Smith yelled after he smacked me across the chest. I didn't say anything, but my mind was running a fast break. "Should I hit him, or shouldn't I?" I didn't know what to do. Finally, I said to myself, "Nah."

SONNY SMITH: *Finally, he said, "Coach, don't hit me anymore." That's all he said. He never made it an issue. The next day it*

*was like nothing ever happened. Oh, yeah, Alvin decided that
he really didn't like running the backdoor play.*

Even in the midst of the team's internal tension, we were
winning basketball games, particularly at home where we beat
conference foes Ole Miss, Florida, and Georgia before the end
of January. We lost by only 2 points to Alabama. By then, the
school had already started trying to capitalize on our success by
promoting our biggest asset: me.

That's when I started hearing the nicknames. David Housel,
the school's sports-information director, thought it was a great
idea to stir up interest by billing me as the Round Mound of
Rebound or Boy Gorge. I hated most of the names, and under
most circumstances I might have punched anybody who called
me Boy Gorge. But I played along, even to the point of performing ridiculous stunts like posing for pictures with boxes of
pizzas and plates full of chickens. There were times when I felt
humiliated, but when you're a young player trying to make a
name for yourself, you can easily be taken in by the hype. It
clouds your ability to choose right from wrong. What I was doing
on the court was right, but allowing myself to be taunted as an
overweight freak was wrong.

SONNY SMITH: *I think we did Charles an injustice at Auburn.
Basketball, you see, was not the main thing at the school, but
Charles was unique. So in order to get publicity for the program,
we used Charles. He never weighed as much or ate as much as
we said he did, but we publicized the fat thing. We started all
that Mouth of the South stuff, etc. I wish we had never done it,
making him do those extroverted things that gave him the reputation he has right now. We created a monster.*

Coach Smith could never accept my weight, even though I
had come to accept my size and felt comfortable with it, long
before I came to Auburn. Whenever I gained weight, it was
never because I wasn't playing hard—though I only played as
hard as I had to, which usually wasn't very hard at all. Players
who defended me always tried to use their weight against mine;
they often bragged about how they would use their strength to

beat me up. It was the macho thing to do. It was also dumb—
not because of my size and strength, which usually outlasted
anyone I played against, but because I learned early in my career
to rely not on my weight but my quickness.

No matter what I weighed, I was always quick, and quickness was the key to my game. My basketball philosophy has
always been this: you can't hit what you can't catch. I'll never
stand still. When I keep my feet moving on the offensive end of
the floor, there aren't many big guys who can keep up with me.
It was my speed and quickness that always surprised the guys
who guarded me. Maybe they saw my size and figured I had to
be nailed to the floor. Maybe they thought I was as slow as an
elephant. They believed the hype. Once again, dumb. While my
opponent was leaning toward me, I was gone. They were leaning
on air.

By midseason, the word on Charles Barkley was starting to
circulate around the league. I was already the best rebounder
in the conference, averaging 9.9 boards a game. I was also scoring
double-figure points almost every night, much of which was the
fruit of my work on the offensive boards. And we were drawing
crowds. Slowly but quite surely, basketball was becoming *the*
thing to do on campus—after football, of course, but still the
thing to do. And I was the team's unquestioned star, nicknames
and all.

SONNY SMITH: *Charles Barkley was Auburn basketball. He
turned the entire program around by himself, as well as a few
other things. This is a true story: Charles loved to dunk the
basketball. Now, he knew that it drove me crazy when he would
snap the breakaway rim; I even had a rule that you couldn't do
it in practice. But Charles would snap the rim just to make me
mad, even when he knew I'd make him run.*

One time, Coach Smith was fuming about my snapping the
rim. "If you pop that damn rim one more time, I want your ass
out of here."

Next time down the floor, I popped the rim. Boom!

"Get the fuck out of here," yelled Coach Smith.

SONNY SMITH: *Well, once he dunked the ball so hard that he moved the entire basket support, which was held in place by two 300-pound cement blocks. I'm cussin' and tellin' everybody to come over and help get the blocks back in place, when Charles pushed me out of the way, walked to the goal, and moved the blocks himself! He then straightened the goal and put both of those 300-pound blocks back in place. It was an unbelievable physical feat. That's how Charles Barkley gave us an identity. We became a team people physically feared. We were exciting and drew a lot of attention, especially on the road. Charles was the reason for every bit of it.*

None of my contributions to the team seemed to matter to Coach Smith. He didn't like the way I played with such inconsistent effort, even though I was embarrassing the best centers in the league, guys like Mel Turpin of Kentucky, a future NBA first-round draft pick. And he wouldn't let go of the great weight debate. Sonny said I needed to lose weight, but I resisted. "Fuck off," I once told him. "The way I'm rebounding and scoring, shit, I don't have to play any harder."

Or so I thought at the time. It was the rationale of a stupid, arrogant nineteen-year-old freshman. What I didn't realize at the time was that if I could lead the league in rebounding at 270 pounds, then I could be an even better player if I lost weight. (I play at around 250–255 today.) I also didn't realize that my weight was contributing to the back problems that had started to plague me in high school. I was just too stubborn to look beyond the next game, the next rebound, the next opponent—the next sucker. My only thought concerning Coach Smith was, "To hell with him."

I carried that childish attitude through two years at Auburn, and it was why Sonny Smith and I never became close while I was at the school. Years later, I finally realized that our problems were as much my fault as they were his. I would never have admitted that while I was at Auburn. I was young, strong, and I could do no wrong. I was also selfish and stubborn, and that's a bad combination.

We finished that first season with a record of 14–14, the team's best effort in six years. We won seven conference games, but still finished seventh in the league. I thought we had had a pitiful season. I was embarrassed. But the Auburn coaches and the players who had been there before thought we, had had a great season. The previous year's team had finished at 11–16, which was typically mediocre for Auburn. After we were trounced by Kentucky, 89–66, in the second round of the SEC tournament to conclude our season, someone announced in the locker room that we should have a party to celebrate our success. I thought the guy was joking.

I MUST DIVERGE a bit and talk about a gross misconception concerning athletes that irks the hell out of me: all athletes are dumb. From the time that most young students begin to excel at sports, too many of them are unfairly labeled academically inferior to other students, the nonathletes. By the time the athlete reaches junior high school, his teachers are already expecting less of him. Even his parents become satisfied with the athlete's subpar academic performances, as along as he performs—and performs well. This breeds an athlete who expects less of himself. Then, when it comes time for the athlete to study, his classmates avoid him like he's got a disease—unless, of course, those same classmates need tickets, or if they just want to be "friends" with the athlete, hangers-on who get their kicks by being in the star athlete's hip pocket. Invariably, the athlete will run into a wall, one that comes crashing down upon him—a wall of bricks labeled *You're stupid*.

Let me set the record straight: there are certainly a lot of athletes who receive—and deserve—bad grades throughout school and who leave college without coming close to earning a degree, but *there is no such thing as a dumb athlete*. None whatsoever.

To perform athletics at the highest levels of skill requires more intelligence than most people will ever know.

This is the problem: most athletes are lazy. Athletics can be a draining pursuit, emotionally and physically. And the pressures that college athletes endure—from coaches, fans, alumni, teammates, and even from themselves—can be overwhelming. Young athletes are expected to produce like professionals, without compensation, in front of thousands of people who want to win every night. After some games when I played particularly badly, I just wanted to crawl into a big, dark hole and disappear. I couldn't. Whether I was in uniform, in class, at a restaurant, or just walking around the Auburn campus, I was always *Charles Barkley, basketball player.* I couldn't hide.

Facing that kind of pressure, athletes often have little energy after the end of a game. So when you come to the classroom, you often just don't *try* as hard as you did in the arena, stadium, court, or pool. As a result, your grades suffer, and you now have to expend even more energy in the classroom, energy you just don't have anymore.

Young athletes, starting at the earliest stages of their athletic development, need to be told that if they're smart enough to play football, basketball, or any other sport, then they're smart enough to understand math, science, history, anything. But they won't get an education without expending the same kind of effort they expend in their sport. And they need to be told, every day if necessary, that their chances of becoming a successful adult are helped more by an education than by a jump shot.

From the moment I arrived at Auburn, the athletic department discouraged me academically. They claimed they didn't want me to be "overloaded" with classes. Still, they tried to make sure that the athletes were taking courses that would help them earn a degree.

I didn't want to be a typical athlete, majoring in physical education, so when I returned to Auburn for my sophomore year, I signed up for a pretty difficult major: business management. Mainly, I liked the way it sounded.

I actually took a couple of business courses, and I enjoyed them; I enjoyed the challenge. When people, including Coach Smith, told me that I wouldn't pass any of the most difficult courses on my schedule—courses like psychology and business law—I took it as a personal challenge. To me, these nonbelievers were as strong a motivator as Mel Turpin. Some people thought I would flunk out that semester, but I enjoyed shutting up everyone who doubted me. I passed those courses.

In the end, though, I couldn't sustain my academic motivation—just like I had done at Leeds.

Anyone who wants to get an education at Auburn can get one. I'll give the school credit for that, which is more than you can do for a lot of schools. One of my teammates on the 76ers, Kenny Payne, is always getting teased by the rest of us because he attended Louisville, where we say he majored in Dunking 101, Dunking 102, and Dunking 103, all tutored by Professor Denny Crum.

Too many schools are still not stressing academics nor trying to help their athletes earn degrees, no matter what they're saying. They aren't trying to teach kids anything—except how to stay eligible, and how to get the schools to bowls and tournaments so the schools can make more money. Then when the athlete stays eligible for four years but doesn't even come close to getting a degree, the school says, "Hey, it wasn't our fault!"

They're transferring the blame.

The athletes have to accept some of the responsibility for their academic plight, but if the schools aren't on their case about it, they won't get it done. I'm living proof.

At Auburn, I just tried to stay eligible. For most of my three years in college I managed to keep my head above water academically, but just barely. Sure, I could've killed myself and signed up for some more challenging courses. But why? None of the other star athletes at Auburn were taking biophysics. In fact, none of us took academics seriously until we were juniors, if then. We were all just getting by.

SONNY SMITH: *We would take him to class, absolutely walk him to class, but Charles would walk out of the door and beat us back to the room. So we got up at six or six-thirty and ran. He never balked at it. I think he'd rather run than go to class.*

The worst thing a college can do is to tell an athlete that a particular class isn't mandatory. Nonmandatory classes were my best classes. I was on the nonmandatory dean's list. The golden rule of college athletics is eligibility. Hell, it's the only rule.

Obviously, I didn't make a commitment to academics during my years at Auburn. I was supposed to attend summer school after my junior season, but I attended the Olympic Trials instead because I knew that I was going to declare myself eligible for the NBA draft. So even if I had changed my mind at the last minute and decided to return to Auburn, I would have been academically ineligible to compete. I haven't gone back to school to obtain my degree; it's my single biggest regret about my years in high school and college. I have no doubt that I could have earned A's and B's at Auburn if I had really put forth the effort. And I know I could have earned my degree. Instead, I just got by—and I was too damn lazy to do anything about it.

Actually, I was extremely lucky. A lot of my teammates at Auburn also struggled through classes, but most of them didn't end up as millionaires. Every guy on the team thought he was going to play in the NBA, but only Chuck Person, Darrell Lockhart—one season with San Antonio—and I made it; just three out of the twenty-five players I played with while I was at Auburn.

Hindsight's great, isn't it? If I could do it over, I would have studied harder both at Leeds and at Auburn. I probably wouldn't have become a scientist or a math genius, but if I did it over again, I probably wouldn't be an NBA player, either. I've beaten the odds once. Lightning never strikes twice, you know.

THE MOMENTUM OF our freshman season carried into the following year. By then, we were campus heroes. I was actually pretty amused by it all, considering that our 15–13 record that season didn't make anyone forget about any of the teams in the Top Ten. Still, it was a long way from the day I had come to Auburn, when nobody on the campus gave a damn about basketball. Back then, there had been only two important sports seasons at Auburn: football season and spring football season.

But winning changed all of that. It's like laughing gas. It makes everyone happy. The older guys on the team had been so anxious to win that nobody seemed to care about which of us received the most attention.

Nobody except Chuck Person.

Like me, Chuck was from a small, rural Alabama town, a place called Brantley. He had been one of the best high school players in the state, the kind of guy who never would've come to Auburn before I came to the school and helped make the basketball program respectable. When he arrived, in 1982, he was a nice, quiet kid from the country. He was obviously talented, having averaged 33 points and 20 rebounds as a high school senior. He was also a cousin of Dwayne McClain, who would later be a starter on Villanova's 1985 national championship team.

Chuck was recruited to be the designated scorer who would complement my rebounding, and we worked well together precisely because our games were exact opposites. Sonny made him a starter seven games into his freshman season, my sophomore season. About a month later, he scored 17 points and had 10 rebounds when we beat Kentucky 75–67 for Auburn's first victory ever over the Wildcats in Lexington. That same night, I had no mercy on Mel Turpin. Mel was a legitimate load who—along with teammate Sam Bowie, another seven-footer—never got the respect he deserved at Kentucky because the school had been used to winning while they were still in diapers.

The Wildcats were perennial challengers for the SEC title who were expected to fight for the national title every year. But just because a team has two big, talented centers doesn't mean it'll automatically win. I was much quicker than Mel, which made me a tough matchup for him. But to tell the truth, Mel didn't have a chance against me because of the Kentucky fans. In Lexington, fans taunted me longer, harder, and louder than any other fans in the country. They brought pizza boxes and generally said anything they could about me, the more vulgar the better. Rude and obnoxious fans always brought out the best in me. Or the worst. And unfortunately for Kentucky fans, I always took my anger out on Mel.

SONNY SMITH: *Charles just intimidated Mel Turpin, absolutely drove him nuts. It was mostly talk, but he was so quick that no matter what Charles said, Mel couldn't have caught him anyway. Another of Charles's favorite targets was Bobby Lee Hurt, which dated back to the high school all-star game that Charles dominated. We were playing Alabama at home when Bobby Lee dunked over Charles on the run to put the Tide up by 2 late in the game. Well, Charles took the ball, jumped over the top of Bobby Lee, dunked, and was fouled. He turned around and stuck a finger in Bobby Lee's face, as if to tell him that he had brought it on himself by dunking on Charles at the other end. If you did*

something to Charles on one end of the court, then you knew it
was going to come back at you.

Despite our growing success, it became pretty clear that Chuck
was the only person on the team who was jealous of my popularity
with the media and the fans. He played a lot as a freshman, more
than 22 minutes a night, and enjoyed big performances against
talented teams like Alabama and Florida, as well as Kentucky.
Confident after those initial efforts, he kicked it into gear as a
sophomore and led the team in scoring with 19.1 points a game,
second in the league. By then, we were one of the most feared
tandems in the conference. I finished first in the race for SEC
Player of the Year, Chuck was second. I was Mr. Inside, grabbing
almost 10 rebounds a game, and Chuck was Mr. Outside, pa-
trolling the perimeter so that teams couldn't focus all of their
attention on me. But at the same time, Chuck's overall attitude
changed. Our designated scorer became our designated jerk.

It didn't matter to Chuck that almost all of the publicity I got
focused more on my weight than my performance. I was the
Prince of Pizza, all that shit. I was being ridiculed for my size
as much as I was being praised for my skills. And I tried to tell
him that I had nothing to do with writing the articles.

But Chuck didn't care. He was a little crazy. All he knew was
that he was playing extremely well, but—in his mind, at least—
getting absolutely no recognition for it. No "pub" at all. He
resented the lack of attention and thought I was getting entirely
too much ink. And it turned him into an ass.

We didn't get along at all during the two years we played
together, but there was more than enough blame for both of us.
We were two stubborn, pigheaded country boys, and neither of
us handled the situation well. Rather than discussing the problem, we just tried to do whatever we could to piss each other
off. And we did.

Chuck was, and remains to this day, extremely cocky. Any day
and every day, he would get in my face in the locker room and
tell me what a great player he was; he would challenge me
verbally during practice, saying he was better than me; and he
would stop me anywhere on campus and tell me I didn't deserve
all the publicity I was getting. Like I said, he was an ass. Chuck

was always a helluva player; his success in the NBA with the Indiana Pacers since he was picked in the first round of the 1986 college draft has proven that. Back then, though, he wasn't the player that he thought he was: the best player in the SEC. I was.

I never gave much thought to any of Chuck's attitude. I had my own problems to deal with, particularly Coach Smith, who continued to berate me throughout my sophomore season—so much so that at the end of my year I decided that I had had enough. I wasn't going to take any more crap about my weight—not from Sonny Smith, not from Auburn, not from anyone. One afternoon, I walked into Coach Smith's office and told him that I wanted to transfer to another school, even though it meant that I would have to sit out an entire year before I could play again. At the time, I thought a year away from the game would be a small price to pay for getting away from him. "Later for you and your program," I said. "And get this: I'm going to Alabama."

Well, that really pissed him off. Coach Smith was in his fifth year at Auburn, and after struggling every season before I arrived, he finally had a team with some talent, a team capable of challenging for the SEC title. Now, he thought, Charles Barkley was going to screw it up.

So did the other coaches. Tevester Anderson, Roger Banks, and Mack McCarthy were all furious because if I left Auburn, they thought that their reputations would have been trashed. Headlines blaring "Charles Barkley Leaves Auburn" would have told every top high school player in the country that Sonny Smith was not a good coach to play for, and that none of his assistant coaches stepped in and remedied the situation.

For each of those men, but particularly Sonny Smith, my leaving Auburn after my sophomore season would have been professional suicide.

SONNY SMITH: *Yeah, it would have been a career-ending thing for me if Charles had left Auburn because of his problems with me. But my first thought was that Charles should be happy, no matter who was his coach. Before Charles came along, I didn't have a real good reputation as a coach. Afterward, I went from being an unknown to what you might call a high-profile coach,* *and Charles was the reason. Nonetheless, I was going to be the boss even if it meant that I might lose him, so when he got upset with the way I treated him, I'd call him into my office, get out the Blue Book that listed every college in the country, and say, "Pick a school, any school, and I'll call the coach and recommend you with my blessing. You don't need to be here." He said, "But I want to play for you. I came here to play for you." "Then you're gonna do things my way," I said. Actually, I was kind of stupid.*

I was so frustrated that I didn't give a shit what happened to Sonny Smith. I was gone, an ex–Auburn Tiger. I packed up all of my belongings and marched right out of the athletic dorm. To where? I didn't really know.

In my heart, I didn't really want to transfer to Alabama. I knew that I'd be able to start for them, even though Bobby Lee and Ennis were living up to all expectations. Over in Tuscaloosa, the coaches and players were going crazy thinking that I was going to transfer. It wouldn't have happened, though, because I didn't really want to give up the year of eligibility. I knew I wasn't ready for the NBA, but still I gave serious thought to that option, too. I thought about going hardship strictly because of Sonny Smith. I considered that perhaps a year out of basketball might eventually hurt my chances to become a high draft choice, or even hurt my skills, so why not give it a shot now? I even talked to a couple of agents about it.

Actually, I had already been, shall I say, "involved" with these guys for several months. These were not mere random acquaintances, either. These guys had been subsidizing me with money, dress shoes, clothes, and other such necessities during most of my last two years at Auburn. One of the agents had only provided me with shoes, but given that I wouldn't have otherwise been able to afford dress shoes, his contributions were enough to make me feel like a Big Man on Campus, especially since I was also able to provide free shoes to everyone on the team.

The other two guys made sure that I always had money in my pocket. And not just pocket change. I must have accepted over $20,000 from them while I was at Auburn. They really took care of me—to the tune of at least $100 every week, most often delivered to me at the dorm in small envelopes. I didn't always know who made the deliveries, and I didn't really care. All I knew was that because of them, I didn't have to worry about spending money. I always shared the cash with my teammates, usually by taking them out for pizzas or buying a couple of rounds of beer.

The agents and I always understood that the money was a loan, which is why I didn't consider the payments to be an NCAA violation. At the same time, though, I was careful not to sign anything because I didn't want to be beholden to anyone for anything other than the cash.

When I signed my first contract with the 76ers and received a $150,000 signing bonus, I repaid each of the agents every dime I owed. Of course, the loans weren't simply a goodwill gesture by the agents. They were actually part of their own investment plan, something that the NCAA, in all its infinite wisdom (read: stupidity), fears the most: an agreement between a hungry agent with cash and a young, susceptible college athlete without it.

The agents always hope that the final "interest payment" would be the athlete's signature on a contract allowing the agent to become the athlete's financial adviser and contract negotiator. If I had decided to declare myself eligible for the NBA after my sophomore year, my "patrons" were certainly hoping for a cut— 10 percent. But signing an agreement would have been stupid. Accepting money from an agent is against the NCAA rules, though it remains a regular occurrence at most of the nation's top schools. If an athlete is careful, the only way he'll get caught is to make a mistake.

Signing anything is a mistake.

Some agents try to con athletes into signing an agreement before their eligibility expires, but that will get an athlete banned from college sports and tainted forever as a money-grubbing lowlife. I may have been young, but I wasn't stupid. The money was there, so I took it. But don't think for a minute that I was alone.

The NCAA is committing grand larceny by not paying college athletes. The schools are using the kids for financial gain, and it's been going on long enough. They take in millions of dollars a year, mostly from the TV networks, for the right to show us sweating out there on the courts or on the football fields. CBS

is paying *$1 billion* for the right to broadcast the NCAA tour-
nament for the next seven years. That's more than the fifty largest
colleges have spent on athletic scholarships in the last *twenty*
years. So don't tell me the schools aren't making big profits.

And the schools aren't stressing academics, either; they're selling wins. The athletic director goes flying around in first class
and getting a big bonus at the end of the year. The coach is
pocketing hundreds of thousands of dollars from a contract with
a sneaker company, a television show, and his summer camp.
Some of that money ought to find its way to the athletes. Besides
being the right thing to do, it might help keep some guys from
blowing their eligibility by accepting money, cars, apartments,
whatever—all of it a pittance compared to what the school's
making off our work.

The NCAA, college programs, athletic directors, and coaches
can go for the gold, but if an athlete reaches for even a sliver of
silver, he's a bum. For some reason, athletes are held to different
standards of behavior from even regular students. If a nerd from
the computer department wanted to talk to IBM about his worth
in the marketplace, would he be declared ineligible for school?
Hell, no! But an athlete, even in this so-called era of reform,
must sneak around like a criminal if he wants to discover his
worth. Face it, fellas at the NCAA, you're all a joke.

It should be no surprise that the agents who had me on their
payroll were encouraging me to go hardship. They said they had
already spoken to a few teams and determined that I would
probably be drafted by the Washington Bullets late in the first
round. The Bullets had two first-round picks that year, the tenth
and twenty-second spots in the draft. "That's good enough for
me," I told one of the agents. "I'm going."

In a few days, though, I realized that being drafted so late,
even in the first round, would cost me about a million dollars.
That's the difference in the earnings of a high first-round pick
and a player taken just a few picks later. More importantly, I
realized that the only reason I was leaving Auburn was that I
couldn't get along with Coach Smith. I couldn't stand the man.
But my feelings alone weren't reason enough to justify throwing
away the amount of money I might lose over the long run. So I
called one of the agents and told him that I'd changed my mind.

"I'm not ready," I said. Not surprisingly, he wasn't happy, but what could he do about it? Not one damn thing.

The Bullets eventually chose two guards with their two first-round picks: Jeff Malone of Mississippi State and Randy Wittman of Indiana. They could have had Jeff Malone and Charles Barkley. I guess the Bullets, in retrospect, weren't too thrilled about my decision, either.

Even though I knew I was returning to Auburn for my junior season, I didn't want to tell Coach Smith right away. I still had to make my point to him and the rest of the coaches about Sonny's rude treatment. So I decided to make them sweat. I wanted them to beg me to come back. What did I do? I hid out for two or three days at the apartment of my roommate's girlfriend, who lived only a few blocks from campus.

It worked.

For all of the chaos, commotion, and controversy I created by laying low, you'd have thought I was David Janssen of "The Fugitive." Sonny Smith and the coaches looked for me all over Auburn. They grilled my teammates about my whereabouts, but my guys weren't giving it up. They were, in fact, having a blast watching Coach Smith squirm and curse his way through practices during my absence. He must have seen his entire coaching career crumbling before his eyes. I received daily reports of Sonny's anguish and loved every minute of it. I had been tired of Coach Smith's constant shit about my weight, and I just wasn't going to listen to it anymore.

Finally, after a few days on the lam, I returned to the dorm and called on Coach Smith. I could see the relief in his eyes when I said I was coming back to Auburn. But I also told him that we had to have a serious discussion about his attitude. "You've been an asshole," I said. "That's got to change."

We sat down in his office right then and talked everything out.

"You've got to treat me like a person, not just a basketball player," I said. "If you think I'm overweight, you can say, 'Charles, maybe if you lost a little weight, you might be a better player,' rather than screaming at me in front of my teammates and calling me 'fat ass,' 'fat boy,' things like that all the time."

He just looked at me and didn't say a word.

"And it's not just me. The other guys aren't happy about the way you treat them, either. Why don't you invite us over for dinner sometimes? Don't just look at us as players in your program, not just pieces of meat—a bunch of guys who're going to help you get a better job or take you to the Final Four. Look at us as human beings."

"Okay, I'll try."

A few years later, Coach Smith told me that our conversation helped him as much as it did me. I've always wanted to be treated as a person first, and then as an athlete. That's all I ever asked of Coach Smith, or anyone else. From that point on, I started having tremendous success and so did he. Since then we've gotten along better than we ever did when I was in school.

SONNY SMITH: *After Charles's sophomore year, I never had any problems with him. I'd like to think that I reached him, but I don't know. I just don't know.*

During my junior season, the Auburn Tigers were our team. They belonged to me and Sonny Smith, in that order. And I was finally starting to earn some recognition outside of Alabama for more than my size. People were starting to recognize what my opponents already knew, that I could flat-out play this game. Suddenly, after nearly every game, I was the first player every reporter wanted to interview. I was in demand after practices, too. I was hot, and I was loving every moment of it. Suddenly, the NBA was a reality, not a pipe dream that I fantasized about like any other kid. Through it all, though, the most important aspect of my success was always that the team—the once lowly Auburn Tigers—was finally kicking some butt.

The 1983–84 Auburn Tigers were expected to be good, and we were, although it took us a few weeks to get ourselves together, and we remained probably the most inconsistent team in the SEC. I started the season with back problems, a lot of which were directly related to my weight. The pressure I had been putting on my body was starting to take its toll. We lost two of our first five games of the season, which might not have been so tough to stomach if they hadn't come against in-state rivals Alabama-Birmingham and South Alabama. Even worse, I couldn't play against South Alabama because of my back.

SONNY SMITH: *We lost the game to South Alabama for one reason and one reason only: because Charles Barkley couldn't play. I knew he had to be hurting, because when Charles was hurt, he usually never showed it and he would do anything to win. Our guys had come to depend on him so much that they absolutely couldn't play without him. When he wasn't able to play, they were lost. So one time he suited up, started, and just walked up and down the court. He couldn't do anything but get an occasional rebound. Hell, he could barely walk. But we won the game simply because he was out there; we won with one guy just walking up and down the court. But that guy was Charles Barkley.*

Later in the year, we stumbled through a period when we slumped to four losses in six games, including a home loss to SEC-rival Tennessee and disheartening 1-point losses to Louisiana State and Mississippi, two other league opponents. Yet we still managed to establish ourselves as legitimate challengers to Kentucky, the league favorites, by kicking the Wildcats' asses. On one joyous night at Auburn, we absolutely buried them by 19 points.

The rubber match with Kentucky came just when everyone thought it would—in the final of the SEC tournament. It was the biggest game in Auburn basketball history because the team hadn't won the SEC title in twenty-four years. We knew we had a tremendous opportunity, but we also knew that we wouldn't be able to surprise Kentucky, which by now knew that we were the one team in the conference they couldn't intimidate.

On the contrary, against Kentucky we were the intimidators, and with the game being played on a neutral court in Nashville, we were convinced that we would win. The game remained close throughout, and with just a few seconds remaining in regulation, the score was tied. At worst, I thought we would go into overtime where I thought we would have an advantage because Kentucky, as the favorites, might tighten up.

But then, with time expiring, Kenny Walker, Kentucky's all-

American forward, received the ball after springing free behind a screen and launched a prayer from about eighteen feet out. Well, the ball swished through the net. After a moment when time seemed to stand still, the reality of the defeat became too much to bear.

SONNY SMITH: *Charles hated losing, absolutely hated it. When we lost the SEC championship in Nashville, he just sat on the floor at the other end of the arena and cried. He sat there for five minutes and cried like a baby. I'd never seen anything like that before.*

The pain of that defeat was eased somewhat when it was announced that the team had qualified for the 1984 NCAA tournament, marking the first time Auburn had ever reached the NCAAs. But we didn't handle our newfound glory very well. We were upset in the first round by the University of Richmond, an unheralded team that had beaten Rider in a preliminary-round game but was largely not well respected. We didn't really know a single thing about Richmond until we stepped on the court at the coliseum in Charlotte, North Carolina. That's when we found out that they were called the Spiders, which was a pretty good description of a bunch of guys who were all over us like pests for the entire game.

It wasn't long after tip-off that we discovered that we had been too overconfident. We took Richmond too lightly, didn't prepare for them at all. Nobody read the scouting reports. Instead, we were looking forward to playing Indiana in the next round. Richmond? They were just a rest stop.

None of us had even heard of any of their players; the Richmond center was a 6'9" stiff named Bill Flye. When I first saw him, I laughed. Before long, though, their best player was lighting us up. It was Johnny Newman, a skinny small forward who later played in the NBA for Cleveland and the Knicks before signing with the Charlotte Hornets as a free agent before the 1990–91 season. Johnny was their leading scorer before intermission, at which time we were stunned, trailing 39–22. We came to our senses and woke up after halftime, but we still lost the game, 72–71. Johnny ended up with a game-high 26 points.

JOHNNY NEWMAN: *For some reason, they played zone against us when all we had were jump shooters. On top of that, Charles was lazy. When the ball would come to his side, he wouldn't step out and cover the man. So that became our strategy, and I was open all night. Later, we heard that they had been looking ahead to playing Indiana in the second round. I hope they got to watch it on TV.*

SONNY SMITH: *Charles had an unbelievable second half against Richmond, but he didn't play at all in the first half because the other center was so bad. He couldn't get himself motivated. All told, we didn't know how to handle the NCAA tournament. I didn't know what we had to do to prepare for the pressure. We could have been the darlings of the tournament, too. The Eastern press came to our practice in masses, and they ate us up: Charles and Chuck had me down on the floor, calling me Sonny and having a great time. We were a real story. Then we go out and get beat. You know, I turned Johnny Newman down when he tried to get me to recruit him. He was working one summer for a veterinarian in Auburn when he asked me for a chance to come play for me. I wouldn't take him. I'm still kicking myself.*

I think that if I had another chance to coach Charles Barkley, I wouldn't promote him as a fat kid. I would try to be more in touch with him personally, more of a friend.

A lot of the players, including myself, took the loss hard. We thought we had blown our chance for national recognition, botched it completely. I cried afterward, but not because we lost the game. I cried because I was thinking about how much money the loss had cost me.

In my heart I started to think that I had played my last game for Auburn. I didn't want to take any more chances with my body, which was already beginning to show signs of wear. I had averaged 15.1 points, 9.4 rebounds, and shot .638 from the floor as a junior. I was no longer a secret. Every major publication in the country, including *Sports Illustrated,* had sent reporters to Auburn that year to watch me play. No question, it was time.

I was going to the NBA.

On top of all that, I'd had enough of Auburn.

During my final season, Chuck and I hardly talked to each other, not even on the court. Sometimes we wouldn't even pass the ball to each other. Ultimately, our pettiness was probably a factor in our loss to Richmond, but by then Chuck and I absolutely despised each other, and it was tough to put those feelings aside when the pressure was on in a tight game. In the locker room after the Richmond loss, he and I didn't even look at each other. The entire team, including the coaching staff, was in shock over the loss. Our entire season, once so successful, was suddenly wasted.

Looking around the room at the sad and stunned faces, I started to believe that my college career was over. Something inside of me knew that when I took off my Auburn uniform that afternoon in Charlotte, it was for the last time.

5

MOSES AND DOC: THE WONDER YEARS

LEADERSHIP is the most overblown, overemphasized, overdiscussed characteristic in sports. Unfortunately, it's also the yardstick by which the best athletes in the world are measured at some point in their careers.

I'm no exception.

Ever since Julius Erving retired from the NBA at the end of the 1986–87 season, my capabilities as a leader have been examined, questioned, analyzed, and debated more than Philadelphia's considerable budget deficit. I've always had one simple rule when it comes to being a leader: from the opening tap until the final buzzer, a leader must play with the same enthusiasm, effort, intensity, and intelligence that he expects from each of his teammates. It's that simple. Nothing more. But there have been times when my critics talked like I spent my first three seasons in the league with my head tucked between my legs.

Wrong. I was observing, listening to, and learning from two of the NBA's most effective leaders ever—Moses Malone, who was traded after my second season, and Julius Erving.

Doc was a legitimate leader by almost anyone's definition. He played hard, avoided controversy, and was always popular with the public. On the court, he led by example; other players could only hope to command a game like Julius Erving.

But to place him on a pedestal as one of the greatest sports leaders of all time is wrong. Doc was no more of a leader for the Philadelphia 76ers than Moses, Maurice Cheeks, or Bobby Jones. Behind closed doors, he was quiet, not inspirational. At times, he was even aloof.

One of the fellas?

Never.

During our three seasons together, I never saw Doc do anything that people describe as a "leadership" trait, nothing other than the fact that he played hard every single night. He didn't make speeches. He didn't try to encourage slumping teammates. He didn't talk to the head coach—Billy Cunningham during the first two seasons, then Matt Guokas—on behalf of players who were on the coach's shit list.

He wasn't Mr. Inspiration. He was simply Julius Erving.

What the public saw of Julius on the court—the all-business, charismatic Dahk-tah, Julius *Errrrrr-ving*, as the 76ers' late, great public address announcer Dave Zinkoff used to call him— was pretty much the person that he allowed his teammates to see. Nothing more. To us, there is no other side to Julius Erving. He was Dr. J on the court and Dr. J in the locker room. He gave his best effort every night, and he expected us to do the same.

The public never expected anything more from Doc.

Why?

Because we were winning. The Sixers won an average of 52 games each season in the three years I shared with Doc. Our best playoff performance was when I was a rookie in 1984–85 and we reached the Eastern Conference finals before losing to the Celtics four games to one. During my last three seasons, through 1990–91, the Sixers won an average of 48 games each year, and we reached the conference semis twice, in 1989–90 and 1990–91. Does the difference in those two periods mean that Julius Erving was a better leader than Charles Barkley? In a word, no.

Say what you will about my attitude, my mouth, anything else. I've always played hard, and I try my best to win. I dare anyone to argue with me about that. But what I constantly hear in Philadelphia is that I'm not the leader Julius Erving was. Look, I played with Doc and I was there in the locker room with him night after night. Believe me when I tell you that Julius's leadership consisted of going out and playing hard night after night—nothing more. Is there anyone out there who thinks I don't do that, too?

I'm not saying that what Julius did isn't leadership. It is. But I'm offended when I hear people say that I'm not a leader, and then those same people kiss Julius's feet for having done nothing more than what I do every night. Julius was a leader, but if you want to talk about the kind of intangible, off-court leadership that brings a team together and inspires you to play your best, the true leader of that Sixers team, the best one I ever played with was Moses Malone.

During our two seasons together—my first two seasons in the league—Moses filled a gap in my life that had burdened me since my father abandoned my family. From the moment Moses called me fathead during the summer before my rookie season through June 16, 1986, the day he was traded to the Washington Bullets—one of the saddest days of my life—Moses was always there for me. He was there with advice, a joke to calm my moods, or a simple pat on the back to ease my frustrations. And he was there to listen to me when I needed to discuss my problems. Or more exactly, to discuss my *problem:* Billy Cunningham.

As a coach, Billy C. was pretty much like he was supposed to have been as a player—competitive, hardworking, and intense. I loved playing for him, but I also hated the way he treated me: like shit.

Billy knew that he could intimidate his players. He was Billy Cunningham, the Legend, while I was Charles Barkley, the Rookie. He used that against me at every opportunity. He told me I never worked hard enough. He told me I played like I thought I was still in college. He cursed. He fumed. He stomped his foot like a madman. He was on my ass so much it drove me mad.

During practices or games, if I made a mistake, Billy was on my ass before I knew anything was wrong. But if Doc committed the very same mistake, Billy wouldn't say a word. All of a sudden, Billy C. was Ray C.—Ray Charles. When I screwed up, it was World War III. I'm talking everyday harassment so constant that

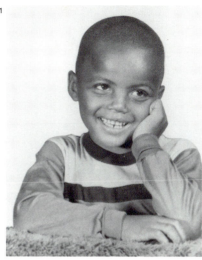

Here I am at age four—how's that for a winning smile?

The same smile, years later, on prom night.

Going up strong for Leeds
High School.

4

With my family: my grand-
mother Johnny Mae Edwards,
my brother John, my mother,
me, and my brother Darryl.

3

This is the kind of crap I put up with to get some ink for our program; this charming photograph ran in *Sports Illustrated*.

With coach Sonny Smith at Auburn; he's probably yelling at me, as usual.

6

5

As you can see here, I may
have been heavier than
Coach Knight wanted me to
be at the Olympic Trials,
but that didn't keep me
from dominating play all
over the court.

Under the boards with my
mentor and friend,
Moses Malone.

Me and Doc—some people in
Philly still won't forgive me for
overshadowing him.

11   Exchanging views in a friendly debate with my old buddy, Bill Laimbeer.

Me and Michael; I'm probably telling him how I'm going to shut his ass down.

Bumping with my favorite teammate—oops, ex-teammate —Rick Mahorn.

Me and
Maureen in
1989.

14

Me with the light of my life, my baby Christiana.

15

I began to hear Billy stomping his foot and screaming my name in my sleep.

I might have been able to swallow the abuse if Billy had balanced it with at least a little public praise, but during the first few weeks of my rookie season the closest he came to offering me a public compliment came in December when he described me to a reporter as "a big kid having a good time."

"When he realizes it's a little bit more of a job, yes, he could be a monster talent," Billy said. "But I'm not going to let up on him until he progresses to the point where . . . well, there's so much that he already does and so much more that he is capable of doing that if he ever gets the determination of a Moses Malone or a Julius Erving or a Bobby Jones . . ."

BILLY CUNNINGHAM: *This team was so talented that it wasn't going to embarrass itself and lose a lot of games. But we could all see that if we were going to do anything in the playoffs that year, Charles was going to be a very important part of it. When you're lucky enough to coach a team like that, you have short-range and long-range goals. Our long-range goal was to hope that Charles would come around and do the things we needed in order for us to win a championship. That's why I was on him day and night. Actually, I got tired of yelling at him. I know that Andrew Toney was glad that Charles was there because all of a sudden I wasn't yelling at Andrew anymore.*

When Charles's career is over, maybe he'll understand why I treated him the way I did, but when a coach sees a player that has a great deal of talent, it's his job to get the player to reach his potential. And Charles was the type of player you had to stay on during practices, games, anytime, in order to make sure that he was running, getting back on defense, all of the little things necessary to succeed. I was trying to get him to develop good habits. A lot of it depends on a player's personality. You've got to embrace some guys, like Maurice Cheeks.

Charles you had to hit over the head with a two-by-four.

Like any rookie, I was eager to please my coach. But like any rookie, I was also insecure. I wasn't "the man" anymore. I was just another player, and Billy's constant insults only caused me to become gun-shy and even begin to doubt my skills. Without Moses I would never have survived that season. When everyone else was more concerned with going their own way, as was usually the case on our mostly veteran team, Moses always had something kind to say to me.

That's real leadership. It was Moses, not Doc, who encouraged me to hang in there when I became so frustrated that I didn't want to come to practice.

It was Moses, not Doc, who somehow convinced me that Billy only wanted me to become the best player I could be, even though he had a funny way of showing it—by keeping me on the bench.

I quickly became a pawn in what may have been the beginning of the power struggle between Billy and the team's owner, Harold Katz, that eventually led to Billy's resignation at the end of my rookie season. During training camp, Harold told Billy that he wanted me to play a lot of minutes. He even wanted me to start. But Billy didn't start rookies, period. So for the first ten games of the season, the Sixers starting lineup included four All-Stars—Moses, Doc, Maurice Cheeks, and Andrew Toney—and Marc Iavaroni, a mediocre third-year 6'10" forward who had averaged only about 4 rebounds a game.

Harold is the type of owner who considers himself to be a basketball expert. His qualifications? Four years of high school basketball, and many years as a Sixers season-ticket holder. He's always treated his coaches well, but he makes it clear that he's the boss, not them. It's his team, and he can do what he wants.

That became apparent from the outset when he didn't let up against Billy. He came into the locker room before and after games and got into heated discussions with Billy behind the closed door to the training room. I knew they were talking about me because Harold would always tell me he was fighting for me, that he was on my side, and that everything would eventually be all right.

Still, I was frustrated. It seemed like Billy didn't have any confidence in me. During the first couple of weeks of the season, I didn't believe that I necessarily deserved to start because I was usually nervous in games and I committed too many stupid fouls. But I thought I should have been playing more minutes, and after a couple of weeks when I finally got rid of the jitters, I knew I should be starting. Even Doc stunned me by telling reporters, "We need Barkley if we're going to win the title."

Billy was stubborn, though, and he stayed on my ass. He even called me lazy. That was my breaking point. In an instant, I went from being frustrated to plain pissed off.

CUNNINGHAM: *We knew Charles was a gifted player, but with the type of kid he was, I didn't want to start him early in the season because I didn't want him to feel as if he had achieved his goals. I always wanted him to push himself. He deserved to start, but he was just a kid. I had the feeling that if I started him, it wouldn't help him to have a long, successful future in the NBA. For that, I thought he needed to push himself.*

Soon, Billy made sure everyone knew just who ran the team by replacing Iavaroni in the starting lineup with someone named Sam Williams, a guy who was so far on the end of our bench that he almost had to pay for his seat. Sam started for five games and accomplished absolutely nothing—other than to prove that I should've been the team's starting power forward.

Finally, after a few nights of this farce, Billy walked up to me just as we were about to tip off against Washington and said, "If you play well tonight, you'll start the next game."

That was all I needed to hear. I was a madman that night. By the end of the evening, Billy knew that he had no other choice than to change his starting lineup. A few days later, on November 30, 1984, I started my first game in the NBA. The Portland Trail Blazers were the lucky losers as I finished with 16 points and 13 rebounds in 32 minutes.

Even though Harold had made his point and won the battle, he couldn't resist the chance to submarine Billy two weeks later. He traded Iavaroni to the San Antonio Spurs for a third-round draft choice. It was basically a charitable donation, a gift to the Spurs; the real purpose of the trade was to let Billy know who ran the team.

After I became a starter, my rookie year was pretty uneventful off the court. I was pretty quiet, and a little reluctant to express myself to outsiders, especially reporters. On the court, I was my old expressive self, the person my mama always told me to be.

"Let your emotions out," she said. "Don't be repressed." The basketball court was the only place where I was comfortable.

Otherwise, I was a typical rookie. There were two of us on the team and each of us was assigned to serve one of the veterans. Andrew was toughest on his rookie, Leon Wood. During training camp, he made Leon bring him warm milk every night and a newspaper every morning. He also sometimes made his rookie do 500 sit-ups and push-ups before he could go to bed. I always thanked God I hadn't been Andrew's rookie.

Julius's rookie during camp was Butch Graves, a graduate of Yale whose father, Earl Graves, is the publisher of *Black Enterprise* magazine. He had to fetch Julius a morning newspaper.

Moses was my boss. I had to carry his bags and get him drinks whenever he wanted it, whether it was at a club or in the middle of the night. Actually, I was luckier than the other rookies. Moses didn't have much of a thirst.

In later years, I never really worried about having a rookie. If I need something, like a soda during practice, I'll just pick a random rookie and ask him to fetch it for me. But generally, I'm pretty soft on them. I carry my own luggage, get my own newspapers. Andrew probably thinks I'm a wimp.

Besides Julius and Moses, my first Sixers team was composed of individuals who were so different from their teammates that I often wondered how we kept from killing each other. It wasn't that we didn't like each other; we got along really well. It's just that when so many different personalities are forced to smell each other's dirty jockstraps for more than seven months, well, it can get real foul—unless everyone is focused on the same goal: winning. These were the principals:

Bobby Jones: He was the ultimate man. If you wanted to create the perfect man, he'd be Bobby Jones. He was an extremely religious man who took his faith seriously without waving it around like a phony, and he never did anything wrong, on or off the court.

I didn't think anyone in the NBA could survive an entire day without using at least one word of profanity. Forget an entire season. But somehow, Bobby managed to live profanity-free. He was the closest thing to a saint someone can be and still play

professional sports. No one was ever concerned about using offensive language, unless Bobby was in the room. Anyone who
cursed around Bobby felt like shit.

On the court, Bobby was just the consummate pro. He worked
hard and never complained. Some of our veteran players didn't
practice often, but Bobby practiced every single day, no matter
how bad he felt. He changed my attitude about practice more
than anything Sonny Smith or Billy Cunningham ever said to
me.

Bobby was also the type of teammate who was approachable
and always willing to offer great advice. But only if asked. His
most important advice to me was simple: work hard and stay out
of trouble.

One out of two isn't so bad.

Maurice Cheeks: I never understood the importance of playing
with an intelligent point guard until I played with Maurice
Cheeks. I'd played with a couple of decent point guards in college—Byron Henson and Paul Daniels, neither of whom ever
played in the NBA—but from the day Maurice arrived at training
camp, playing with him was an unbelievably different experience. He has a sixth sense for the game, an intelligence that
allows him to make the game easier for anyone who shares the
floor with him.

He knows exactly how to pass the basketball to you so that
you don't have to travel or take any awkward steps to complete
the play.

He knows when to give his teammates the ball, whether far
from the basket or in the lane, depending upon your ball-
handling ability.

And he knows where they like to catch it, at the chest or above
the shoulders.

Maurice made me understand the science of the game, the
angles and spaces that can determine whether a play succeeds
or fails. Playing with him made basketball an extremely simple
game. That's why I believe that among all of my former and
current teammates, he was the very best player I ever played
with. He was the most important player the Sixers ever had;
without him, Julius and Moses would never have gotten their
championship rings. For that reason alone, Maurice deserves to

finish his career in Philadelphia, something that, barring a dramatic trade in the next couple of years, just won't happen.

On August 28, 1989, Maurice was sent to the Spurs in a five-player trade that brought us point guard Johnny Dawkins. At the time, Johnny was a three-year veteran from Duke whose most important quality, as far as the Sixers were concerned, was that he was seven years younger than Maurice.

Any player can be traded—especially if he plays for the Sixers—but Maurice deserved to be treated better than he was on the day he was sent out of town. He learned about the trade from a television reporter who stopped Maurice in his driveway and asked him how he felt about leaving Philadelphia after eleven seasons in the city. No one from the team had called him. (Something that would become a pattern in other deals, particularly those involving Mike Gminski and Rick Mahorn, two of my best friends on the team.) The camera was rolling. Maurice was stunned. When I saw the report on the news that night, I could see the hurt in his face, the shock of it all. Maurice was never a very good poker player. As I watched the screen, I cried for him.

Philadelphians never really got to know Maurice. He wasn't comfortable talking with outsiders, especially the media. But during our five seasons together he and I often had conversations that lasted well into the morning after games. We were especially close during his last two seasons in Philadelphia, the two worst seasons in his time with the Sixers. The 1987–88 season, my fourth year in the league, was a real disaster. Our starting center, Tim McCormick, was only an ordinary player; our coach, Matt Guokas, was fired halfway into his third season; the team won only 36 games and we didn't make the playoffs, the only time that's happened since I came to Philadelphia.

It was a painful season for all of us, but especially for Maurice, one of the team's last links to its 1983 championship, along with reserve center Mark McNamara and Andrew, who suffered through the final stages of foot injuries and was forced to retire at the end of the year. Though it might be tough to believe, considering how quiet Maurice was in public, he did most of the talking during our late-night conversations.

He was philosophical; he always liked to talk about life, about how most professional athletes never appreciate the good we experience until it's gone.

He talked about the team's good old days, about how it felt to play great every time the team stepped on the court. We used to vow that we would help the Sixers regain that feeling. But before we got the chance, the best teammate I ever had was gone.

Andrew Toney: Maurice was the best player I ever had for a teammate, but Andrew had more pure talent than anyone. Actually, he was the best teammate I *never* had.

It didn't take me long to realize that he was clearly the most talented player on the team. Forget Julius, Moses, Bobby Jones, and even Maurice. Andrew Toney was in a class by himself. By the end of the opening practice at training camp, I was stunned by his skills. That night I even called my brother back home in Leeds and told him, "I'm playing with Doc, I'm playing with Moses, I'm playing with Maurice, I'm playing with Bobby Jones, but I can't believe how good Andrew Toney is!"

He was only 6'3" and weighed about 185 pounds, most of it in his upper body. Andrew was so strong physically and, more importantly, mentally that he felt he could score on anybody, anywhere, and at any time. That feeling of invincibility was the source of his strength. He also had the most dynamic jump shot I've ever seen.

All told, Andrew Toney was as close to unstoppable as any player in the league. No guard was strong enough to handle him down in the low post close to the basket, where he played like a power forward. During scrimmages at practice, he often tried to post up Moses and even me! Andrew wasn't afraid of anybody.

It was a shame that his career ended like it did, painfully slow and without much dignity. Andrew limped through twenty-nine games in 1987–88 before the pain in his feet became too much to bear. When he played his last game for us, he was still so young, just thirty years old. That was three years after he had first complained that his feet—his "dogs," as he called them— were hurting. None of the players had believed it, though, because the doctors he went to said they couldn't find any evidence of an injury that would keep him out of the game.

Management thought Andrew was faking, trying to get a new contract, and they managed to pretty much turn the whole team against him. We were struggling and we needed his production. Meanwhile, the only reports we were reading in the newspapers said, "Tests Prove Negative."

The feud between Andrew and the team grew nasty, and it began to have a negative effect on all of us. Andrew didn't help himself with his demeanor. He had always kept his problems to himself, and he only became more reclusive when his teammates doubted him. All he ever said to us was, "I'm going to the doctor." Again and again, that was all we heard.

As a result, nobody believed Andrew was really injured. He had played in seventy games in 1984–85; that was the fewest games of any season in his career to that point, but it was also more than someone who was supposed to have stress fractures in both of his feet. I certainly didn't believe him because I didn't think anybody could play with that kind of pain. (I later found out for myself about what the human body can endure when I played the last week of the 1990–91 season, and the playoffs, after suffering torn ligaments in my knee and a stress fracture in my ankle.) He wasn't the same Andrew, though. A 53 percent shooter the previous season, he fell to just 49 percent that year.

During the following season, Andrew's feud with the team came to a head. He played in only six games, but because the team didn't think he was injured, he was forced to sit on the bench in uniform for most of the season. Having him there while we were out there bustin' our butts made the tension between us even worse. The players talked about Andrew behind his back. We questioned his integrity, which is about the lowest kind of criticism one athlete can level at another athlete.

All the while, Andrew never said anything, except that he was hurting.

He returned the following season and struggled through the first two months of the year. He played in sixteen of the team's first thirty-one games before the pain again became too much. He went on the injured list and remained there for five games until the end of January.

By then, the Sixers had signed another guard, World B. Free, the onetime all-star who had changed his name from Lloyd because, he said, his friends on the playgrounds back home in Brooklyn called him All-World. Give me a damn break. Free had always been an explosive scorer, but by the time he got to Philadelphia he was light-years past his prime and damn near ready for retirement. He lasted only twenty games for us, about twenty games too long.

Part of the Sixers' motivation in signing Free, I think, was to inspire Andrew into a comeback. It worked. Andrew limped through fifty-two games, scoring only about 10 points a night, something he could probably have done with two broken legs.

For a while, though, he was almost the Andrew of old. During his first four games, he was shooting the ball with confidence again and passing it to us for easy scores. Andrew scored 61 points and had 18 assists in those games. For a moment, we thought he was on his way back.

One night, though, I finally learned the truth about Andrew's pain. We were sitting next to each other on the bench when I accidentally bumped into one of his feet. I hardly noticed it, but Andrew winced. Then I looked into his eyes, and I saw that he was crying. From the pain. That's when I knew it was over for him.

I also learned something else that night. I learned that when a true professional athlete says he's hurting, then he's hurting. I learned that doctors don't know everything; they're not infallible.

In Andrew's case they simply screwed up. But so did Katz. And so did the players. All of us were wrong. When we found out that he had really been hurt, everybody went crazy. We thought we had been conned by management. I felt guilty for a long time. One of the saddest aspects of my career will always be that I never really got the chance to play with a healthy Andrew Toney. He was the best.

ALTHOUGH, AS A rookie, I was surrounded by all that talent, I was still closely scrutinized by the Philadelphia media and the fans. Everyone had an opinion on what might be called the Barkley Questions: Is he too fat? Should he start? Is he the best player on the team?

All in all, my performances were respectable. I averaged 14 points that season, along with almost 9 rebounds in just 28.6 minutes a night. I wasn't the dominating player I wanted to be, but I was contributing, and the team was winning. A lot. In fact, the Sixers played much of that season in cruise control.

Our problem was that we were too good. With Moses in the middle between Doc and myself, Maurice and Andrew—even a one-legged Andrew—in the backcourt, and Bobby coming off the bench, we believed we were going to win every game no matter how we played. We knew we could win most games even if we showed up during the national anthem and played the first half in our street clothes. So almost every single night, we screwed around for the first three quarters then won the game in the fourth quarter.

Our inconsistent efforts didn't cost us—we were 58–24 that year—until the Eastern Conference finals when, after beating the Washington Bullets 3–1 in the first round and crushing Milwaukee 4–0 in the conference semis, we went to Boston for a date with the Celtics. That series turned out to be my coming-out party, even though Billy sent me back to the bench before game one, replacing me in the starting lineup with Bobby Jones.

CUNNINGHAM: *By the end of the year, Charles was a pretty important part of the team. There was no question about that, but to expect a rookie to start against that Boston team was crazy. Remember that their frontline guys—Kevin McHale, Robert Parish, and Larry Bird—were all in their prime, and Charles was a kid who was still learning how to play the game, how to use quickness and strength to his advantage. He would have had major problems.*

Or so everybody thought.

The Celtics were the league's defending champions. Most importantly, they were the 76ers' biggest rivals. We hated the Celtics, something I discovered just before we left the locker room for a preseason game against Boston that first year. Doc never showed any emotion in the locker room, but at that moment, he changed. He went from being The Doctor to being Mr. Hyde. His entire attitude changed. He started to fume. He scowled. He started talking about how we just *were not going to lose to these guys!* I was shocked. I didn't want to go near Doc. I was already freaked over playing the Celtics for the first time. I didn't show it outwardly, but on the inside I was thinking, *Oh, my God, I'm about to play against Larry Bird!*

After Doc's outburst, I went to the bathroom.

In the playoffs, the Celtics were clearly a better team than we were. They finished the regular season with the league's second-best record, and they had beaten us three times in six games that season, with each team winning on its home court. They didn't miss a beat in the series either, beating our butts in the first three games, the third loss coming by 11 points at The Spectrum. It was an embarrassment.

I scored 23 points in game three, which was a lot of points for me then because I hadn't yet started to think of myself as a scorer. Not on a team with Doc, Moses, and Andrew, three of the greatest scorers in the history of the game. Instead, my forte was rebounding, and that night I grabbed 11 boards. In effect, I was delivering a statement: *Hello, Larry. My name is Charles. I'm gonna be your worst nightmare for a while. For about ten years.*

In the locker room after game three, I got the sense that my teammates were resigned to losing the series. No team in league history had ever come back after losing the first three games of a playoff series, and nothing I saw in that locker room gave me any indication that the 1984–85 Sixers were going to be the first. At the same time, though, I felt that there was no way we would get swept in front of our home fans. That would have been too much to stomach. No one in the locker room said anything about it, but in those moments after game three I finally felt, for the first time all season, that my teammates were mad.

It wasn't a cure-all, but it worked for one game. Billy started me in game four and I played like a wild man. Besides my 20 boards, I had 15 points and 3 steals, most of it against Kevin McHale, the Celtics' long-armed forward who was in his fifth NBA season out of the University of Minnesota. At 6'10", Kevin is six inches taller than I am, but his long arms make him seem at least another six inches taller. During warm-ups for games against the Celtics, we used to tease Kevin, telling him that with his broad shoulders, long arms, and square head he should have bolts in his neck. It was all in fun.

I've always respected Kevin. In fact, until someone comes along and proves otherwise, I'll always believe that Kevin McHale is the best player I've ever played against. He's smart, and he knows all of my moves. I counter him with my quickness, but I also have to be more focused against him than any other player in the league. Kevin is the reason why I've always played well against the Celtics. He's one of the few individual challenges that becomes as important as the game itself. Throughout my career, I've known that if I've kicked Kevin's butt, we've probably kicked the Celtics', too.

The Sixers won game four pretty easily, 115–104, but we lost the series four games to one, losing a tight game three days later in Boston, 102–100.

The series marked a significant moment for the Sixers. After eight seasons, Billy Cunningham retired from coaching with a record of 454–196, one of the best winning percentages in league history. He had won two NBA championships with the Sixers— as a player in 1967 and as a coach in 1983.

The series also marked the beginning of the end of another era for the Sixers, for when it ended everybody on the team knew that Doc was no longer the team's best player. Even Doc knew.

I was.

CUNNINGHAM: *Basketball is a very easy game for Charles. If he could shoot the jumper consistently, he's Michael Jordan. In 1987, I saw Sonny Smith at the Final Four in New Orleans. He told me, "God, you did a great job coaching Charles. How do I know? Because he hates you."*

I always respected Doc, but he was simply different from the rest of us. I sensed that even before I arrived at my first training camp. I was never concerned about whether or not I'd be able to compete in the NBA. I knew I had talent. But I lay awake at night worrying about what I would say when I first met Julius Erving. No way I was going to call him Julius. That wasn't even an option. Back home in Leeds, I was always taught to refer to my elders as Mr. or Mrs., and Julius was definitely an elder. Even so, I thought that "Mr. Erving" would be too formal for a teammate, and "Doc" was too familiar, too casual, too disrespectful. This was heavy stuff for a kid from Alabama who wanted to get off on the right foot with the most important player on the team, and it turned me into a total wreck.

Fortunately, Julius made it easy on me. As we were getting dressed in the locker room prior to my first practice, I looked up from tying my shoes and there he was reaching out to shake my hand. "Hi," he said, "I'm Doc."

I was never more relieved in my life.

Julius and Moses were completely different individuals whose opposite personalities gave the Sixers the kind of emotional balance that every NBA team needs in order to survive an entire NBA season.

Moses was never serious; he was the team comedian, the practical joker. Whenever things got tense, Moses would do something completely crazy, something that reminded us that basketball was only a game.

Doc, on the other hand, was always calm and unemotional. He never lost the cool that was at the heart of his image.

Well, almost never.

Hardly anyone will ever forget the night of November 9, 1984, just a few days into my rookie season, when Julius Erving and Larry Bird became the unlikeliest main event for Fight Night in the NBA.

By the middle of the third quarter that evening, everyone knew that something was going to happen on the floor because you could have cut the intensity inside Boston Garden with a dull knife—and it was all coming from Doc and Larry. They were going at each other like enemies on the playground, like none of the rest of us were even on the court. And Larry was kicking Doc's ass.

Bird was on a roll, scoring from everywhere and talking big trash all at the same time. I respect Larry as much as I've respected any player, but in his prime he was the biggest shit-talking guy in the league. That night, he and Doc were having verbal warfare:

"Take that!" Doc would say, even though he was struggling.

"There's one for you!" Larry shot back.

But Larry was the only one who was on fire. He scored 42 points, mostly against Doc, who managed just 6 points in return. Bird hit 17 of his 23 shots, grabbed 7 rebounds, and had 3 assists as the Celtics built a 20-point lead, 95–75, and the Garden went wild.

At the time, I didn't really know what happened to spark the fight because it happened so quickly and I wasn't looking in their direction. It didn't help that referee Dick Bavetta worked most of the game alone because his partner, Jack Madden, had suffered a knee injury in the first half and couldn't continue. I do remember Bavetta calling Larry for an offensive foul when he elbowed Doc as he tried to take a shot. Moments later, as the two guys crossed midcourt, Larry elbowed Doc again, and that was it.

I turned around and saw Larry and Doc staring at each other face-to-face. Suddenly they started swinging and had each other around the throat. I was standing behind Larry, so I just reacted and grabbed him around the chest. I actually went in there to help break it up. But while Moses and I held Bird, Doc flailed away on him. He must have punched Larry three or four times while I was holding him, even though that's not what I intended to happen.

When I found out a few days later that I was going to be fined $1,000 by the league for fighting, I tried to explain that I had just wanted to break up the fight. But someone showed me a tape. It was nasty, even worse than I had remembered. I really hadn't seen any of the punches Doc threw until I watched the replay. Doc just pounded Bird while I had my arms around Larry's shoulders, holding him for an easy target. I sat there watching.

"Oh, man, this does look bad," I said.

After a while, I almost laughed; Doc was throwing some pretty good combinations.

Both players were ejected, of course. And for the remainder of the game there was an eerie feeling in the Garden. Everyone seemed stunned. People were in shock that Larry and Doc had gotten into something so beneath them as a fight, and it was strange to be playing without either one of them out on the floor.

The Celtics eventually won, 130–119, but no one seemed to care.

Over in the Boston locker room, Cedric (Cornbread) Maxwell joked that neither player should have been thrown out because "neither one of them could bust a grapefruit."

Down the hall in our locker room, Doc was out of it. He was sitting in front of the hook where his clothes still hung. It had been a long time since the ejection, but he was still dressed in his uniform. He was subdued, saying nothing. He wasn't embarrassed about what he had done. Every player in the league realizes that at some time or another they'll probably get into a situation where they've just got to fight. I think he was simply shocked because *The Doctor wasn't supposed to fight.*

Julius took it in stride. He was, after all, a competitor who knew the risks of intense competition.

But Doc? He was ashamed.

Doc never wanted any controversy in his life. So, he always tried to just roll with the punches—expect when they were thrown by Bird. If a reporter asked him a question that he either couldn't answer or didn't want to answer, he would smile and say, "I don't think I'll answer that."

Can you imagine me doing that? I'd get crucified by the media in Philadelphia. But Doc was able to get away with it because no reporter anywhere in the country, especially the ones who worked for the Philadelphia media, wanted to piss him off. Doc *was* Philadelphia. Hell, Doc was the NBA.

WHEN I JOINED the Sixers, the scoring responsibilities belonged to Julius and Moses. Andrew was the third option in Billy's pecking order, followed by Maurice. I pulled up the rear, which was fine by me because throughout my basketball career I had never really wanted to score a lot of points. When I came to the NBA, I envisioned myself averaging 10 points and 10 rebounds for my career. That was my goal.

But that slowly began to change after my rookie season. I averaged 14 points a game that first year, about what I had averaged at Auburn. That was more than enough to satisfy my taste for scoring. I had gotten to the NBA because of my rebounding, and that was all I was concerned about. Even as a rookie, I realized I could dominate the glass at the NBA level as much as I did in college. I finished the season averaging about 9 rebounds a game, and there were some nights when I'd get well into the teens, monster nights. I wasn't playing a lot, either, less than 29 minutes per night, well below the 38.0 minutes I would average during the next five seasons of my career through 1990–91. But what I had found in the NBA was freedom from the zones that clogged up the floor in college.

In the pros there was room to roam. And because I was always one of the quickest guys on the floor, I could get to open spots underneath the basket before anybody could block me out. For me, the NBA was basketball made in heaven.

Scoring was gravy, which is why I was stunned at my second training camp when Matty, in his new role as head coach, asked me to score more than 20 points per game in a new offensive scheme that was more structured. He wanted me to change my game and I wasn't very happy about it. As a rookie, I had gotten at least 6 points a game off the offensive glass, all because under Billy I had been able to roam. Players who are called upon to handle most of the scoring for their teams usually have to stay within the offense—meaning they had to stay in specific parts of the floor like chess pieces until their play was called. Billy didn't give a damn where I was, as long as I was out of the way. Under Matty, all that would change, but not smoothly.

I had never been a good outside shooter, and that caused us some problems. Doc and I were both in the starting lineup, but neither one of us could shoot very well from outside, which meant that we were easy prey for defenses. All anyone had to do against us was sag into the middle and cover Moses and watch me and Doc bang away from the perimeter. Add to that the fact that Andrew was hurt and pretty much useless, and that Maurice *wouldn't* shoot unless it was an absolute emergency, and well, we were fucked.

I was basically lost and angry. I didn't think it was fair to ask someone—me—who had been just an average scorer to become one of the team's leading scorers, especially when I only knew how to score inside. The points I got were hard points because

I was always posting against guys who were taller and heavier than I was. But most of the time, I was hesitating, thinking too much. *When do I shoot? Do I shoot now? From here? Over there?*

It was a frustrating but gradual learning process that would eventually allow me to explode offensively. But mostly I fell on my face, which was all the more frustrating because, suddenly, people in Philadelphia expected me to play well every night.

Slowly, I began to get a new feel for the game. I developed my outside shot and became more confident in my ability to score against anyone. By the end of the season, I felt I was ready to handle the new responsibilities—even if Doc wasn't completely ready to give them up.

Some of my first contentious moments came during this season. Early in the year, Matty fined me for getting ejected two minutes into a game against Atlanta. (He didn't fine himself, though, for getting a technical in the very same game.) We lost the game and he was right: I couldn't help the team if I was in the locker room. Since then, I've never intentionally tried to get thrown out of a game, although my best intentions haven't always worked.

Then, midway through the season, I turned down an invitation to participate in the league's slam-dunk contest during the All-Star break. Reporters around the country ripped me for being arrogant, but I didn't care. I was exhausted. I had already played a full college season and I needed a break. By the end of the season, I had earned 23 technical fouls, a clear indication that my career was in full swing.

But I truly believe that a lot of my troubles in Philadelphia began because during my second season some of the reporters covering the Sixers resented my success, as well as my emergence as the team's new star. It was as if they wanted the spotlight to continue to fall on Doc because he was close to retirement. They still wanted the Sixers to be "Doc's team."

Anything but "Charles's team."

That may have been why I was criticized for an incident that only highlighted the primary difference between myself and Doc. We had started the season slowly, winning only half of our first ten games. I decided that we needed to hold a team meeting.

Actually, I only suggested the meeting to the players and they all agreed that we needed it, including Doc. "We're playing like shit," I told Doc. "We need to talk."

Doc paused for a moment. Finally he responded, "Maybe that's a good idea."

Well, when the local media found out that I had called the meeting, they went crazy. A columnist at the *Philadelphia Daily News* wrote, "Who does this young fella think he is? This is Doc's team. Not Charles Barkley's."

I had asked Doc to lead the session because I didn't want to infringe upon his turf. But just before it began, I looked up and saw Doc walking toward me from the other side of the locker room. I didn't know what he was going to say. I thought he was going to tell me to shut up and not say a word. Instead, he shocked me. "You handle it," he said. "I know you can."

I told everybody that there had been problems, and that the only way to change things was for everyone to say what they had to say. I went around to everybody in the room and asked them to say what was on their mind. There was a lot of complaining, mostly about how some of the starters were cruising through the games like they were bored, not giving a full effort. Not everybody was happy about what was said, but the meeting turned out to be the ultimate cure, and in the end, I was vindicated because we went on a 9-game winning streak to give the team a 20–12 record. After that, I didn't hear anything about the "young fella" anymore.

By the end of the regular season, the Sixers' new order was clear. Moses was still our main man. He averaged nearly 24 points and more than 12 rebounds a game. But I was a close second, well ahead of Doc, who had announced that he was going to retire after the following season. I reached Matty's scoring goal, averaging 20 points a game, without compromising my rebounding. In fact, with an average of nearly 13 rebounds a game, I finished second in the league behind my good friend Bill Laimbeer. I was the talk of the league. And no one was calling me names anymore.

Except one: Sir Charles.

That season, I also learned the key to survival in the NBA: shortcuts. I learned to avoid all strenuous activity away from the

court, even at home. All I ever needed was a television and a
bed, so my new lifestyle was no different from the one I had had
in Leeds. Only now it was a necessity, because I discovered that
the NBA was even more demanding mentally than physically.
In college, the best players can get by with their skills, but in
the pros, one player is as good as another so you have to have a
mental edge in order to reach your peak every night. That means
mind games.

It shouldn't be surprising that some of the best players in the
league are the best at playing mind games. Michael Jordan, Larry
Bird, Dominique Wilkins, and Chuck Person talk more shit than
anyone in the league. It's mostly playground stuff. Hardly ever
vulgar. Well, not *too* vulgar. It's harmless fun among competitors
that helps us remember that it's just a game. Nothing more.

Sometimes, though, it works. Especially when one guy can
damn near psyche out an entire team. I knew the 1991 NBA
Finals were over after game two when the Lakers started complaining about Michael's jaw. They said he shouldn't have been
talking trash to the Lakers' bench while he was kicking their
butts. By complaining, the Lakers—particularly Byron Scott,
who was last seen on the side of a milk carton—showed the world
that Michael was getting to them. They were whining about him
like babies, knowing that there was nothing else they could do.

SURPRISINGLY, DOC TOOK the changes in his status well. He
never begrudged me the attention I started to receive, and near
the end of the season he even called me a "superstar," saying I
was a combination of Darryl Dawkins, the former Sixers' center
who was better known for his flamboyance than his performances;
Hall of Fame center Wes Unseld, one of the legendary defensive
and passing pivotmen; and Nate (Tiny) Archibald, maybe the
best point guard of his era.

Needless to say, I was flattered.

The Sixers finished the season with the league's fourth-best
record, 54–28, but we were having our troubles coming together
as a unit on the floor. It showed in the first round of the playoffs
when we needed five games to eliminate Washington in a best-
of-five series. We had to go into the playoffs without Moses, who

had suffered a serious eye injury during the final month of the season. It shouldn't have mattered because the Bullets were also without their starting center, Jeff Ruland, who had missed fifty-two games with knee and ankle injuries but was supposed to be ready if the series went to four or five games.

Before the series started, someone asked me if I was worried about Ruland recovering in time to turn the series around for the Bullets. Please. The question itself even pissed me off. I called Ruland a joke. He was a good player—during his best season, 1983–84, he averaged more than 22 points and 12 rebounds a game for the Bullets and was an All-Star—but there was no way he was going to be able to help the Bullets beat us. *That* was the real joke.

Ruland did return for game four, which the Bullets won 116–111 to tie the series, but we finally got rid of them, winning the decisive game without much of a struggle, 134–109.

The story was very different in the conference semifinal series against the Bucks. Without Moses to worry about, they were able to concentrate on beating me up with a succession of guys. I didn't endear myself to the Bucks' fans when I was quoted prior to the series as saying that Milwaukee had "only two first-class" players, Terry Cummings and Sidney Moncrief. What I had really said was that they had only two great players and that all of the other guys were role players.

I didn't consider my characterization an insult, just reality. Nonetheless, the fans in Milwaukee got their jollies by watching the Bucks pummel me with three guys: Cummings, who's 6′9″, and reserves Charles Davis, who's 6′7″, and 7-footer Paul Mokeski. The Sixers management tried to provide us with some incentive by telling us that Moses might be able to play if we managed to reach the conference finals. But I knew better. My grandmother had been a nurse and she told me that with the type of injury Moses had, there was no way he would be able to return until the following season. Again, Granny was right.

TOWARD THE END of the regular season, I spoke out about something that had bothered me throughout the year. I had watched as two loyal Sixers—guard Clint Richardson, who had played on the championship team, and Leon Wood, a former first-round draft choice who was picked tenth overall in the same year I came into the league—were traded for useless draft choices and players who would never help us at all. And I was incensed.

Just before the start of the season, Clint, a 6′3″ reserve, was traded to Indiana for two draft choices (one a second-round pick; the other a third-rounder), picks that brought us a memorable pair of players, Hansi Gnad and Derek Strong, neither of whom ever played one minute for the Sixers. Then in January, Leon, a 3-point specialist and member of the 1984 Olympic team, was traded to Washington for forward Kenny Green. Call this an I'll-take-your-first-round-bust-if-you'll-take-mine trade.

In April of that season, I lashed out at Harold Katz, telling Mike Bruton of *The Philadelphia Inquirer,* "The only reason we're not as good as we could be is an attitude. If you enjoy playing for an organization, you'll give a little bit more. I don't think anybody enjoys playing for Harold, and that hurts our performance."

Harold has always been fair to me, especially to my bank account, so I've got no problem with him personally. But I still feel that a lot of players don't like playing for him because they don't feel like there's much loyalty here.

There have been a lot of trades and waivers since I arrived in Philadelphia. Talented guys like McCormick, Sedale Threatt, David Wingate, Mike Gminski, Rick Mahorn, and Maurice have all been shipped out. In 1989–90, the Sixers won 53 games and finished at the top of the Atlantic Division, but instead of building on that, Katz tore it apart. By the end of the 1990–91 season, seven of the players who had contributed to the 53-win season were playing for other teams—including Gminski, forward Bob Thornton, and guards Scott Brooks and Derek Smith.

I understand that the Sixers are Harold's team, and that he can do what he wants. But with all of the great teams and players the Sixers have had under Katz, only Bobby Jones and Doc have finished their careers with the team, and Doc just a couple of years before his retirement almost got traded to Utah! That would have been the worst front-office move since the Nets sold Doc to the Sixers for—what was it? A box of new uniforms?

Players thrive when the franchise has a sense of loyalty that lets them feel, at least to some extent, that they'll be around for a long time. I'd love to finish my career in Philadelphia, but you never know. Kareem Abdul-Jabbar was traded, so were Oscar Robertson, Walt Frazier, Dave Bing, Earl Monroe, Wilt Chamberlain, Pete Maravich, all of them great players.

You never know.

AT THE TIME I made my comments, I didn't know that just a few months later, the concept of loyalty would sink to new depths in Philadelphia when the Sixers made *the* worst trade in the history of the franchise. The team traded Moses and Terry Catledge, a hardworking power forward who didn't mind being in the background, to the Bullets for Ruland and Cliff Robinson, a 6′9″ forward who had played for New Jersey, Kansas City, and Cleveland before going to the Bullets on the day I was drafted.

For me personally, the trade was devastating. Mentally, it screwed me up a great deal for some time because in losing Moses, I lost another father figure, someone who was more important to me than anyone in my life, except for my mother and grandmother.

The trade occurred on the day of the 1986 draft. I had called the Sixers' offices twice that morning after hearing rumors all night that Moses was going to get traded. I didn't want to believe it, but I knew that Moses's departure, despite four productive seasons in Philly, was a real possibility. So did Moses, who was sitting at his home in Houston, waiting for the news.

What set the stage for the trade was a stroke of good fortune for the Sixers, which they then turned into shit. In 1979, the team traded forward Joe Bryant, who was nothing more than a journeyman, to the Los Angeles Clippers (who were then based in San Diego) for a 1986 first-round draft choice. No one ever accused the Clippers of being brain surgeons. It was a stupid move, trading their future—in this case, a player who was then only a high school freshman—for a player who would last only three less-than-memorable seasons with their club.

Well, that particular high school freshman was sharpening his skills down in someplace called Swannanoa, North Carolina. His name was Brad Daugherty.

The draft choice obtained by the Sixers turned out to be the No. 1 pick in the entire draft, thanks to the luck of the NBA lottery. The Sixers looked at the pick as their chance to establish our future, as well as our present. It's rare that a team as good as the Sixers winds up with the No. 1 pick. The draft is designed to help bad teams get better, so teams with the worst records usually pick ahead of those that won more games. It doesn't work, though, when bad teams sell off their future. That's how they remain bad teams.

That's also how the Sixers ended up as the beneficiaries of the Clippers' misfortune.

At least, we should have been.

By doing nothing but drafting Daugherty, who had grown up to become a 7' center from the University of North Carolina and one of the best college players in the country, the Sixers would have undoubtedly had one of the scariest front lines in the league: Moses at center, Brad and myself at forwards. With that combination up front, we would undoubtedly have won another championship by now.

Instead, Katz not only traded Moses, but on the very same day also traded the No. 1 pick to Cleveland in exchange for Roy Hinson, a 6'9" forward who had averaged almost 20 points and 8 rebounds for the Cavs the previous season.

Why?

It seems the Sixers, along with several other teams, thought Daugherty was "soft." He wasn't an intimidating shot-blocker like Patrick Ewing was when he came out of Georgetown. He was just a solid player, a second-team all-American with a nice jumper. But that wasn't good enough for the Sixers. They wanted what they thought was a sure thing: a solid three-year veteran.

Well, it all bombed. The Sixers thought the two trades looked good on paper, but paper doesn't play games.

Ruland's bad knee never completely healed, and he would play only five games for us before retiring after the 1986–87 season when it was apparent that he would never play pro basketball again.

Robinson was never more than an ordinary player for the Sixers, a major disappointment.

And Hinson never truly fit in with us; we traded him to the

Nets a year and a half later, along with McCormick and a 1989 second-round draft choice, for Mike Gminski and Ben Coleman, a reserve forward who was gone after the end of the following year.

Moses, meanwhile, went on to several more productive seasons in Washington and Atlanta, while Daugherty become a two-time All-Star in his first five seasons. By the end of the 1990–91 season, he was the third-best center in the Eastern Conference behind Ewing and Robert Parish of the Celtics.

It all happened on June 16, 1986, the worst day in the Sixers' history.

The logical thing to do that day was simple: if you trade Moses, don't trade Brad Daugherty. You don't make both moves.

Once the 1986–87 season began, it wasn't difficult to see how much we missed Moses. His ability to score and dominate our opponents near the basket forced teams to focus on him, which made it easier for the rest of us to do our thing offensively without worrying about being double-teamed.

Moses's presence made the game easier for everyone. Without him, it quickly became a nightmare.

Our problems that season—mine in particular—began during training camp when I sliced my heel during a locker-room scuffle with someone who shouldn't have even been there, a guy named Peter Moss, whose brother Perry was about to be waived by the Sixers. Pete had bragged that he was the strongest guy in the world. I had to remind him that he was at least No. 2. He pushed me against a locker, and the resulting cut cost me nine stitches.

It also started a run of bad luck for the Sixers: Ruland went down for the first time. Bad knee. Then he went down again. Same knee. Roy got hurt. Another bad knee. So did Cliff. Bad ankle. Then on November 4, just five days into the season, I hit the floor hard trying to snatch down a rebound against Indiana, and for my effort, I suffered a ruptured spleen. I had never even heard of a spleen, didn't know what it did, that it helped clean the body. Three weeks later, I wished that I'd never heard of the damn thing.

The pain of that injury was the worst that I've ever felt because I couldn't escape it. It hurt when I breathed, which meant it hurt all the time. Looking back now, I have to thank Dr. Julie Grosh, an expert on spleens, for saving my season. Every other doctor who examined me told her to operate, to "rip the guy's spleen out." Surgery would probably have knocked me out for most of the season. I might not have completely recovered until the following year. But Dr. Grosh said no. She prescribed rest, saying that the organ would heal on its own. She was right. I missed nine games before I just couldn't take sitting out any longer.

In my first game back, I played 23 minutes against the Houston Rockets in Philadelphia and scored 12 points, grabbed 8 rebounds, and passed for 5 assists. It was a decent return, but I was scared to death during the game. One good shot to the ribs and I could have been out for the season with internal bleeding, which would have been even more severe than the original injury. Thankfully, I survived. I owe Dr. Grosh a lot. She took a chance with me, even risked her reputation. I appreciate it more than she may ever know.

All of those events set the tone for the 1986–87 season—Julius Erving's last year in the NBA.

Towards the end of Doc's career, there was talk throughout Philadelphia that he resented my becoming the focal point of the team. Stories in the local media tried to pit Doc and me against each other. I never felt any resentment from Doc, but the entire team suffered from the controversy and other maladies. We won only 15 of our first 29 games and finished the season with only 45 victories. It was the Sixers' worst season in twelve years.

With a team in disarray, Matt Guokas had his hands full. Matt was a good coach, but he was too laid-back to be effective in the NBA. When Billy Cunningham got mad, you knew. Not so with Matt. He had to struggle to get mad. When he threw a tantrum, you could tell that he was uncomfortable. For much of the year he just begged me to carry the team. It was impossible, but Matt kept pushing.

We were eventually eliminated in the first round of the playoffs, three games to two by Milwaukee. Matty lasted only 43 games into the next season before Katz fired him, but he was just a scapegoat for the team's real deficiencies. That Sixers team just didn't have the talent to win consistently. But hey, you can't fire the players.

But all of these problems were only sidelights to the focal point of the season, Doc's Farewell Tour. The year started out fun for everyone. We were witnessing history and no one minded the parade of appearances, ceremonies, well-wishers, and gifts that preceded every game during our last trip of the season to a particular city. At first, Doc was embarrassed by all the attention, but as the season passed, he improved his speeches and became a gracious honoree. What became difficult for him—for all of us—was the basketball.

Doc's frustration came from many fronts. At thirty-seven years old, it was difficult for him to warm up and get loose, complete the pregame ceremonies, and then try to play basketball. It didn't help that he had been moved to guard, a move that was made because at 6'6" Doc was being outmuscled by some of the league's bigger and stronger small forwards. While he was the second-best-conditioned athlete on the team, behind Andrew, he wasn't quick enough to guard most of the players he was matched up against. So on most nights his performances were almost embarrassing.

Memo to Sixers: No matter how much I get beaten up by bigger and stronger players as I grow old, chasing guards around all night is something I never want to do. Never.

Eventually, Doc grew tired of everything. The ceremonies drained him. During one stretch of the season, Matty just stopped playing him for too many consecutive minutes. His body and mind just couldn't deal with it all. Doc wanted to play more, and after a few games he and Matt got into it. They shouted at each other behind closed doors in the locker room, within earshot of the entire team.

We all knew what was really happening: Doc was struggling and Matty was doing what was best for the team. I felt sorry for Doc, but at the same time I was quite happy for him. While physically he could probably have played at least one more season—he truly took care of his body—Doc knew it was time to leave the game behind. We should all be so lucky.

I never believed Doc had anything against me, except perhaps that I embodied the reality that life was about to take a major change for him. He wanted to be the team leader to the end, but it just wasn't in him.

The only real problem I had with Doc during our three seasons together was that he was never one of the fellas. The other players on the team always felt like they had to control themselves when Doc was around. Not like you controlled yourself around Bobby Jones; around Bobby you felt like you *should* control yourself. Around Julius you felt like you had to. No practical jokes. No craziness. No loud arguments or fooling around. Nothing. Not around Doc.

You could relax around anyone else in the room, including the coaches, but Doc never allowed himself to come "down" to that level. Not even in the privacy of the locker room, the players' inner sanctum. He never walked over to any of his teammates and said, "Let's go have a burger and a beer," something everyone else did with regularity. Everyone except Doc. You'd never find him at a restaurant or nightclub with the rest of the team. He stayed by himself.

Still, I was honored to play with him. I brag about it every day. Hell, I'm one of the few guys in the world who can say, "I played with Dr. J."

Sometimes I wonder, though, if I ever really knew Julius Erving.

I think I only knew Doc.

6
ANYTHING YOU WANT

ANY NBA PLAYER who says he goes directly to bed after games is lying.

Correction: Any NBA player who says he goes directly to *sleep* after games is lying.

It's no secret that life as a professional athlete means never having to spend the night alone, not even if you're the ugliest, scrawniest, no-playingest rookie on the Nets or Clippers. It doesn't matter if you're at home or on the road, everybody is your best friend in the entire world. Or at least, they want to be.

At some point during their career, every professional athlete has to contend with the allure of his profession. And some athletes are getting a taste of it now as early as high school when many of their schoolmates begin treating them differently from other students simply because of their athletic skills. Boys want to be their best friend, while girls want to be their playmate.

For professional athletes, the toughest game away from the game is separating genuine friendship from genuine garbage. In our social lives, just as in our professional lives, the stakes and pitfalls of friendship are much higher than they were when we were in high school and college because there's much more for the outsiders to gain, and more for us to lose.

A pro athlete is almost always trying to weed through the variety of willing candidates vying for his attention—and/or his affection. But most of us realize why we're so adored, and it has nothing to do with whether or not we're wonderful human beings.

If I weren't earning more than $3 million a year to dunk a basketball, most people on the street would run in the other direction if they saw me coming.

The same can be said for almost any professional athlete, but particularly black athletes, who must realize that without their athletic skills most people in this country would consider them just another nigger. Yet for far too many of us, it's easy to forget that reality, easy to enjoy the thrill and perks of being a celebrity, particularly for athletes who are insecure about themselves. Or for rookies who are experiencing their first moments away from the rules and regulations—like curfews and mandatory training tables—that cramped their lives in college.

For most of us, it isn't long before the allure wears thin and the constant attention becomes a real pain in the ass, because people care less and less these days about respecting our privacy. To them, our high-profile status overshadows our right to live normally outside of the public arena, to walk through a shopping mall, attend a movie, or simply to be alone with our families and friends without being scrutinized for everything from how we dress, speak, and act to how our wives or girlfriends look.

How we handle it depends upon how badly we need our egos stroked, and how much help we need to cope with the ups and downs of our profession. Every professional athlete I know understands the precarious nature of our profession. On some nights we're everyone's hero; on other nights we're the biggest bums in town. But too many players fall for the extremes. They believe the hype. One day they think they're as good as they are on nights when they play like All-Stars. But the next day, they wonder if they're as bad as they are on nights when they play like dogs. These swings are almost impossible for anyone to deal with.

The truth, of course, is somewhere in between.

I know that I'm never as good or bad as any single performance. I've never believed my critics or my worshipers, and I've always been able to leave the game at the arena. Once I take a shower, the game goes down the drain. Unfortunately, some players can't put the night's frustrations behind them so quickly. They slip the game into their gym bags, along with a couple of beers, then carry it out into the dangerous night where anything can happen.

Practically every player in the NBA is an insomniac. The odd rhythm of night games and morning practices the following day means that we keep incredibly strange hours. I hardly sleep at all on the nights before games because I'm too excited thinking about how much pain I'm going to inflict upon my opponent the following night. That makes for eighty-two restless nights—not including the playoffs, when I hardly sleep at all. I don't sleep much after games, either. Can you come home from a full day's work and go directly to bed? It's no different for most NBA players.

I've always found it practically impossible to get rid of two hours of intense competition against bigger, stronger guys with just a late-night snack and a few beers with my teammates. I need several hours to come down from the emotional high of competition and reach the point where I can fall asleep. By the time I cool down physically and calm down emotionally from a night of bumping bodies with guys like Buck Williams, Charles Oakley, Derrick Coleman, Kevin McHale, and that gentleman of gentlemen, Mr. Bill Laimbeer, it's usually at least two o'clock in the morning, sometimes three o'clock, and maybe even later before I can think about going to sleep. That's another eighty-two nights with ESPN.

Most games end each night at around nine-thirty P.M. That's about eight hours after I've had my last real meal, usually a large lunch at home; if I'm on the road, it's room service alone or, during the last two seasons, with Rick Mahorn, perhaps my best friend in the league. Sometimes, I'll have lunch with friends who live in that particular city.

Among NBA players, I count very few as friends. I didn't really know Rick well when he signed with the Sixers before the 1989–90 season. When he was with the Pistons, we enjoyed our battles, and we almost always talked, usually over dinner after games. We talked about our respective families. And I learned that, like me, he's very close to his mother. That was extremely important to me, and it said that despite the "Bad Boy" image, he was an extremely good person. In fact, Rick's a very sensitive guy who relies on his tough-guy image only as a way to survive in the NBA.

Besides Rick, perhaps my closest partner is Utah forward Karl Malone, another country boy, which makes it extremely difficult to perform against him. I don't like playing against friends because when I prepare myself to face someone, I also prepare myself to hate them—at least for a night. That's the way it has to be, but it's hard when it's a friend.

The player, though, with whom I share most of my frustrations is Michael Jordan. He and I have been close ever since we met at the Olympic Trials in 1984. During the 1987–88 season when the 76ers won only thirty-six games and failed to reach the playoffs for the first time in thirteen years, Michael helped me through what was the most frustrating period of my career.

I played well almost every night that season. Statistically, it may have been my best year—a career-high 28.3 scoring average along with 11.9 rebounds, which was sixth in the league. But as a team nothing was happening. Nothing but losing.

Michael had experienced the same frustration during his first couple of years in the league when the Bulls weren't a great team yet. He told me to hang in there and that things would change, but only when the Sixers surrounded me with better teammates. Things were just then beginning to change for the Bulls, who finally won the NBA title three years later. I knew Michael was absolutely right about my predicament, but to hear the best player in the league admit that without his teammates he was nothing made my own frustrations easier to accept.

On the whole, it's hard to have friends among your teammates, especially in Philadelphia. After Moses was traded and Andrew retired, I tried not to get too close to the people I play with because it only hurts even more when they're gone. They were the two closest friends among my former teammates, a group that became three when the Sixers released Rick.

Most of my true friends are away from the game, people I knew long before I reached the limelight. My best friend is Joseph Mock, a former high school teammate who played center at Leeds and is currently a Navy fighter pilot. He'll be my best friend until the day I die.

I don't like to socialize with strangers on the road because I

don't like surprises—of any kind. I try to stay around my teammates and a few friends. If I don't go clubbing with them, I don't
go at all.

Being around my teammates, particularly on the road, has
always helped me keep my sanity in this league. Some of them
have also helped me find a good meal. I've got nothing against
the cities of Milwaukee, Indianapolis, and Cleveland—it's Rich-
field, really, twenty miles south of Cleveland, which I've actually
seen only once—and certainly nothing against the Bucks, Pacers,
and Cavs. But I hate those places! They roll up the sidewalks at
ten o'clock every night, which means that there are no decent
restaurants open by the time the team leaves the arena. And
after games, NBA players are like hungry animals on the prowl—
always for food, and often for companionship, too.

This was one of the first things I discovered about the pros:
finding suitable female companionship was perhaps the easiest
aspect of our profession. It was the true road "game."

On most occasions, an athlete only has to open his eyes or
simply check into the hotel in order to find a friendly face. It
wasn't long into my rookie season that I started receiving stacks
of messages on the road from people whose names I didn't recognize—women whose names I didn't recognize.

Moses had already warned me. "Watch out for the freaks," he
had said during training camp, speaking in the Southern drawl
that was so deep that most people who didn't talk to Moses every
day couldn't understand one damn word that came out of his
mouth. Moses also sometimes talked with a look on his face that
made it seem as if he was trying to test your gullibility. So when
he said, "Watch out for the freaks," I didn't know whether he
meant to leave them alone or to Watch out for the freaks! as in,
Go for the gusto!

I was, after all, still a country kid from Leeds who was amazed
at being handed a bunch of messages from women in every city.
There were messages for most of the players, but especially the
rookies and other players who were still relatively new to the
league.

Most of the 76ers' veterans were married men who had either
already established that they didn't fool around, or they just kept
"regulars" in every city that they called upon every time the

team stopped through. That left us rookies and young single players. Fresh meat. It was open season on us. Hunting season.

Athletes are easy targets for friendly women, a reality that most of us have had to contend with since our hormones started raging in junior high, long before we were mature enough to understand why women were so eager to taste our affections. There have always been women—groupies, freaks, whatever you want to call them—who are willing to spend the night with an athlete, or any other so-called celebrity. And many of us have accepted the invitations. For me, there's seemingly always been a limitless group of women who are anxious to meet me, talk to me, spend time with me, anything, just because I played for the Philadelphia 76ers. Among the mail delivered to the Sixers' offices, or to the locker room at the Spectrum in Philadelphia, I have received boxes filled with roses, candy, cookies, cakes, and even underwear. On the road, such deliveries are regular occurrences, like mints on my pillow. It's a scream. Dominos Delivers Desire.

I could fool myself by thinking that these women want to meet me because I am such a wonderful guy. But that's just what I would be doing: making a fool of myself.

Like any rookie, I was curious about the kind of woman who would leave a message at a hotel for someone she didn't even know. I even answered some of the messages just to see what kind of friendly conversation they might have had in mind. Most of the responses began pretty innocently. "I just wanted to come down and meet you."

"And?"

"Anything you want."

It sounded real tempting. I'm not going to lie and say that I've always been a saint when it comes to the opposite sex. But at the same time I was still only a few months out of Alabama and still too damn scared to do anything but resist temptation—no matter how much I might have wanted just to see what the caller looked like. "A little peek wouldn't hurt," I often said to myself. But it would have been stupid, an invitation to trouble.

NBA wives are, in general, pretty secure. They have to be. Women will regularly disrespect them in public, pushing them aside in order to get to their husbands.

In Philadelphia, my wife, Maureen, and I have been subjected to vicious rumors and lies concerning our relationship ever since we were married. If I'm just seen in Philadelphia talking to another woman, people assume I'm screwing her. I've seen female friends of my wife around town, stopped and talked to them for a few minutes, and soon it's back to Maureen that I'm out picking up women.

As a test, I once started a rumor about us just to see how long it would take to get through the grapevine. I told someone that Maureen and I were getting divorced. The rumor got home before I did.

I've come to the conclusion that people are generally miserable, so they want your life to be miserable, too. If people in Philadelphia spent as much time worrying about their own relationships as they do about mine, everyone in the city would be happy.

Socially, times for me were never so hard that it clouded my sense of reason. I knew why most people wanted to meet me—men with their no-lose, get-rich-quick investment schemes, and "sick cousins" who just needed a couple of thousand dollars for medicine, or an invitation to a party that was "live."

Only because I was an NBA player.

Only because I could dunk a basketball.

That's sad. And scary.

For a lot of players, though, the temptation can be too great. Surprisingly, I've only had one teammate who was ever slapped with a paternity suit—although many of us have often sweated out the possibility—and I've never had a teammate whose marriage broke up over some silliness caused by another woman. That's primarily because I played with so many veterans, like Doc, Maurice, Bobby Jones, and Rick, as well as quiet young players like Hersey Hawkins, guys who hardly ever partied and never answered unsolicited "messages."

Other than Moses and Andrew, two guys who would have made anybody's all-star party, and Maurice, who joined us on the club circuit on rare occasions, the Sixers have never been known as one of the league's real party teams. As contenders, the Sixers players have, for the most part, always taken their job seriously. The business of basketball is something the veterans

I've played with carry with them into every game and every practice, which helped set an example for me. Their goal was simple: win the NBA title. They did not come to party.

But I'm not going to lie; sometimes we did just that.

I've already called Moses my basketball mentor. Well, he didn't do such a bad job of teaching me the right moves for those clutch performances off the court as well. While I've never been one who preferred to go to many parties, Moses and I both loved to dance and have a few drinks at a local nightspot, but only after games. Almost never on nights before games. Even athletes need limits.

Or rather, especially athletes.

I've had many teammates who got caught up in the anything-goes lifestyle in the NBA and allowed it to hurt their careers. Where's Cliff Robinson? David Wingate? Both of them truly enjoyed being in the NBA, and I think it affected their progress as players. But they were by-products of the Sixers' change from a veteran, professional team during my first few years in the league to a younger team in recent years.

Young and sometimes stupid.

It's so easy for us to take advantage of the hours we keep. Practices don't start most days until ten o'clock in the morning, which leaves most of our afternoons free, with games at night. A player can stay awake until two A.M. and still sleep seven hours before having to be at practice or shootaround the following morning. But too many of us are fooling ourselves and enjoying the good life to the extent that it detracts from our ability to perform. Those seven hours of sleep starting at two A.M. aren't as effective as seven hours obtained, say, between midnight and seven o'clock in the morning.

What difference does it make over the course of an 82-game season and three months of playoffs? Plenty.

Who are the culprits? That's easy. Usually it's the players who are flashes in the pan; one season they're all-everything, and the next they're struggling in the CBA.

Such temptation is just one of the reasons why most rookies crawl through their first pro season. For the most part, they're immature and especially susceptible to the pitfalls of the league's good life.

It's as if some of them were let out of a cage, hungry and ready to prowl. They're usually the last ones to wander back to the hotel after games, and on most occasions they're accompanied by a new "friend." Not even Superman can play *that* game every night, especially after playing fifteen to twenty-five minutes against NBA veterans who are using every tactic imaginable, from talking trash to physical intimidation, to make the rookie's life hell. A night of that kind of punishment, plus midnight gymnastics, takes its toll on rookies, particularly during the last thirty or so games of the season.

Check the numbers: most rookies have never played more than forty games in any season of their lives, so by January—at about the time the league reaches the halfway mark—they're sucking wind; their numbers are dropping and they're starting to get frustrated because teams have finally figured out how to play them. They'll tell reporters that the reason for their decline is the greater number of games, that the season is longer than what they're used to playing. "I'm still learning," they'll say.

Well, that's bullshit. An NBA season on the road will kill a rookie faster than kryptonite kills Superman.

Despite all my best efforts, I was on empty myself after about thirty games during the 1984–85 season, my rookie year. Most of it was mental not physical, because I wasn't getting any playing time worth crap. Billy Cunningham just wasn't playing rookies, no matter what, so my butt was on the bench. I finished my rookie season averaging less than 29 minutes per game, the lowest total of my career. Still, by January of that season I was tired, tired of playing basketball every day, tired of even looking at a basketball. Three months of the season were gone, but there were still three months left. If basketball had become a chore during my final season at Auburn, it was now a bona fide job in Philadelphia, and I wasn't always happy about it.

But thanks to Doc, Moses, Maurice, and Bobby, I learned the secret of NBA survival: conditioning of the body *and* mind.

It's no secret that among professional athletes, the No. 1 priority should be to maintain our physical condition. But even the healthiest body will only survive about forty games. For the next twenty games, an NBA player exists on will. These are the season's dog days, times the body must rely on the spirit in order to perform near its peak.

Games played in the month of February seem like they're played in a Twilight Zone, so far from the start of the season that teams have devised defenses for the opposition's best players, and too far from the end of the season to seem important. Yet we have to look at every game as if it's the key to the season, the game that will determine whether or not the team will qualify for the playoffs, or allow us to maintain the homecourt edge for one or more postseason series.

Until recently, the players haven't gotten much help from the owners, who were too cheap to pay for single rooms with king-size beds (each player pays the difference between the double and single rate) and only started flying the players first class (ever seen a seven-footer try to squeeze into a coach seat on the morning after a game? It's not pretty) in 1988 when the union made first-class travel on flights that last longer than an hour a part of its collective bargaining agreement with the league.

Finally, a few years ago, a few smart owners began to realize the benefits of taking travel comfort to another level by chartering, leasing, or even purchasing their own planes. It quickly proved to be a wise investment because it allowed the teams to dictate their own travel schedules. Teams started traveling to the next destination immediately after the game rather than on an early-morning flight that required a five A.M. wake-up call. And rather than having to contend with crowds of autograph seekers and planeloads of passengers, teams had some privacy, starting when the team bus drove directly onto the tarmac and continuing on the plane when the players, coaches, and staff could relax without having to worry about being scrutinized by the public.

The benefits are many: (1) players get out of a city on a night when they might otherwise be out chasing the town; (2) everyone begins to relax as soon as they board the plane, which is spacious enough for players to spread out in an area by themselves, play cards in groups, view films with the coaches, or even receive treatment from the trainer, all while also enjoying a hearty meal; and (3) rather than enduring an early wake-up call, players are allowed to enjoy several more hours of sleep the following morning, which translates into more energy for games.

Some owners finally realized that the difference between making the playoffs or not, and between having the homecourt advantage or not, is often only a few games. And both of those accomplishments can be critical to the two bottom lines: winning the title and making a profit. The expense of chartering, leasing, or purchasing a plane more than comes back in wins and dollars because the players are rested.

It's no coincidence that the first team to purchase its own plane was the Detroit Pistons. They purchased *Roundball One* before the 1988–89 season, the year they won their first championship. Last season, the Bulls flew their own plane all the way to the title.

I wasn't exactly jealous of the Pistons because I knew that Harold Katz was too cheap to purchase a team plane. Why worry over something you can't have? But by the middle of the 1990–91 season, eight teams either owned or chartered their own planes, including—besides Detroit and Chicago—Portland, the Lakers, Phoenix, and Boston, some of the league's best teams. Other teams chartered on nights when they played back-to-back games in different cities, including—sit down—the Sixers!

It wasn't until we started chartering during the 1990–91 season that I finally got upset about the whole issue. What took us so long? Now, after seeing how much difference it makes in my own physical condition, I can see why the Pistons and Bulls were winning titles and winning more games than everyone else after they started using their own planes. Of course, the Sixers would have to win the title *before* Katz would spring for a plane.

Anyway, on those nights when neither the body nor the spirit is willing, it's probably the team's fourth game in five nights. Those nights are a waste of the players' time and the fans' money. Teams should never play more than three games in any seven-day period so players can perform at their peak and recover from the bumps, bruises, and other minor injuries. Too often, something minor becomes a more significant injury because it wasn't given the proper time to heal. But I'm not naive. Such a change in the schedule will never happen as long as the league insists on playing eighty-two games. I think the ideal schedule would last about sixty games, which is approximately the number of games in which the average team has all twelve of its players in uniform, healthy and energized to play. The other twenty-two contests are a farce.

Let me say something else. The owners insist that in order to reduce the number of games, the players would have to take a pay cut of equal proportion to compensate for the loss of revenue. Well, contrary to the stance taken by the players' union, I might be willing to take a pay cut in order to play fewer games. Why? Because twenty-two fewer games per season means twenty-two more games that I would be able to add onto the end of my career when I'll earn more than I do now.

The longer I play, the longer I'll be able to earn millions for playing basketball. At the current rate of salary increases in professional sports, I should be more than able to make up for any current loss of income with future earnings received long after I might otherwise have retired.

Case in point: Kareem Abdul-Jabbar, who claimed in a lawsuit that he lost nearly all of his money because of an unscrupulous agent in a scam that came to light in 1985, sixteen years into Kareem's NBA career. At the time, Kareem was thirty-eight years old and there was talk that he should have been on the verge of retirement. He played three more years, however, retiring at the age of forty-two as the oldest player in league history. Between the time his financial problems surfaced in 1983 when his home burned to the ground, and his retirement following the 1988–89 season, Kareem earned about $12 million in salary alone, more than enough to right his financial condition and start a new life.

Due to medical advancements and better conditioning programs, players are lasting longer than they have in the past, but if the league had long ago subtracted a couple of dozen games from the schedule each season, maybe players like Magic and Larry Bird—players I'm sure Commissioner David Stern would like to see play forever— would still be in their prime rather than on the downside of their careers.

But until the league and the union agree to shorten the season, fans should always check their favorite team's schedule. If they're playing their fourth game in five days, go to a movie.

●   ●   ●

OF COURSE, staying in condition is now the least of anybody's worries about life on the road. Last November 7, everyone in the league was shocked back to reality about the danger of our lifestyle. That was the day Magic Johnson stunned the world by announcing that he had tested HIV-positive, which means he has the AIDS virus.

Which means that he is going to die.

I was shocked like nothing had ever shocked me before. I hurt for Magic, and for a long time I was actually shaking.

The news was like an earthquake in the NBA, where a lot of guys are not only promiscuous but share the same women in some of the cities. I'll bet every player in the league cried for Magic and his family. And at the same time, I'll bet just about everybody damn near had a heart attack, too.

Magic said that his doctors had recommended that he retire, and so, just like that, he was gone from the league. The end of his career. It was all too sad for me to take.

And suddenly, AIDS wasn't just somebody else's problem. It was our problem. Up until then, it hadn't really registered when I'd heard about somebody getting AIDS. It wasn't my problem, I thought. Now it's hit close to home, and I feel bad for everybody who's contracted the virus or come down with the disease— every one of the 200,000 people in the United States who has been diagnosed with the disease, the 1 to 1.5 million people with the virus, and the 1 million who have the virus but don't even know it because they won't get tested.

I now understand that AIDS is a major problem in the black community, and that black men in particular had better stop being so macho about the disease, because if we don't we're going to let our communities be destroyed by it.

I think most NBA players practice safe sex—at least, I'm sure they do now—which was Magic's message to everybody on the day he retired. But I'll be surprised if he's the only player infected with the virus. Real surprised. Most guys think they're invincible. They think they'll never have a serious injury, never be involved in a serious accident, never get caught if they use drugs. And most of all, they think they won't get AIDS.

Now we all know that's wrong.

In the fall of 1991, I had my blood tested for AIDS because, like Magic, I had gotten a new life-insurance policy that required me to get tested. The test came back negative.

Sometimes I wonder, if it had come out positive, if I'd have wanted to know. And if it had, I doubt I'd have handled it with the strength Magic has. I'm wearing number 32 this season to remind people to think about him, and what he's going through.

THERE'S ALWAYS BEEN a lot of talk about drug use in the NBA and the fact that we, as professional athletes with a lot of time and money on our hands, are often targeted by the temptations that might lure someone to the kind of places where illegal drugs are taken like appetizers. The league has had its share of drug problems despite an antidrug program that gives players three chances before they're banned from the league for life.

Near the end of my second NBA season, we were in Chicago when we heard that Micheal Ray Richardson of the Nets had been thrown out of the NBA because of drugs, the most heralded player ever permanently banned under the league's drug agreement with its players. Just over a year later, Lewis Lloyd and Mitchell Wiggins of the Houston Rockets also flunked drug tests and were banned. In all, six players have been kicked out of the league for using illegal drugs, but that's fewer than 2 percent of the hundreds of players who've been in the league since 1984 when I was a rookie.

The very first player permanently banned under the drug policy was former Utah Jazz forward John Drew. Like me, Drew grew up in rural Alabama, in a tiny town called Beatrice, forty-eight miles from Selma. Drew attended Gardner-Webb College, a small college in Boiling Springs, North Carolina, and after an all-American sophomore season he applied for the NBA under the hardship rule. He was drafted in the second round by the Atlanta Hawks and became a two-time All-Star during his eight seasons with the team. Then on September 2, 1982, Drew was involved in one of the most lopsided trades in league history. The Hawks sent Drew, then twenty-seven years old, fifth-year guard Freeman Williams, and $1 million in cash to Utah in exchange for the rights to a rookie, a kid from the University of Georgia named Dominique Wilkins.

Drew played nine games in 1982–83 before his drug use caught up to him in the form of a telephone call from Jazz trainer Don (Sparky) Sparks. Sparks asked Drew to come to the room of head coach Frank Layden, and when the player walked in, they told Drew the truth that he didn't want to hear. "John," Sparks said, "you've got a problem with cocaine."

Two hours later, Drew was on his way to a drug rehabilitation center in Baltimore where he remained for two months, when he returned to Salt Lake City to try to start a new life. It didn't work.

He played only nineteen games during the 1984–85 season before the cocaine finally took over again. On December 6, 1984, John earned the dubious distinction of becoming the first player ever permanently banned from the NBA for using illegal drugs. I took the news particularly hard because I had met him when I was a sophomore at Auburn. He was just a few months out of rehabilitation, and one of the first things he told me nearly knocked me off my feet. "Don't ever use drugs," he said.

He then proceeded to tell me how cocaine had ruined his life. "I've snorted ten Mercedes-Benz up my nose," he said. "I've beaten women and I've got twelve kids all over the world. It's made me do crazy things, and it will get anybody. If I had it to do over again, I would never ever have done cocaine."

John told me about a weekend in 1980. He had been named to the All-Star team and was supposed to catch a seven A.M. flight to Washington, D.C., where the game was to be played. Well, in order to celebrate, the All-Star decided to do an all-night—with a pipe. John smoked so much cocaine that he missed his flight. So he called the airlines and rescheduled for the nine-o'clock flight. He missed that one, too. He also missed the twelve o'clock.

"I couldn't move," he said. "I made reservations for six flights and didn't make any of them. That's how good the coke was to me."

A few years later, I ran into John again, even though I didn't know it at the time. Suddenly this guy comes up to me, grabs me, and says, "Charles, it's me." It was John. He looked so bad that I didn't even recognize him. He had been in jail for writing bad checks and looked like he had been living on the streets, living nowhere. He had lost it all. He asked me for some money. He said he was hungry.

John had always been good to me, so I offered him what I had. Now I realize that it was probably a mistake, that more than likely he used the money for drugs.

I've never seen any NBA players do drugs, and I've never played with anyone who had gone through rehabilitation. I once thought that I'd never want to play with someone who could topple back into drug use at any time. I didn't want to depend on that type of person for my success. But I've since changed my mind—and it's a good thing, because right after the end of the 1990–91 season, Harold Katz went out and signed two players with drugs in their pasts: Charles Shackleford and Mitchell Wiggins.

The 1989–90 season was Shack's second year in the league. He was a reserve center for the Nets who missed a lot of games with injuries. While he was out, Shack was arrested for possession of marijuana when some cops stopped him for speeding. As for Mitchell, he was one of the few players who've been banned from the league for testing positive for cocaine. It happened in January 1987, and after cleaning up his life he was reinstated in July of that year.

On the whole, I'd still rather not have teammates who tend to get into any kind of trouble, especially trouble involving drugs, but I can't judge someone who's sincerely trying to correct a mistake.

Actually, I believe the league has a larger problem than cocaine: alcohol. Teams are required to have beer in the locker rooms after games and practices, and I'd say that 99 percent of the players have at least one beer whenever it's available. It's one thing to have a beer or two on a day when there's a heavy workout, but it's also easy to get into the habit of having a few beers every day—workout or not. And that's a dangerous habit to have.

The league goes out of its way to warn players about the dangers of drug abuse. They should start talking about alcohol, too.

Starting in about 1986, I became extremely curious about cocaine. I wondered what it felt like to get high and why it had such a strong hold over people. But I never allowed my curiosity to get the best of me. I never tried cocaine.

I'm scared I might like it.

We've all been told that drug addiction is a disease. I don't agree. Using drugs is a choice. It's a conscious decision that people make every day of their lives. Not just athletes, either. That's why I think it's bullshit to think that we're more susceptible to drug use because we spend a lot of time on the road, earn a lot of money, and have a lot of free time.

I've been offered drugs only three or four times since I came into the NBA, each time at restaurants in Philadelphia. The first time it happened, someone offered me pot; the second time, cocaine. I've never been offered drugs at the hotels where players have supposedly been approached. Drug dealers are good at what they do; they know who uses and who doesn't, so they don't waste time with people like me.

Of course, I'm not very comfortable with strangers I meet on the road. I'll party hearty in Philadelphia at places where I know everybody, but never on the road where I might not know more than a handful of people in the room. It's safe. It's my choice.

There were times when I chose to use drugs. I smoked pot a couple of times when I was at Auburn. A few of my teammates were regular smokers, so I thought, why not give it a try? I hated it. I didn't get high and the taste was awful. Thank God.

Cocaine was easy to get, even on a college campus in rural Alabama. But I was always afraid of it. I wondered what it did to people; so many kids were using it. I figured it must be pretty damn good for people to risk their college careers for it. It was a few more years—the date was Friday, June 19, 1986, to be exact—before Len Bias, one of the best college basketball players in the history of the game, dropped dead from an overdose of cocaine. But people knew the dangers of drug use. Even at Auburn we knew that you could use cocaine once and die.

When I speak about drugs at schools, summer basketball camps, or drug rehab centers, I ask everyone one question: What can drugs do for you?

The answer: Nothing good.

No one's asked me, but I think a lot of the reason that our

children are still being consumed by drugs is due to the problems of the criminal justice system. As juveniles, kids under sixteen years old know that no matter what they do they can't be sent to jail. They don't care about the risks because they know that whether they're caught with illegal drugs, or running drugs from the dealers to the salesmen, or holding dangerous weapons, or selling drugs or holding drug money—no matter what—they can't be kept in jail for long. Not if they're juveniles.

Maybe it's time to start treating kids as adults if they get involved selling drugs. No more juvenile sentences for drug offenders. If they do the crime, they go to jail, period, no questions asked. There will always be kids who are lured into the drug industry, but maybe it'll cause at least a handful of them to think twice if they know they'll go to jail. Now, too many kids don't give a shit about the law. And we're all suffering for it.

(By the way, I've read recently where some cities and state governments are starting to release inmates because of overcrowding and poor living conditions.

Wait a minute. I didn't realize prison was supposed to be comfortable. They can stack them in there like sardines as far as I'm concerned!

Like I said, no one asked me.)

When I speak to kids about drug abuse, there are always skeptics, those who don't think I know what I'm talking about simply because I don't use drugs. I can always find them in the audience; they're the ones with the look that says, *You're a fool, you just don't know.* I don't care how old they are, I look them right in the eye and get their attention.

"You don't believe me, do you?" I ask.

"You think I'm full of crap because I don't live in a place where they sell drugs on the streets and because I don't need money.

"Well, *you're* full of crap."

That's when I start to tell them about my younger brother Darryl. In October 1989, he suffered a paralyzing stroke that was caused by drugs. He was twenty-one years old.

We don't know when and where Darryl started using cocaine, though my mother and grandmother began to have their suspicions in 1988 when he began hanging out with some people in Leeds who were known drug users.

He and I were close but different, and our differences grew even wider after I left Auburn in 1984 and joined the Sixers. From the moment I signed my first pro contract, Darryl seemed to be jealous of my accomplishments. My mother says he wouldn't even watch me play on television and wouldn't play basketball with any of his friends. She says he constantly complained that all he ever heard around Leeds was "Charles this, and Charles that."

Darryl never indicated to me that he had any problems with my accomplishments. When I called home and spoke to him, he said, "Everything's cool."

But there must have been some sort of deep, hidden resentment that, in his mind, he wasn't keeping up with his big brother. Darryl still lived with our mother and grandmother. He struggled at school and after dropping out after ninth grade, he struggled through one year at vocational school. He wouldn't talk to my mother or grandmother about any of his new friends, but they both knew what was happening: Darryl was trying to compete with me by running in the fast lane.

I didn't know whether he was involved with drugs, though through the grapevine—a very short grapevine; in Leeds, everybody knows everybody else's business—I knew he was doing the sort of things that could lead to drug use. He was hanging out late, all night at times, and being seen with the wrong people.

Darryl didn't care. He had made his choice.

We finally found out the truth in the spring of 1989—during the 76ers' first-round playoff series against the Knicks—when Darryl was arrested outside the FoodMart grocery store in Leeds and charged with selling drugs to an undercover narcotics agent at a local club.

More than anything else, more than sympathetic, more than sad, I was really, really mad over the incident. One of the prices of celebrity is unwanted notoriety. If someone in my family gets in trouble, I'm in trouble. Just prior to the arrest, the police had notified the local television stations that they were going to bust "Charles Barkley's brother." As the police arrived at my grandmother's house, helicopters circled overhead. But no one was home. My other brother, John, was at school, my grandmother was out running errands, my mother was in Philadelphia, and Darryl had just left for FoodMart to buy some beer.

The police arrested him just outside the store. They tore apart his car, but found nothing.

The following day headlines throughout Alabama read, "Charles Barkley's Brother Arrested," not "Darryl Barkley Arrested." Had it been anyone else but Darryl, the arrest wouldn't have made the eleven-o'clock news and the police wouldn't have chased him down with damn near the entire force. But because it was Charles Barkley's brother, everybody with a camera and a badge wanted a piece of it.

CHARCEY MAE GLENN: *We still didn't know whether Darryl was actually using drugs, and we didn't know how to approach him about it. We didn't want to lose him, have him go off on us and stay out all night again. But finally, my mom, Johnnie Mae, decided to give it a try.*

"Darryl, are you using drugs?"

"Of course not, Grandma."

"Well, I really want to believe you Darryl. I really want to believe you, so would you take a drug test just to satisfy my curiosity?"

Of course, Darryl said no. But I spoke up and said one of the hardest things I've ever said.

"Darryl, you've got no choice. Either take the test or get out."

After several minutes, he agreed to take a test. Since we didn't want to create a scene by going somewhere in Birmingham, we looked in the yellow pages and found a drug center in Decatur, seventy miles from Leeds. When he got there, Darryl took the test while mother and I waited in another room. Before Darryl joined us, the doctor came in and gave us the bad news. The sample had traces of cocaine and marijuana.

Well, that was the worst moment of my life. I turned to my mother and cried. I told her, "I can't believe this, not after as much talking about drugs as we've done. Not after everything."

The doctor hadn't told Darryl yet, so when we confronted him we asked him again: "Do you use drugs?"

He denied it again and continued to deny it until the doctor showed him the results of the test.

He refused to stay at the clinic, so when he got home, we told him that he had two choices: he could either get help or he could move out. He looked at us. "I'll move out."

Well, we all sat down together and cried and talked and cried and talked. Finally, I said that since he wasn't going to get help, he had to pack his clothes because we weren't going to have any drug users in the house. "I want the keys to my house and to your car," I said. "The car stays in the garage." He was shocked, but not enough to get help.

All the while, my heart was breaking. To myself, I said, "Lord, I'm turning my child out in the street and I don't know what's going to happen to him." I tried to be tough.

At last, he said he'd go to rehab. We drove back to Decatur the following morning.

Rehabilitation alone isn't worth shit. To stop using drugs, a person has to change his life completely. He's got to forget about the people he thought were his friends, the ones who used drugs around him and gave him drugs whenever he asked for a fix. As far as a reformed drug addict is concerned, those people are dead.

Darryl never got that far. He stayed in rehab for only two weeks, and it didn't help. He wasn't a heavy drug user, maybe only for about two or three months, so he didn't go through severe problems in getting the cocaine and pot out of his system, but about three weeks after he left the rehab center, he had an attack and was rushed to the hospital. He was suffering a stroke.

The doctors said he had an enlarged heart and that the cocaine had become too much for it to bear. It couldn't pump fast enough to allow the blood to flow through the valve and to the brain.

Darryl survived. The stroke left him slightly paralyzed, but he can take care of himself now. He was married in December 1990, to Melanie Jerald, someone he's known since they were kids.

There was no reason for what happened to Darryl to have occurred. None. Except that Darryl made a choice. He chose drugs. In some strange way, maybe the stroke was the best thing that could've happened to him. Maybe it was a cruel blessing in disguise. Drugs have different ways of interrupting your life. He could've been killed in a dispute with another dealer. He could've been caught with pounds of cocaine and been sent to prison for life. Or he just could've died from an overdose. Given those options, a stroke isn't so bad. I guess.

As it's turned out, he hasn't used drugs since the attack and he's changed 180 degrees. He's completely different now, quieter, less angry than he was before. He joined me at the 1991 All-Star weekend in Charlotte and shared with me one of the most memorable times of my life. Despite playing on a stress fracture in my left ankle. I grabbed 22 rebounds and scored 17 points for the East team and was named the game's Most Valuable Player. That afternoon, Darryl was right there in the stands.

In past years, he wouldn't have been there. He had been very ungrateful for the things he was able to have because of my success, and very selfish about doing good things for other people. All he wanted to do were things that made our mom and grandma miserable.

He was almost a lost cause. But he's 100 percent different now. Death scared him. The fear of going to jail for maybe the rest of his life scared him. Hell scared him.

I don't know why it hasn't scared everyone else. Drugs are as popular as ever. People are still using cocaine, selling cocaine, and getting killed because of cocaine.

Len Bias, I'm afraid, died in vain.

7

WIMPS AND COMPLAINERS, YOU KNOW WHO YOU ARE

THERE'S NOTHING WORSE than a sorry, pitiful, whining teammate, someone who constantly complains about anything and everything under the sun, the moon, and the stars.

These guys complain about not getting enough playing time. They complain about not getting enough shots. Some of them even complain about not getting enough "pub" in the media.

In the years between my rookie season in 1984–85 and the 1990–91 season, I played with exactly sixty-six different teammates. I've never been afraid to criticize any of them when it's been necessary, and it's gotten me into a lot of trouble. People think I'm out of line when I criticize my teammates. "It must be tough to play with Charles when he's doggin' you all the time," is what I hear a lot. Well, that's bullshit.

I'm no different from Larry Bird—one of my idols—Magic Johnson, and Isiah Thomas, guys who kick their teammates' asses when it needs to be done. I've heard Larry scream at Robert Parish, Danny Ainge, and Kevin McHale. I've heard Isiah scream at John Salley, Mark Aguirre, and Bill Laimbeer. And I sat in my den at home in Philadelphia during the 1991 NBA Finals and watched Magic scream at Vlade Divac. I knew exactly what he was feeling: he was working his ass off and his teammates weren't doing a thing. He was out there all by himself.

But did anyone criticize Magic for screaming at Vlade? Not one word.

If it had been me, I would have been crucified.

My job as team leader is to get these guys, my teammates, to play to their potential, because the bottom line, the only thing Sixer fans really care about, is how well the team plays. But when I've yelled at my teammates through the years—including at the end of the 1991 playoff season when I said that with our current roster, the Sixers just could not win a championship—I've been whipped like a dog and charged with being disloyal.

When Larry, Magic, and Isiah yell, it's called leadership. When I do it, I'm an asshole.

Explain that to me.

THERE'S NOTHING IN the game more important to me than my teammates. They're the guys I go to war with every night, so if you want to test my limits, disrespect one of my teammates and see what happens—or ask the fan in Indiana who insulted Mike Gminski on April 16, 1988.

Most of my teammates over the years have been tremendous, hardworking professionals who really wanted to win. Some of them were stars, guys like Maurice, Doc, Moses, and Bobby Jones, all of whom were the kind of teammates any player would be thankful to be able to pull on his jockstrap next to. But most of them were simply good players who wanted to contribute: guys like Terry Catledge, a strong, sound, hardworking power forward who was a good player, but not a great one; Gerald Henderson, a smart, scrappy point guard who worked hard every night, someone I enjoyed playing with; Marc Iavaroni, a good friend who was traded for no other reason than that he was caught in a power struggle between Billy C., who didn't want me to start, and Harold K., who did; Albert King, who was the best player in the world when he was on a streak, whom I never really got to see in his glory; and Leon Wood, a great friend and a good shooter, better from 3-point range than anyone I've ever played with. I'm surprised Leon isn't still in the league.

But I've also played with my share of jerks. A few of them were real players, guys with legitimate NBA talent, but they couldn't accept their roles behind guys like Doc, Maurice Cheeks, Andrew Toney, and myself. Some of them were starters, guys who didn't have one damn thing to complain about. But all of them found something to complain about: not enough of fill-in-the-blank.

Most of them were nothing more than pains in the butt whose main accomplishment was to disrupt the team and in most cases bring it down to their low level.

Thankfully, there have been only a few guys during my days in Philadelphia who've been real lowlifes—guys who were less concerned about playing than getting paid twice every month. As long as their paychecks came, they were happy. They didn't care if they won or lost, whether they played or not. They just enjoyed being in the NBA and making a lot of money. Being a professional athlete wasn't a job to these guys, it was an episode of "Lifestyles of the Rich and Famous." It's no coincidence that very few of these guys are still in the league.

As I've said, Cliff Robinson and David Wingate truly loved being in the NBA. But they didn't love being a professional, and it hurt their careers. Cliff, a 6'9" forward with a nice shot, left the University of Southern California following his sophomore season and joined the Nets as a first-round draft pick—eleventh overall—at the young age of nineteen. That was his first mistake, leaving school before he was mature enough to handle the re-sponsibilities of a job.

He played seven seasons in New Jersey, Kansas City, Cleve-land, and Washington before coming to the Sixers in the deal that ruined my life, the deal that cost us Moses. He played three more years, but never fulfilled the potential of his skills. Cliff loved the good life, so much so that the Sixers simply never called him when his contract expired after the 1988–89 season. Neither did anyone else. He had wanted to sign an all-cash deal with no incentives. Guys like Cliff need incentives, or they're worthless. For once, the Sixers did something right—but only by doing nothing.

David was drafted by the Sixers in the second round of the 1986 draft, just after four great years at Georgetown when the Hoyas reached the Final Four three times, and won a national title. We thought we had gotten a steal. David was a tough, hard-nosed, and aggressive 6'5" guard with great defensive skills. But just like Cliff, he was scoring for everyone except us. We fixed our mistake by sending him to San Antonio in August 1989 in the deal that brought us Johnny Dawkins, who would become one of the up-and-coming point guards in the league before blowing out his knee four games into the 1990–91 season. As for David, he lasted three seasons with the Spurs before being cut.

When I think of Cliff and David, I think of wasted talent.

Jay Vincent, who was with us for one year (1989–90), was just a waste. He was a great talent but he was truly lazy. He also had an attitude problem.

Then there was Sedale Threatt, a hard-playing, scrappy guard who liked to party more than he liked to play. He should have worked harder on his game.

And I'll never forget Chris Welp, our first-round draft pick in 1987 who was a small forward in a center's body. He was 7' and 245 pounds, but didn't want to play basketball. He only did it because of his height. Instead, he would rather have gone fishing.

YOU WOULDN'T BELIEVE some of the things that guys will bitch about while earning millions of dollars a year for playing a damn game. For the most part the complaints are about kid stuff, like who gets the best seat on the plane, who gets his ankles taped first before the game, and who gets the most writers around his locker after the game.

Garbage like that doesn't win basketball games, but it can lead to the kind of bad feelings that can *lose* games. When one player starts complaining, a team can ignore him. But when a second player joins him, it can get ugly. Two guys doesn't sound like a lot, but two of twelve is a pretty high percentage of unhappy people. Add one more and you've got a real mess. The whole soap opera then becomes the team's focal point; the other players begin talking about the drama rather than concentrating on the games. Suddenly, what began as one minor complaint is now poison.

It's difficult enough—damn near impossible, in fact—to blend twelve guys, and their twelve egos, during a seven-month period when they're living together in hotels, on airplanes, and in arenas throughout the country. Even the most successful teams are a delicate balance waiting for one simple event to tear it apart. Those petty issues can become major problems and turn a legitimate contender into an expansion team.

The 1986–87 season, my third year in the league, was the beginning of a two-year period when the 76ers, by our standards, might as well have been an expansion team. It was Doc's final season, and I still wasn't completely comfortable with my new responsibilities as one of the team's first options as a scorer, but I was confident that I could do anything I wanted to do on the court.

Doc had been "the man" on the Sixers for ten years. So when Matty Guokas asked me step into Doc's shoes, I knew that I was about to become the most-hated villain in Philadelphia history: the guy who pushed Doc out the door.

But Doc saved me. He knew his time was up. Just a few weeks into the 1986–87 season, he understood that the emotional toll of his farewell tour was affecting his game. If the NBA had let him alone, rather than making such a big fuss over his retirement, he might have gone out stronger. His heart was with us, but there were times when his mind was elsewhere.

But Doc's diminishing skill wasn't our biggest problem. It was those damned trades that set the Sixers' franchise back at least five years. We lost Moses, Catledge, and our shot at Brad Daugherty, for Jeff Ruland, Cliff Robinson, and Roy Hinson. I really feel that, among all of the problems caused by the two trades the Sixers made prior to 1986–87, one of the biggest—even bigger than Ruland's knee, which allowed him to play in just five games in a Sixers uniform, and Cliff's attitude—was Roy Hinson.

Roy was a better-than-average player, a 6'10" power forward with solid low-post moves, a nice jumper, and awesome shot-blocking skills. During his three NBA seasons prior to joining the Sixers, he averaged almost two blocked shots per game. Also, he was not a bad guy. He was a quiet family man whose temperament was reasonable and controlled. He was perfectly suited to play a prominent role on any team—but not too prominent. The Sixers expected him to start at power forward, where he would rebound and play defense while Ruland and I handled most of the scoring.

That was the dream.

The nightmare was something altogether different.

Ruland might have been the best center I ever played against. He was awesome. He was huge (6'11", 275 pounds) and strong and took up a lot of space. We always had to double-team him, but it didn't always work because he was such a great passer. He and Moses had some bouts that were so serious I found myself standing around watching. Afterward, Moses was always out of it. On those few nights when Moses got his ass kicked, it was usually Ruland who did the kicking. It was unbelievable.

But when he got to Philadelphia, he suffered a blowout. His left knee, which had limited him to only thirty games for the Bullets in 1985–86, just couldn't handle the pounding and the pain. The five games he played for us in 1986–87 were the last five games Ruland played in his career. He had three knee operations and seven months of rehabilitation after the final procedure, before he finally accepted retirement. He was unable to play, barely able to walk. Doctors said his knee belonged to a sixty-year-old man. His absence forced us to move Roy into the pivot. The result was a disaster.

It was pretty simple, really: Roy was just never comfortable with the expectations that came with being the starting center on a successful NBA team. Centers are always in the spotlight. It comes with the territory; they can't avoid it. I don't care if you're Patrick Ewing, Sam Bowie, Vlade Divac, or Mark Eaton, an NBA center must thrive under the pressure of being one of the twenty-seven best centers in the world. If not, if they shy away from the responsibilities of having a team built around their skills, it crushes them.

Roy was crushed. He had the talent to be the Sixers' starting center, but it was as if he would've rather been playing for some terrible team, like the Nets. (That's just what he eventually did when the Sixers sent Hinson, McCormick, and a draft choice to New Jersey for Gminski and Coleman; Roy later suffered a serious knee injury that has all but forced him to retire. He played in only nine games in the 1990–91 season.) He never played like we expected him to. He never even played for us as well as he did when we played against him before and after he was with the team.

In Philadelphia, he ran away from the pressure. And if a team's center plays hide-and-seek with himself, it leaves a hole in the middle that nobody can overcome.

Roy scored a respectable 13.9 points and blocked 2.1 shots a game during his first season in Philadelphia, but he managed to grab just 6.4 rebounds a night, an embarrassment for someone with his kind of athletic skills. At the same time, Moses was kickin' ass for the Bullets, averaging 24.1 points and 11.3 rebounds for the season. And in Cleveland, the player whom the Sixers would have chosen if they'd kept that No. 1 pick, Brad Daugherty, was making a lot of people look stupid.

The next season, most of Roy's numbers got worse: 11.6 points, 5.8 rebounds. He was still blocking 2.3 shots a game, but it was clear that if we were going to continue to be contenders after Doc was gone, we needed a *real* center. So just twenty-nine games into 1987–88, Roy was gone.

ROY HINSON: *Sometimes, Charles gets so wrapped up, gets so into a game, he won't see anyone else. That's not good because no matter how great he is, you still have to play with four other guys. It's difficult for guys who don't want to watch. A lot of times I felt it was like I was just watching. If the coach called out five plays, four of them were for Charles. We'd try to get some motion, but when the ball got to Charles, it stopped.*

Well, Roy, let me say this: stop trying to cover up for the fact that you didn't play well. You simply couldn't play in a winning environment. You didn't have the killer instinct necessary to intimidate your opponent and put him away. When you were losing in Cleveland, you played well. And when you were losing in New Jersey, you played well—until your knee gave out. But when you came to Philadelphia, with a team that expected to win, you couldn't cut it.

Actually, Roy, I felt bad for you. I don't know if your knee was hurting, if you were playing with pain. But you also left me puzzled. You should have been a better player, and I've never been able to understand why you weren't.

. . .

FIVE YEARS. THAT'S what those two deals cost us. Had they not been made, I'm convinced that I'd have at least one championship ring by now, if not more. Instead, I've had seven seasons of struggle, frustration, and disappointment. With the exception of the 1989–90 season, when we won 53 games and reached the conference semifinals, we simply haven't had enough talent to compete for the NBA title. That's how important one deal can be. Or in this case, two stupid deals.

If I were building a team from scratch—which is just about what the Sixers were forced to do after the 1990–91 season—I would start with only one goal in mind: to find talented, hardworking guys who know their respective roles, but more importantly, have the will and determination to win.

Secondly, I would go to the team's superstar and ask for his opinions about players and possible trades. I'm not talking anything radical. The Celtics have done it with Bird for years; Jerry West of the Lakers doesn't go near the telephone without going to Magic first; the Pistons run just about everything through Isiah, and do you think Jerry Krause goes out to lunch without letting Michael pick out the restaurant? Hell, no.

But has Harold Katz ever asked me one damn thing about a player or a trade? No. I know he's not obligated to; it's his team and he can do anything he damn well wants to. But I think I've earned the right to be respected for my basketball knowledge. I should be consulted when it comes to building the Sixers. Instead, I hear things through the grapevine and have to dig around for my information just like a reporter.

For instance, if I'd had my way, the Sixers would have signed Cliff Levingston after the 1989–90 season. After eight seasons in Detroit and Atlanta, Cliff became a free agent at the end of the year. Cliff's a classic role player, someone who accepts what's offered him and doesn't bitch about what he doesn't get. Cliff had averaged more than 8 points and 5 rebounds off the bench during his last two seasons in Atlanta, and he was someone who could have been a strong addition to our second unit, who could have taken some of the load from Ron Anderson, our sixth man.

But no one asked me. Instead, Cliff signed with the Bulls. And now he's got a championship ring.

One of our problems is that Harold enjoys making deals, and yet he knows about as much basketball as any fan who sits around watching games all the time: not much. A good owner has knowledgeable basketball people around him whenever he's making any deals. That's how the Lakers (West), Pistons (Jack McCloskey), and Bulls (Krause) made themselves contenders.

Harold didn't have anyone around him when he shipped off the No. 1 draft pick and Moses in the same day. But even if he had had a basketball person with him, I don't know if he would have listened to him.

Jimmy Lynam, the Sixers' current coach, has a great basketball mind. He's been around the game for damn near his entire life. He played college ball in Philadelphia for St. Joe's, where his coach was Jack Ramsay, another great basketball mind. He then coached in college for ten years before moving to the NBA, where he's coached two years for the Clippers—so, everybody makes a mistake—and four years for the Sixers.

I trust Jimmy Lynam more than anyone I've ever been associated with in the game. But does Harold listen to him? I don't think so.

And who pays for Harold's stubbornness?

The Philadelphia 76ers.

The Roy Hinson soap opera was just one of the low points of the 1986–87 season, which was the start of the most painful period of my career. We won only forty-five games that year, lost the division title to the Celtics, and were eliminated three games to two in the first round of the playoffs in an emotional series with Milwaukee that marked the final moments of Doc's career.

The following season was basketball hell. The team finished with an embarrassing 36–46 record, was a disgusting *fourth* in the Atlantic Division—thank God for the Nets!—and ended up with our butts at home when the playoffs began.

It was during that two-year period when I probably earned most of my reputation as a controversial figure. Much of what I did and said during that time was caused by the frustration of losing, losing, losing almost every night, and the reality that I was playing on a team that simply wasn't good enough to compete with the top teams in the league.

I learned one particular lesson during the 1987–88 season: that so-called fans can be total jerks when their team doesn't win. Despite struggling through 1986–87, we still reached the playoffs for the twelfth straight year, a league record. But when we didn't make the playoffs the following year, we caught hell. In the streets, people looked at us differently. They acted differently. And they made stupid remarks.

"Hey, Charles, you guys cost me some money!" said one guy.

"I didn't cost you shit," I said. "You shouldn't have made any bets." (See, I didn't need Commissioner Stern to teach me any damn lessons about that.)

The year had been tough enough on me even without that kind of abuse. But I confess: I played my part in the disaster.

It began when I announced during the exhibition season that I should be the 1986–87 Most Valuable Player. That came right before I signed a renegotiated contract and extension worth a guaranteed $12.05 million through the 1993–94 season, an average of $1,506,250 per year. It was the deal that would set my family for life, and for being able to do that I was truly grateful to Harold Katz.

But if Katz thought that he'd bought my silence, he quickly learned he was wrong. There were still a lot of bad feelings among the players about losing Moses. Of course, no one wanted to come forward and say anything, figuring that he might be the next one out the door. But I didn't care. I had to speak up. During training camp I blamed Katz for the Sixers' decline, saying that his vocabulary seemed to be missing a word—*loyalty*. "I don't think anybody enjoys playing for Harold Katz and that hurts performance," I said.

Four years later, that statement is still true.

I EXPERIENCED SOME physical problems in 1986–87 that began with my preseason scuffle with Perry Moss's brother Peter when I cut my heel against a locker. I suffered an injury that needed nine stitches to close and caused me to miss several practices and a few exhibition games. Katz and Matty were furious. One day later, Perry Moss was cut. As Arsenio Hall might say, "Hmmmm . . ."

That injury was a prelude to the nicks and bruises, physical and mental, that I would suffer throughout the season, the worst being my bruised spleen. I missed only nine games, but the injury absolutely scared me to death because it wasn't a muscle, a knee, or some other joint, the kind of injury every athlete must contend with.

Later that same month, I caused an uproar throughout the East Coast when I told Steve Bulpett of the *Boston Herald* that Larry Bird was "an asshole." The Celtics were the defending NBA champions, but I also said they were beatable because management hadn't improved the team's personnel since the end of the previous season. "Everybody knows it," I said. "Teams are gaining on them. They're going to lose at least ten more games than last year. They're cocky and they're arrogant."

As it turned out, I was almost right on target. The Celtics won *eight* fewer games (59) in 1986–87 than they did the previous season, which also happens to be the last time Boston won the NBA title. The 1986 championship was the beginning of the end for the Celtics' mystique; since then, they haven't even been the best team in the East, not since Detroit and Chicago started beating them up.

My comment about Larry's being an asshole was only meant to be a dig between friends. During the 1985–86 season, Larry had blasted the entire Sixers organization, saying the team's management would screw up our first-round draft choice, the infamous No. 1 pick in the entire draft. He turned out to be on the mark.

What I had actually said to Bulpett was that Larry was an asshole for making that comment, not that he was an asshole, period. Maybe I should also have said that Larry was right.

IT DIDN'T TAKE long for the losses to mount in 1986–87. We won 13 of our first 19 games, then collapsed. Everyone's weaknesses began to surface, as did everyone's frustrations. By late December, our record was a pitiful 15–14 and we were already going into the tank.

On Sunday, December 28, 1986, the Lakers crushed us by 26 points, 111–85, in Los Angeles. They seemed to sense our problem and preyed on it. They knew we were upset with each other—twelve guys going in twelve different directions. How could they not know? We hardly spoke to each other on the court. When we did communicate, we screamed at each other.

Personally, I was in a funk. I wasn't used to going into games with absolutely no shot of winning, all because of our conflicting personalities, and I didn't like it at all.

In the second period of that game, I missed a dunk and sparked a 10–0 run by the Lakers. We were done for the night, and I didn't handle it well. I played hard, but I didn't get another basket for the rest of the night.

After the game, Matty described my missed dunk to reporters as a "momentum changer." It sounded to me like he was blaming me for the loss, and I exploded.

"Anybody who would say that is an asshole," I told the reporters who had come running to me with Matty's statement. "All parties included."

I wasn't stupid and I hadn't lost my mind. I knew that calling the coach an asshole was like asking for a stiff fine. But Matty didn't overreact to it. He knew damn well what was going on. He knew I was leading the league in field-goal shooting and rebounding, while several other guys on the team weren't doing their part. We were a powder keg, and Matty didn't want to be the spark that set it off.

He left that job to me.

I'VE ALWAYS GOTTEN frustrated when guys at the end of the bench whine and complain about a lack of playing time. A coach can't play everyone. Most teams are carried by nine or ten guys during the regular season, even fewer in the playoffs. The other guys should thank God they've got jobs that pay them more money than 99 percent of the people in the world. The minimum salary in the NBA will be $130,000 for the 1991–92 season. *Minimum!* I'm offended when these guys start bad-mouthing the starters, guys who are busting their butts every night. Or when they start talking about what they would do if they got some playing time. If they aren't doing it, then they should just shut the hell up!

There are two types of complainers: those who have a right to complain, and those who don't. Those with the right to complain still come to the arena every night ready to work and do the job every time they take the court. The ones who don't, simply don't deserve to play.

We had two guys on that team who had no business even opening their mouths: Kenny Green and World B. Free.

Green, who played college ball at Wake Forest, was a bust of a first-round draft pick for the Bullets. They had picked him twelfth overall in the 1985 draft, just ahead of a big, muscular, quiet kid out of Summerfield, Louisiana, and Louisiana Tech. His name? Karl Malone. (Now you know why the Bullets haven't been in the playoffs in about a hundred years.) They pawned him off on the Sixers only a few games into Green's rookie season. At 6'7", he's known as a " 'tweener," someone who isn't big enough to play forward, but who can't handle the ball well enough to play guard.

Kenny had talent, but because most of the minutes at small forward, his best position, were divided between myself and Cliff Robinson, Kenny couldn't get off the bench. One afternoon before practice, I was sitting in the locker room listening to him bitch about how he should be playing ahead of Cliff. I looked around and said, to no one in particular, "Yeah, right."

World wasn't happy either, and he never hesitated to let everyone know about it.

His original name was Lloyd. While growing up in the Canarsie area of Brooklyn, New York, Lloyd dominated on the local playgrounds, so much so that he was called All-World. So in 1981, Lloyd changed his name to World B. (The "B" stands for, well, "b.") He must've believed the hype.

In the NBA, World was one of the best shooters in league history. He had a powerful upper body and launched his shot with one of the highest arches I've ever seen. After leaving the Sixers in 1978, he scored more than 20 points a game for eight straight seasons in San Diego, Golden State, and Cleveland before becoming a free agent at the end of the 1985–86 season when he had averaged 23.4 points per game in seventy-five games for the Cavs. It says something that he was still available for us to sign two months into the season. He was thirty-three, just past his prime, and with Andrew Toney's status uncertain because of his injured feet—he played in only six games in 1985–86—management thought World was the perfect player to fill in, even as a starter, if needed.

I'm not sure that was the brightest move the Sixers could have made, because we then became a team with *too much* talent.

It's not easy for most former All-Stars to accept a lesser role near the end of their careers, no matter how much their skills have declined. They don't want to believe that they're not the player they once were, that they can't jump as high or get their shot off as easily as they did in the past. So they become bitter and frustrated, and they take every opportunity to dog the guys playing ahead of them. That kind of attitude only creates problems, the kind of problems we just weren't strong enough to handle that season.

I think World's arrival forced Andrew to try to play sooner than everybody expected, no matter the pain. Whatever the reason, Andrew was back, and as he shook off the rust of having not played regularly for more than a year, he began playing better and better. He only averaged 10.6 points per game for the season, but he played more than 20 minutes a night, more than any of us ever expected.

Quickly, World became the odd man out. Considering the alternative—unemployment—sitting on the bench wasn't such a bad life, but World bitched and moaned about it every chance he got. As it turned out, he bitched himself right out of the league.

By mid-February, I couldn't take it anymore. The team sucked—we were 29–22—and when you're losing, nobody wants to hear any shit about playing time, especially from the people who don't even take off their sweats.

That's why on February 17, 1987, I stood with a group of reporters after practice in Philadelphia, with several of my teammates standing close enough to hear every word, and made what became known as the remarks heard round the world—or at least in every NBA city: "We've got so many bitchers and complainers on this team. We've got guys who have complained,

complained, and complained. That's why we haven't moved ahead. We don't have total unity. Everybody's got to stick together. We've got a lot of pussies on this team. They don't realize that we're all in this together."

At the time, I didn't mention any names. But everyone on the team knew who I was talking about, including the guys involved: Kenny Green and World B. Free.

Just over two months after the Sixers signed World, they waived him. He played in twenty games for Philadelphia and averaged about 14.3 minutes a night. He should have played more about as much as my grandmother should have put on a uniform. World B. Free was World B. Off-Target. A 46 percent career field-goal shooter, he shot only 32 percent for the Sixers. I rest my case.

As for Kenny Green? He played in nineteen games over the course of the season, which is probably nineteen more games than he should have played. He shot 36 percent from the field, and that might have been the *best* thing he did for us. After that season, Kenny never played in another NBA game. We haven't missed him.

At the time, I made my statement out of frustration, and I was just beginning to understand that as the team's best player, it was my responsibility to speak up whenever necessary. That's my idea of a leader: someone who plays hard every night and kicks his teammates' butts when it's necessary. I was sick and tired of hearing Kenny and World whine, and public embarrassment was the only way to shut them up.

Despite our record at the time, I still felt reasonably good about the team and most of my teammates—guys like Doc, Maurice, and Andrew, of course. And I felt bad for the guys who were injured and unable to play: Jeff, Roy, and Cliff. I was really proud of guys like Tim McCormick, a 7' center from Michigan who got every ounce of talent out of his body every night. (Tim is a career backup, which is nothing to be ashamed of. The 1990–91 season was his seventh year as pro; he now plays for the New York Knicks and will probably be around for several more years. He's smart, and he works his ass off. I can only respect a guy like that.)

At the time I made my comments about Kenny and World, it

was a critical period for the team. We struggled to stay around the .500 mark, and we could have gone either way. I only wanted to go one way, the winnin' way. We needed to be unified for a serious run for the playoffs. If I hadn't said anything about those guys, we might have gone the other way—into the toilet.

So what if I pissed some guys off? That wasn't my concern. I only wanted the team to have the right frame of mind for the last few weeks of the season. It turned out, though, that it wasn't enough.

One game near the end of the season sums up our entire season. We were at home against the Bullets, Moses's new employers. The Bullets had already beaten us three times that year, beaten us to death. And Moses was the main reason why. He and Catledge were making the Sixers the laughingstock of the league. I wasn't surprised that Moses was still putting up serious numbers for the Bullets, the same kind of numbers he'd been racking up throughout his career. But Catledge's numbers—13.1 points, 7.2 rebounds—were like salt in the wounds.

Ruland was at home that night with an injury. It figured. We were also without Doc, Andrew Toney, and Kenny Green. Eight warm bodies. That's all we had at tip-off that night at the Spectrum. Five starters and three reserves. Basically, we were in deep shit.

Sitting in the locker room before the game, I looked around at the people who were there and made a promise to myself: I vowed that we would not lose that night. I was sick and tired of people talking about how good the Moses trade had been for the Bullets, and how bad it had been for us. Okay, it had been. But on this night, I wanted to change everyone's tune, so I promised myself the victory. I didn't stand up and make an announcement. I didn't tell anyone. I wasn't Joe Namath. I simply vowed to do everything I could to win this game. The night before, I had scored 40 points and grabbed 21 rebounds in a 121–112 win over the Bulls, but I wanted to leave everything I had left this night on the floor.

I did, but we didn't win. The score was 106–105, Bullets. As time expired, I threw up a shot from halfcourt but missed. At that moment, I couldn't move. I stood on that spot on the floor with my hands on my knees, exhausted. My numbers that night were solid: 28 points, 17 boards, 8 assists, as well as a couple of blocks and steals in 46 minutes. The fans were impressed. The Bullets were impressed. Even my seven teammates were impressed.

I wasn't. I was crushed.

Moses and Jeff Malone, the Bullets' best guard, came over to where I was standing and put their arms across my shoulders while offering a few words of appreciation. I honestly don't remember what they said. It wasn't important, except that it's always nice when an opponent pats you on the back for your effort.

But it hurt that my effort wasn't enough. It wasn't enough to win, and I never appreciated winning more than I did during those dog days during the 1986–87 and 1987–88 seasons when we didn't do a lot of it.

I FINISHED the next season, 1987–88, as the league's fourth-leading scorer with a 28.3 average, the highest total of my career. I was fifth in rebounding with 11.9 boards a night. And I was playing more than 39 minutes a game, more than I had ever played before. Statistically, it was the best year of my career, but because of our sorry record (36–46) it was also the worst year of my career, the hardest thing I've ever had to go through as a professional athlete.

By late December, the pattern was set: we stunk.

At Boston earlier in the month, we trailed the Celtics by as many as 49 points in a game that we lost by an embarrassing margin. Could you blame me for cursing at the woman behind the bench that night who told me it "wasn't very nice" for me to kick a chair in frustration or curse at my teammates? You'd have to be pretty stupid to mess with me on a night when I'm being embarrassed in Boston.

Later that month, we were blown out by the Lakers at the Forum in Inglewood, California. (Sound familiar?) Even worse, I was thrown out of the game with under three minutes left in the third quarter when I was hit with my second technical foul by my nemesis, referee Mike Mathis.

I'd had my problems with Mathis for a while, beginning in a game in late '85 when he threw me out for calling him an asshole—twice. (Why does that one word always cause me so much trouble?) For the next couple of years I thought Mathis held a grudge, particularly in 1986–87 when he threw me out twice in two months for arguing over calls that he flat-out blew. It got to the point where the Sixers complained to the league office, saying, "We can't have our best player thrown out of so many games worked by the same official."

The protest didn't help. When Mike was on the floor, I felt like I was in a constant no-win situation. Things have gotten a little better between us, but it still drives me crazy when he—like a lot of officials—won't even acknowledge me when I've got something to say to him. I actually think I get along pretty well with most of the league's refs, especially the good ones like Jack Madden, Joey Crawford, and Jake O'Donnell. But too many of them are like robots, and they won't even accept the idea that you've got a stake in the game. They don't let you talk to them or express your complaints at all. (Memo to Darell Garretson, supervisor of officials: If the game's going to work, to be fun for everybody, then there has to be an open line of communication between your guys and the players. Stop telling them to walk away from us. Loosen up.)

This night was a classic example of how a ref can get a player tossed out of the game if he wants to—and I was certain by this time that Mathis was out to get me. But my troubles actually began when I drew a "T" from the other official, Paul Mihalak— a call that was absolutely wrong. I was standing in the lane just as Magic was about to shoot free throws, and I was yelling loudly at Maurice. I was pissed at how my teammates were playing and I was trying to get him to spark everyone. I probably said a few unprintables at the time, but so what? I was talking to my teammate, not to Mihalak. But he was standing nearby, close enough to think that I was talking to him. Boom. Whistle. T. I couldn't believe it.

Almost immediately, Mihalak admitted that he had screwed up on the call. He told me it had been a "snap judgment," thinking that my words were aimed in his direction. But refs rarely reverse themselves in public, so while Mihalak was standing there confessing to me, Magic was shooting a free throw—and Mathis was plotting my exit.

He didn't have to wait long.

I was pissed off and on the verge of an explosion. I was angry about the technical, but I was also tired of getting the shit beaten out of me by A. C. Green, the Lakers' power forward. It was open season on Charles Barkley that year, primarily because the team was so bad that no one gave a damn about us. So just a few seconds after the first T, at the other end of the floor, I snapped. I elbowed Green in the chest right in front of Mathis—an invitation.

I was gone.

I sat in the locker room and steamed. I thought about our season, how we were embarrassing the Sixers' legacy. Just five years before then, the team had won the NBA title. Now, we just sucked. We had lost to the Lakers by the score of 131–115 after trailing by as many as 29 points. We were a pitiful 12–13, and I knew it was going to get worse.

When reporters walked up to me in the locker room, where I sat slumped in front of my locker, I just couldn't help myself. I knew some of my teammates would be insulted by what I was going to say, but I didn't care. I had to speak my mind. "The team is just bad," I began. "Bad team, man. The whole damn team, man. We've got a bad fuckin' team. Unless we play a perfect game, we can't win. And that's a bad situation. It's really bad when you have to play a perfect game to win."

Adding insult to the injury of losing to the Lakers, the Sixers fined me $3,000 for my remarks. In a country that preaches freedom of speech—where nitwit war protesters can disrespect our troops in the Persian Gulf and suffer no consequences—I was fined for telling the truth. We were a *bad fuckin' team!* We were terrible and the Sixers knew it. The truth hurts, and the organization tried to make me feel the pain.

About three weeks later, with the team floating around the .500 mark with an 18–17 record, and me getting my ass kicked by triple-teaming defenses every night, the Sixers finally did something about our condition: they made the trade with the

Nets that got Roy Hinson the hell out of my life and brought us Mike Gminski.

It wasn't enough to turn us around that season—eight games later, Matt Guokas was replaced by Jimmy Lynam—but it solidified us for more than two seasons, until the Sixers screwed everything up on January 4, 1991, when they traded G-Man to Charlotte in exchange for Armon Gilliam. A center for a power forward when the only people we had left to play center were a one-dimensional stick-figure (Bol) and a 6'10" forward (Mahorn) who hates playing the position (and can't)! I guess Katz believes all that shit about how you don't need a center to win anymore. (Memo to Katz: It's a lie. Just watch us.)

The only way to win basketball games in the NBA is with talent. Not coaching. Not anything but talent. If a team has talent *and* it wants to win more than every other team in the league, it will always win. Always. Talent and desire—they're the two most important elements in the game.

I like the Pistons' mentality, even though they went out like chumps against the Bulls in the 1991 playoffs. I would have loved to have played for the L.A. Raiders. Professional sports isn't about who's nice. It's not about people saying, "Well, let's go out and be friendly with the other team." It's about competing. It's about hard work and kickin' butt. For forty-eight minutes, it's about you against twelve other guys and doing what it takes to win, by any means necessary. That's all that matters. Everybody on the other team is your enemy—my enemy.

For two seasons during my career—*only* two, thank God—we didn't have anything close to that kind of attitude. We were passive and tentative, scared of losing rather than trying to win. When we won thirty-six games in 1987–88 and missed the playoffs for the first—and only, I hope—time in my career, I was under tremendous pressure to make up for my teammates' lack of skills. Guys like McCormick, Cliff, and Albert King were asked to play roles that they just couldn't fill.

So I was the team's workhorse. I didn't like the role. Still don't.

I've got nothing against hard work, as I think I've shown throughout my career. And I don't mind being "the man" on the team, the player who scores the big baskets and makes the big plays down the stretch when the game is on the line. But even plowhorses don't work as hard as I did during those sorry seasons, and it didn't serve any purpose—except to wear me down and probably take years off my career.

The way I've got it figured, there'll never be another player like me again. There'll never be another player who is 6'4" and averages more than 10 rebounds a game, scores inside whenever he wants to against bigger opponents, and is quicker than most everybody he plays against. I'm the Ninth Wonder of the World. (Muhammad Ali has already laid claim to being the Eighth Wonder of the World.) But I've always known that I was going to have to pay a price for the way I play.

Every night, I'm pounded, scratched, elbowed, and bruised. In 1986–87 and 1987–88, every night was like three nights because opponents knew that if they beat me up, there was no one else on the team who could respond.

Ideally, I needed to play fewer minutes. And I needed to play with at least two other guys who could score, at least one more serious rebounder, a point guard who knows how to play, and guys on the bench who can give the starters a rest without allowing the opposing team to gain any ground.

Is that too much to ask? With all of the great damn players in the NBA, it shouldn't be. But for those two years at least, it seemed like I was asking for the moon.

8

THE NEXT TIME I GET HOLD OF BILL LAIMBEER...

I would gladly chip in and pay part of his fines every time he smacks Bill Laimbeer.

—FRANK LAYDEN, GM Utah Jazz

AT ONE POINT in my career—at most points, actually—you couldn't have gotten me to sit down at the table and break bread with Bill Laimbeer. Break his neck, maybe. But nothing else. Not for any amount of money. Not even for John Williams's ridiculous $26-million contract—or James Worthy's phone book. Of all the guys I've bumped heads and traded elbows with during my NBA career, I thought Bill Laimbeer was the whiniest, the most despicable, the most disgusting guy in the league.

On the other hand, I've always respected him as a player. He's a 6' 10" white guy who can't jump over a piece of paper, but I thought he was tough. He didn't back down from anyone and would do anything to help his team win—including committing acts of cheap-shot artistry that only someone like me could appreciate. I admire those qualities and abilities in an NBA player. Otherwise, I thought he was a jerk.

My feelings about Laimbeer were never more apparent than on the night of April 19, 1990, when all hell broke loose at the Palace in Auburn Hills. We were making our final appearance against Detroit, the defending champions, for the 1989–90 season, and while the Pistons had already clinched the best record in the Eastern Conference, we were looking for a win that would clinch the Atlantic Division title.

We hadn't won the division in seven years, not since the Sixers won the 1983 NBA title by steamrolling through the playoffs with 12 victories in 13 games. That was Moses's famous "Fo', fo', fo' " championship season. We knew we weren't good enough to win the 1990 title, but winning the division was the first step back toward respectability, our first step toward erasing the nightmare of finishing fourth in 1987–88.

That night, we had other motivation, too.

The Pistons had pretty much dominated most teams in the East that season. And they were 6–4 against the Lakers, Suns, Jazz, Trail Blazers, and Spurs, the teams in the Western Conference with a chance at the title. They kicked the Bulls' asses, winning four of five regular-season games. And they were a combined 8–1 against Cleveland and the Knicks, the second-tier teams. Against Boston, the most overrated team in the league that season, they were 2–2.

But we pretty much owned the Pistons that season, winning two of our three games going into that night at the Palace, all because we didn't fall for that "Bad Boy" crap. After all, the baddest Bad Boy was now a Sixer—my partner Rick Mahorn.

Mahorn had joined the team during training camp that season after being treated like shit by the Pistons. Just days after the team had won the 1989 title, Pistons management slapped Mahorn in the face by leaving him unprotected in the league's expansion draft. Rick was the first player picked, by the Minnesota Timberwolves.

Naturally, Rick was pissed. He refused to join the terrible T-wolves and traveled to Europe, where he was about to sign with some team known as 619XO Verona when the Sixers called. A trade was in the works with Minnesota, but the team wanted to know if he would report to Philadelphia or stay in Europe. Rick may be ugly, but he ain't stupid. He was on the next flight.

It was the best move the Sixers could have made that summer—signing someone who was even a bigger son of a bitch than I was. Having Rick around made things easier for everyone, especially me. He attracted so much attention from opponents that he psyched guys out. Hell, he psyched out entire teams.

While they were worrying about whether Rick was going to kill them when they drove down the lane, I was able to make steals, our center Mike Gminski was able to concentrate on defense and blocking more shots, and the guards were able to cheat out on the break more because Rick was such a smart position rebounder who launched two-handed, overhead outlet passes like Wes Unseld.

Most importantly, though, it was clear that the Pistons missed Rick more than they thought they would. They were still a great team after they let him go. They still had great talent. But there were two main reasons why the Pistons won the 1989–90 championship: (1) Chicago choked against them in the Eastern Conference finals, losing in seven games when Scottie Pippen suffered a migraine headache on the day of the final game. A migraine? Hell, Scottie's a great player, an All-Star–caliber player. But on this day, he suffered from a case of the can't-handle-the-pressures when his team needed him most. In other words, he choked. And (2) Portland wasn't smart enough to close them out after winning game two in Detroit and returning to Portland with a 1–1 tie and three straight home games to play. Instead, the Trail Blazers got caught up in the hype, the Bad Boy hype. Once the Pistons started beating them up on every play and then laughing at them, Portland rolled over and played dead. They stopped doing the things they'd been doing all year, which is exactly the Pistons' game plan. The Blazers were swept three straight at home, which was the most embarrassing thing that could have happened.

It was a charade, though, for the Pistons, and we knew it. The Sixers had the real Bad Boy, and the Pistons knew it. Bill Laimbeer knew it, too. Bill was able to talk shit, cheap-shot guys, and do the Laimbeer Flop all he wanted, as long as Rick was there to get his back—to take on someone, if necessary. But without Rick around, he was just a punk.

In fact, the Pistons missed Rick so badly that they tried to get him back. Before he was released by Philadelphia, the Sixers had made a deal with Detroit that would have sent Rick back to the Pistons in exchange for James Edwards, a thirty-five-year-old center. But Rick's salary was too much for the Pistons to fit in under the salary cap.

There are some unwritten rules among NBA players, one of them being that there are certain guys that you just should not take out with cheap shots. Michael Jordan is one of them, of course. So are Magic Johnson, Larry Bird, and David Robinson. I'm one of them, too. Cheap shots can seriously injure a player, and while I'll always foul a guy hard if I have to—no matter what new rules the league comes up with—I draw the line at doing anything that would injure any player.

Laimbeer doesn't seem to care about the league's "untouchables." He'll take anybody out at any time, any of us. One of the things he does is to use his lower body to knock you off-balance while you're shooting, which can easily make you land in an awkward way, causing an injury, a twisted ankle or knee. He also uses his arms well; he places them straight up in the air like he's innocently holding his ground, but he's really got his elbows in your face. If you happen to break your nose, so be it.

Now, I don't mind being fouled. (But be forewarned: if I take a hard shot from somebody, I feel obligated to return the favor.) I shoot 75 percent from the free-throw line, so I'll take the easy points. But I didn't appreciate it when he would take me out, which he's done so many times during my career that I was convinced that he was trying to hurt me. He had no respect.

By the time we arrived at the Palace that evening, everyone knew that the Pistons were worried about us. They were worried about facing us in the conference finals. Of all the teams in the East, we were the only one who wasn't afraid of them. So we wanted to mess with them from the opening tap, if not before. In the locker room before the start of the game, I wrote a note to Laimbeer and sent it to him through a ball boy.

It read:

Dear Bill,

Fuck you.

> Love,
> Charles Barkley

I never wanted to fight Bill, but the note set the tone for the afternoon. Once the game began, we upped the stakes by taunting the Pistons—particularly Laimbeer—throughout the game.

Rick gave Bill a hard time all day. When we were anywhere within earshot of him, we taunted him with the line from the movie *House Party:* "I smell, I smell, I smell . . . a pussy." And when I was on the bench, I led team cheers: "Hey, fellas? What do we think of the Pistons? *They ain't shit!*"

We were just messin' with him; the Sixers don't take anything too seriously. It's how we keep our sanity. Bill didn't say anything, but we could tell he was pissed. He was pouting and taking deep breaths like he was trying to keep himself from exploding.

He was also frustrated because he was having such a bad game. He finished with only 8 points, well below his average. He played like a, well, you get the picture.

Basically, we embarrassed the entire Piston team. At halftime, we led 53–43 and the Pistons were ready to collapse. Finally, with just 3:40 left in the game, Isiah Thomas, one of the most combative players in the league—don't believe that Babyface shit; Isiah will cut your balls off in order to win—just snapped. He ran right smack into Rick and turned the ball over. But before anything else happened, Isiah took a swing at Rick that grazed Mahorn's shoulder.

Rick didn't retaliate. What a sweet guy, huh? In fact, he looked at Isiah like he was crazy, like he was an annoying insect. Needless to say, Isiah was thrown out of the game.

The play didn't affect us one bit, while the Pistons seemed to give up. They just quit.

There were only a few seconds left in the game when Rick got out on a breakaway and jammed on a play that gave us a 105–95 lead. As we started to the other end of the court, I reached out to tap the ball out of bounds. Bill tried to slap my hand away. I didn't pay much attention to him because the game was pretty much over. But then Bill took the ball and rubbed it in Rick's face. Again, Rick didn't react to the incident. To him, Bill was just another insect.

But for me, Bill's act was the last straw.

My philosophy concerning my teammates has never changed. I would never belittle the military by saying that a basketball game is like war, but every time I step onto the court, the guys on the other team are my enemies. The game's not about making friends, it's about winning. As Malcolm X said, "By any means necessary."

After tip-off, the only people I trust are my teammates because it's us against the enemy. And I'll defend them in any situation. If anybody—*anybody*—bothers any one of them, I'm gonna make them pay for it.

No discussion. No argument.

That's why all hell broke loose at the Palace. It's no excuse for what happened, but Laimbeer was daring us to start something. So, we did. Specifically, I did.

The replays must have run on television a thousand times. It got ugly real fast. I charged Laimbeer and punched him at least twice, including once with a roundhouse left that caught him in the eye.

Everybody was involved in one way or another, pulling jerseys, wrestling guys to the ground, or generally just trying to keep from looking like sissies by staying on the bench.

The biggest coward of all was Piston forward Scott Hastings, who sucker-punched me in the back while I was at the bottom of a pile. The guy should get some playing time before he starts punching people.

Ten minutes after it started, the fight was over. Everyone in the Palace was stunned, but the fans managed to work up enough energy to boo me as I was escorted off the floor—and thrown out of the game—by referee Jake O'Donnell.

For the players, it was the most expensive game in league history. A total of $162,500 in fines were handed down by my good friend Rod Thorn at the NBA office. My bill was an unbelievable $51,700, including the amount I lost from the one-game suspension.

I'm convinced that Thorn goes overboard when he fines me, like he's charging me interest. But I didn't give a damn about the money after the fight in Detroit, and I still don't. It was worth it to make sure that Laimbeer didn't disrespect any of my teammates again. When that's being challenged, Rod Thorn is the last thing on my mind.

When will the league learn? The owners want us to play hard every night, to play with the intensity that gives them their "Fan-tas-tic!" highlights every night. But then they don't want us to ever lose our tempers. Right, Rod. Let's see you post up eighty-two nights a year against guys like Laimbeer and never lose your cool.

There are going to be a few fights every year. But overall, I don't think fighting is a problem in the NBA, not anymore. Fights are down from previous years, but it doesn't have anything to do with the fines. Players now, in general, have more respect for each other than to do the kinds of things that might instigate a fight.

There's less trash-talking going around these days than there has been in the past, unless Chuck Person's on the floor. Only insecure players talk trash. They're insecure because they think that the only way they can compete against a great player is to try and rattle him. But what players like that don't understand is that great players are great because they can't be rattled.

Personally, I love it when my opponent tries to rattle me like that. It only shows how stupid he is. If somebody comes into the game talking about how he's going to stop me, or take me offensively, I just laugh. It doesn't happen much anymore. The last thing anyone wants to do is piss off an angry animal. And when I play, I'm angry.

There are also fewer "take-out" plays, when one player tries to stop an opponent by doing something that might hurt him. That's where I draw the line with my own physical play. I'll do anything to an opponent, legal or not, if I can get away with it, but I'd never do anything to injure an opponent. With the average salary close to $1 million a year, we've *all* got a lot more at stake. Not just the stars. All of us.

The fine from that skirmish with Laimbeer was worth every penny because I stood up for my teammates and punched out a guy who tries to intimidate and harass his opponents to their limits, but then can't deal with the consequences.

On April 19, 1990, I was the consequence.

As for Laimbeer, I left that arena thinking that he was scum. During the off-season, though, I started to feel differently about him.

On the surface, it wasn't that important for us to get along because we don't live together. Unless you live with a person, who cares if you don't get along? If Bill and I lived together, we'd probably have killed each other by now.

Still, I began to feel like I wanted to change things with him, maybe even sit down with him to see if there was a chance we could understand each other better.

I don't know exactly why I had the change of heart. I wasn't mellowing in my old age, nothing like that. Maybe it was just the realization that if one of us didn't try to make things better between us, they might have gotten even worse.

The fight was our low point. It was embarrassing to see ourselves portrayed like that on television and in magazines and newspapers for weeks following the fight. I didn't want to keep playing against him with such hatred, on both sides. Sooner or later it would come up again, and we'd both lose it. Again. And the next time it would be even uglier.

Before the 1990–91 season, I decided that if we ever found ourselves together—just the two of us, away from the court— I'd ask him if he wanted to bury the hatchet. I don't hate anyone, at least not for more than forty-eight minutes, barring overtime. I don't sit around and hold grudges against anyone.

I didn't want to go through life knowing that Bill and I didn't get along because we didn't really try. For my own personal peace, I wanted to put our problems behind us. Hating Laimbeer for the rest of my life just wasn't worth the guilt and aggravation.

When the season started, I didn't know if we would ever get the opportunity to talk. I guess neither of us wanted to be the first to approach the other.

We played the Pistons four times during the 1990–91 season, and not once did I approach the game with an attitude ready to fight. Not once did I think, "Gee, I hope another fight breaks out." At least not with Laimbeer.

I was thrown out of our game at the Palace on November 30, but the incident had nothing to do with Bill. It involved Dennis Rodman, and it was unjustified. Rodman had been beating me up defensively during the entire game. That's his style, and it's earned him honors as the league's Defensive Player of the Year for two straight years—in 1989–90 and 1990–91.

On this night, it was a pain in the butt.

Dennis was built to be a defensive player. He's a lot like me in that he's big and quick, even though at 6′ 8″ he's almost four inches taller than I am. He's also got arms that seem longer than they should for someone his size. But what makes him most effective is the officiating.

Dennis is stronger than he looks, and he uses his strength to hand-check his opponents. It might not seem like much, but the reason the league outlawed hand-checking is that it had become an easy way to control players. By placing a hand on my opponent's waist, I can pretty much guide him wherever I'd like him to go. That's not defense; it's mugging.

A lot of what Dennis is allowed to get away with should be fouls. If anyone else played the way he does, in fact, it would be a foul. Maybe the officials believe Dennis has earned the right to hand-check.

All I know is that at least half of the scratches on my upper body are Dennis Rodman's signature.

With less than a minute remaining in the game in November, and the score still close, I was trying to post up against Dennis when I raised my arms to receive the pass and caught him in the face. It wasn't intentional, and I barely grazed him. Well, you'd have thought Dennis had been picked off by a sniper the way his head snapped back. He also fell to the floor. It was an all-time performance, one that convinced the refs to throw me out.

I was stunned—less at the fact that I had been thrown out than that I didn't get my money's worth for the ejection.

As for Laimbeer, I was still hoping that we could patch things up, maybe agree to a truce that considered everything that had happened between us prior to that season as history. Over with. Done.

I think we finally got it together on February 4, a day before the Sixers played the Pistons at the Palace. We teamed up that afternoon and filmed a scene for the movie *Hot Shots!*

Needless to say, I was at first a little reluctant to agree to do the scene. I didn't know what frame of mind Bill was in, since we hadn't talked. The filmmakers didn't know what to expect, either; they could have been risking their lives and tons of equipment by putting Bill Laimbeer and Charles Barkley within ten feet of each other. But it worked.

Before we started filming, I teased Laimbeer, just to feel out his mood. If he was going to be an asshole, I could play that, too. "If Bill doesn't screw me up," I said to the crew, "I might get an Academy Award nomination." Bill laughed.

In the scene, we pushed each other around, adding a lot of shoving, holding, and shouting. Nothing new for us.

We spent three hours together that day. And there were no off-camera fireworks. Instead, we talked. The conversation centered mostly on our families and our teams. Not that we'll ever get along on the basketball court, but I respect him a lot more now that I've gotten a chance to talk to him.

What I learned that day about Bill was that he's very funny and down-to-earth—even a nice guy.

Jesus, I never thought I'd say that.

I'M OFTEN ASKED to name my toughest opponents, the guys who give me the most trouble. Coaches have spent years trying to figure out how to guard me, and very few of them have ever gotten it right. Do you beat me up with a strong, Charles Oakley–type player? Or do you outquick me with someone like James Worthy?

During my NBA career, I've been guarded by 7′ centers and 6′ 4″ guards. I'm usually doubled-teamed, and sometimes I'm the target of numerous off-the-ball attacks—an elbow to the ribs, a knee to the back, a forearm to the shoulder (especially when I was suffering with my shoulder injury throughout the last half of the 1989–90 season; just ask the Cleveland Cavaliers, who took every opportunity to punch my shoulder during our first-round playoff series, which helped cause my pitiful .580 free-throw percentage during the five games).

No matter. With a 23.3-points-per-game career scoring average, and a .580 career shooting percentage, I've had reasonable offensive success against everyone and any defense that's been used against me. There are still a few guys who always give me trouble—and for different reasons—guys who I know are going to make my evening a nightmare.

The toughest guy I've ever played against is, without question, Kevin McHale of the Boston Celtics.

Kevin is strong and reasonably agile for someone his size, 6' 10" and a barrel-chested 225 pounds. But his greatest asset is his condorlike wingspan. Kevin's arms are so long they look like they should belong to Manute Bol, who's 7' 7" tall. They allow him to use his tremendous reach to make up for what he lacks in quickness.

Kevin can play me two ways, either with a solid body-to-body defense or out on the wing. Though I can usually get past him with my quickness, he's often able to reach back and flick away my shot because of his reach. And he usually does it without committing a foul because his long arms allow him to get to the ball without bumping me with his body.

In five games against Boston during the 1989–90 season, I averaged only 20.8 points, lower than against any other team in the Eastern Conference. I converted an embarrassing 45.5 percent of my shots, well below my 60 percent level for the year, and worse than I did against every other team in the league, except one, the Sacramento Kings. (I don't get it, either.)

The trend changed in 1990–91 when McHale's body finally began to betray him. By midseason, he was thirty-four years old and suffering from a lingering foot injury that would cause him to miss fourteen games before the end of the year. Even when he played, he was pretty much invisible, especially during the Celtics' two playoff rounds.

At the end of the year, Kevin hinted that he might retire. He's another example of what the game does to great players: it breaks us down like old horses until we're useless, then throws us away. Gone.

Playing the Celtics has always given me a high, but I particularly loved playing them during the 1990–91 season when everyone was talking about them as the "new" Celtics, simply because they had been revived by three fresh, young guards: Reggie Lewis, who was in his fourth season, third-year guard Brian Shaw, and rookie Dee Brown. Yet they were still anchored by the old reliable trio—McHale, Robert Parish, and of course, Bird.

The Celtics won the Atlantic Division title by an easy margin, twelve games ahead of us, and their 56–26 record was second best in the East behind the Bulls. But their season was a mirage.

If we hadn't suffered so many key injuries—Johnny Dawkins's season-ending knee blowout in the fourth game of the year knocked us out of the title chase—I'm sure the Sixers would've walked away with the division crown and maybe even challenged the Bulls for superiority in the East. I didn't want to hear about the "new" Celtics. I wanted to prove that in a head-to-head matchup on any night, we were just as good as they were, if not better.

As a result, in four games against Boston in 1990–91, I kicked ass. Without Kevin, the Celtics resorted to normal double-teams. It was cake. Double-teams don't usually affect me because I'm a pretty good passer, and I'm quick enough to get around most anyone. Boston didn't have anyone else who could even come close to guarding me, not Kevin Gamble (at 6′ 6″ and skinny, he's just too small) and not Bird (too slow). I averaged 32.8 points, 9.8 rebounds, and 7 assists against the "new" Celtics. I also hit more than 63 percent of my shots against the "new" Celtics, which in the NBA is in the damn-near-unstoppable category. That's how much of a difference a healthy McHale made for the Celtics, at least when it came to me.

Without him, it's Charles Barkley ass-whipping time.

The other player who gives me fits is 6′ 8″ Dominique Wilkins of the Atlanta Hawks, aka the Human Highlight Film. For me, he's usually a horror movie.

As a team, the Hawks have always been beatable. They have an attitude problem. When they're on a roll, they're a great team, but put a little pressure on them and they crash and burn.

Yet Dominique gives me real problems because he's the only small forward in the East with the right combination of size, quickness, jumping ability, and strength to damn near match everything I can do.

I can't beat him to the basket, so I have to use a lot of fakes to try and get him out of position.

I can't muscle him into the seats, so I've got to try and outjump him.

Right.

In 1989–90, I managed some respectable numbers against 'Nique and the Hawks—26.3 points, 11.8 boards, and a .540 field-goal percentage—in four games. The following season, though my scoring (27.8) and shooting accuracy (.545) went up against the Hawks, my rebounds (7.3) dropped like a rock. (I should've been able to get 7 rebounds in my sleep against those soft guys.) Again, I was respectable. But I never exploded against Atlanta, put up Mandingo-sized numbers—mostly because I was chasing Dominique's ass all around the court.

Enough of praising Dominique, though, because he might also be the most overrated, overhyped player in the league. 'Nique is a great, great scorer, but until the 1990–91 season he avoided rebounds and assists like they had a disease.

I think a player has to be able to do more than one thing extremely well in order to be considered a great player. Anyone can score, but great players also have to rebound, pass, or play tremendous defense in order to be a "great" player in my book. Most people, including the media, don't look at it that way. They get carried away with scorers, guys like Tom Chambers, Tony Campbell, and Reggie Miller. These are one-dimensional players, maybe even All-Stars. But they're not *great* players. There's a difference.

'Nique has made great strides in improving his all-around game, but he's still not as good as the hype would have you believe. Take away his scoring ability and what do you have?

I'VE ALWAYS KNOWN that certain tricks were necessary for survival. You've got to have these gimmicks because in the NBA everybody is just as talented as you are, so you need even the smallest of advantages. At our level, it's a mind game. All pro sports are a mind game.

I also had a great teacher: Moses. He taught me how to step on a guy's toes when he's getting ready to shoot. You can only do that close to the basket where the ref doesn't have a good look at your feet, but it works. Throws off their rhythm and trips them up just enough to where I might be able to strip them of the ball.

If I had to name the league's all-time defensive player, a guy who played defense with sheer guts and little else, it would be Sidney Moncrief.

Sidney played for the Milwaukee Bucks for what seemed like a hundred years—actually, it was ten seasons, starting in 1979–80—before old, tired knees finally forced him into early retirement at the end of the 1988–89 season. He came back, though, and was a valuable contributor to the Hawks during 1990–91 as a reserve, and as a baby-sitter for a team even he said was "too emotional."

Sidney is a true gentleman, someone who was always nice to you off the court, but who would play you like an assassin during games. One year, when the fans in Milwaukee were booing and cursing me the entire game—okay, so I had popped Paul Mokeski in the face during the previous game—Sidney came to me and tried to keep me from getting discouraged. Not many guys in the league would have done that, if any.

Sidney played defense from the old school. On the court, he was a hard, hard brother who would beat me up for three quarters then play with me in the fourth when I was too tired and frustrated to do anything about it.

He was thirty-three years old during 1990–91, and his knees only allowed him to play limited minutes for the Hawks. But Sidney, I've got only one thing to say to you:

Go away. Please.

Strangely enough, the player in the league who comes closest to matching the defensive style Sidney possessed in his heyday— imagine the Teenage Mutant Ninja Turtles triple-teaming me on the block—also plays for the Bucks. Alvin Robertson resembles Sidney Moncrief in many ways. They're both 6' 4" and broad shouldered and extremely strong. And like Sidney, Alvin's one of the best defensive players in the league, even if he is a hatchet man.

That's right. A hatchet man. Alvin is Sidney with a sledge-hammer. Referees let him get away with more hand-checking than a prostitute. The way he plays the game is supposed to be illegal. Instead, he was voted the league's 1986 Defensive Player of the Year. If I hit people as hard as Alvin, Rod Thorn would exile me to the World Basketball League for players 6′ 4″ and under.

Anyone who's ever seen me play knows that I've got nothing against hard, physical basketball. In fact, I'd rather hit a guy than watch him dunk on me. And when I'm on offense, I enjoy drawing a guy into making contact and committing a foul, because most guys in the league aren't strong enough to stop me from getting my shot off. I also enjoy dishing it out.

My strategy is simple: I try to beat up anybody I play against hoping that when the fourth quarter arrives, they'll have nothing left. In the fourth quarter, it's a battle of wills.

Basically, I'll just do whatever it takes to win, to beat my man on either end of the floor. If I'm bigger than my opponent, I'll try to overpower him. If he's bigger, then I'll try to outquick him. I use a lot of quickness around the basket. When someone tries to box me out or hit me, I'm gone. And you can't hit what you can't catch.

When a guy tries to take a charge against me, I knee him in the chest, just a love tap, a little something to knock the wind out of him. One such shot and a player usually won't stand in my way a second time. Like I've said before, athletes aren't dumb.

Some of them, though, are crazy. These are the guys who *love* contact. They give hard fouls and they take them without flinching. Greg Kite has lasted eight seasons in the NBA without an ounce of talent—only guts. He's survived by being a hard-ass for Boston, the Clippers, Charlotte, Sacramento, and Orlando.

Joining him on my all-hard-ass team are Charles Oakley of the Knicks, who probably uses his body better than anybody in the league; the Lakers' Jack Haley, who's not as tough as he thinks he is; and no surprise here, Bill Laimbeer.

One thing these guys have in common is that they'll all try to frustrate the opposing team's best player with physical contact. Instead of playing basketball, they play like frustrated Wrestle-mania stars. It usually works.

Laimbeer single-handedly—or single-*fist*edly—turned around the 1990 NBA Finals when he started throwing the Portland Trail Blazers all over the court in game three. I'll let guys like Bill get their one hard foul, then I'll warn them:

"You've got to cut that shit out!"

Then, if necessary, I'll get in one good solid shot of my own, and that'll take care of that. Usually.

AS FOR MY all-NBA team, I've got a few surprises. Anybody can put Michael Jordan, Magic Johnson, David Robinson, Patrick Ewing, and Larry Bird—as well as myself—on their all-NBA team. But I'm going to be different. I want to point out the guys who play their guts out, who do their jobs every night, but don't get enough credit from fans, coaches, and the media. These guys are usually the ones who make the difference between their team's being a contender or being eliminated from the playoffs in the first or second round. One guy won't win shit in the NBA, not even if he's Michael, Magic, Patrick, and myself all rolled into one body.

That said, here's *my* all-NBA team, an underrated group of players who do the right thing every night, get the utmost out of their skills, and who should be recognized every season as some of the best players in the league in their position:

- *Kevin Johnson,* Phoenix, point guard—The Cleveland Cavaliers kept the wrong guy. Midway through the 1987–88 season, they traded Kevin, their backup point guard at the time, along with forward Tyrone Corbin, center Mark West, and three draft choices, to the Suns in exchange for forwards Mike Sanders and Larry Nance. Instead, they should have traded their starting point guard, Mark Price. Both guys are killers, but there's not a point guard in the league who can keep up with Kevin. More than anybody in the league, he's an assassin.

- *Rolando Blackman,* Dallas, shooting guard—If I've got five seconds to score the winning basket and I've got my pick of anybody in the league to take the shot, it'll be Rolando, the league's best clutch shooter. It doesn't even help to foul him because he's a career 83.6 percent free-throw shooter. As a last resort, I'll tell jokes while he's on the free-throw line. It doesn't help.

- *James Donaldson*, Dallas, cocenter—Who, you ask? Most people thought this huge 7′ 2″, 278-pound center would never make it in the NBA, let alone become a starting center. Two teams traded him before he joined the Mavericks in 1985. For the fact that he can't jump higher than my grandmother, he plays his position as smart as anyone.

- *Robert Parish*, Boston, cocenter—If he doesn't make the Hall of Fame, they ought to tear it down. He'll probably play more seasons than Kareem Abdul-Jabbar, and he might have broken some of Kareem's records if he gave a damn about records. Instead, all he ever cared about since he came into the league in 1976—Jesus, I was in eighth grade!—was winning.

  Too bad Golden State management was too stupid to realize that the Chief was the best thing it had on the roster. More than eleven years after maybe the worst trade of the eighties—Parish and a 1980 first-round draft pick, which became McHale, for two first-round draft picks—the Warriors still haven't recovered. By himself, Bird would not have been able to win three championships during his career with the Celtics. He wouldn't have won even one of those titles without Robert Parish.

  What's most amazing about Parish is his longevity. Most big men don't hang around very long because they get a beating every time down the floor—body against body, elbows and knees banging and forearms in the back. He may not have lasted so many seasons had he played twenty years ago. He's lucky that there are so few true power centers in the game. Twenty years ago, he would have had to play Nate Thurmond one night, Wilt Chamberlain the next night, and Bill Russell the next. Those guys would have been beating him up.

  Now, there are really no power centers. They all run, jump, and dunk, play a finesse game. Even the best centers. Patrick Ewing doesn't play with a lot of power. Neither does David Robinson, Brad Daugherty, or Vlade Divac. Having all of those guys around has kept Parish young.

• *Scottie Pippen*, Chicago, small forward—Might be a toss-up with Dennis Rodman, but Pippen gets the edge for taking and shaking off a cheap shot from Dennis during the 1991 Eastern Conference final. They're both great players. Dennis is still a liability on offense; he's going to have to improve that before he can reach the next plateau. When he gets there, he'll find Scottie waiting for him. Scottie didn't let his embarrassing ending to the 1989–90 season get to him. He came back and proved that it was simply part of his growing process.

Even while he was in the middle of a contract dispute with the Bulls, he continued to play well. And even though he and the team had come to an agreement before the end of the NBA Finals, Scottie was still in a precarious position. He could have hurt himself and played so poorly that the Bulls might have considered reneging on the agreement. Instead, he was the series MVP I-A, as far as I'm concerned.

• *Buck Williams*, Portland, power forward—As I've said, I truly enjoy playing against Buck because whenever we square off, I know it's going to be work. It's going to be a war. On some nights he gets his; on others, I get mine. Either way, we both always walk away feeling good about each other. Honorable mention in this category goes to Horace Grant of the Bulls. I'd love to play with him. He's a rebounding machine, just kicked everyone the Lakers threw at him in the Finals to establish himself as one of the league's new premier power forwards. But his twin brother, Harvey of the Bullets, might eventually be even better.

• *Kevin McHale*, Boston, sixth man—Like I've said before, he's the best player I ever played against. Guards me tougher than anyone. That alone is enough to earn him a place on this team. He hasn't been the same since he injured his foot a few seasons ago, as much as he's probably refused to admit it. And don't think the Celtics haven't missed him. In fact, I think they miss him as much as they miss Larry Bird.

And now, for good measure, here's my scouting report on how I'd play Charles Barkley:

First, I'd assign a quick defender to him, rather than a strong one who might try to beat up on him. Most players try to get physical with him. Check out the photo on the cover of this book. See the scratches on his arms and shoulders? NBA battle scars.

But very few players in the league, if anyone, will ever out-muscle him during the course of an entire game. And most strong guys are too slow to keep up with him, either in the halfcourt game or on the run. You can't guard what you can't catch. Put a big muscle guy on him and you'll be down by 10 at the end of the first quarter.

Then, I'd make him shoot jump shots rather than allowing him to drive into the lane. That means your guy has to back off and give him room. Get too close and Charles will talk to your defender. He'll flat out tell the guy, "Hey, fella, if you're close enough to touch me, I'm going around you." The guy will probably start laughing, but then Charles will do it!

And don't get fooled by his tricks: Charles likes to wear his jersey loose because down in the trenches, down on the low box under the basket, opponents often grab a player's jersey in order to throw off his balance. So Charles leaves a couple of inches of jersey hanging over his shorts and pulls on the front of his jersey to keep it loose. It almost always works; you can grab his jersey, but Charles still has room to get off his shot or move into position.

Those are the plans, anyway. But the fact is, you'd also better be ready to clamp down on his teammates, because while you might slow Charles down, there aren't going to be a lot of nights where you really stop him.

9

BUT, I AM RICH

I don't make a million dollars like you.
> —ZACK HILL, 76ers public relations
> director, to Charles Barkley.

I don't make a million dollars, either. . . . I make
three million.

> —CB

STAGGERING.

That's the only way to describe the salaries professional athletes are earning these days. It's unbelievable. Mind-boggling.

For the 1991–92 NBA season, I'll earn just over $3 million simply for playing basketball—for playing a game—and I'm not even among the league's five highest-paid players. I don't pull down as much cash as several baseball players, including Dwight Gooden of the Mets, who signed a three-year $16.2-million contract before the start of the 1991 season, which will pay him an average of $5.4 million per season; and Boston Red Sox pitcher Roger Clemens, who also signed a new contract, one that pays him $21.5 million over four years, or $5.375 million a season.

And these guys only play about thirty nights a year.

Unbelievable.

The *average* salary for the NBA's 324 players was about $900,000 annually during the 1990–91 season when the minimum salary was $120,000. In 1991–92, the minimum will go up to $130,000. That's what a player will earn just for listening to the

national anthem eighty-two times during the season and for showing up at practice every day. That's what you can earn for being
Scott Hastings.

With average salaries so high, a lot of players can burn $300,000
in the fireplace and still have enough for them and their families
to live better than 99 percent of the people in America. Unless
he's a total nitwit with his money, he's totally set for life.

Unfortunately, too many people are financial nitwits—buying
cars so fancy that they don't know what all the buttons do, expensive clothes they don't look good in, and stereo equipment
they can't operate. Give me a sweat suit and a comfortable pair
of jeans and you've got one happy man.

On top of the financial rewards of being a professional athlete,
there aren't a lot of demands on our time. Pro basketball players
work seven months (if you're the Los Angeles Clippers) to nine
months (if you reach the NBA Finals) out of the year, and we're
obligated to the team on most game days for fewer than four
hours, from ankle taping to shower. It's like a dream. An unbelievable dream.

Are we overpaid? Yes.

But then, so are entertainers, guys like Bruce Willis, who
earned an unbelievable $15 million for just seven weeks' work
on one damn movie, *The Bonfire of the Vanities;* and Arnold
Schwarzenegger, who copped a few million for only six weeks'
work on *Kindergarten Cop.* Since both of those movies bombed,
their salaries should be matched against those of NBA players
belonging to teams that also bombed in 1991—say, like the Nets'
Derrick Coleman ($3 million in 1991–92) and Blair Rasmussen,
formerly of the Denver Nuggets, ($2.2 million in 1991–92).

On the other hand, no one could ever say that Magic Johnson
($3.1 million), Michael Jordan ($3.2 million), David Robinson,
($2 million), and most of the top players, including myself, don't
earn every dime we get. While a lot of NBA players are stealing
money, we're helping the league go to the bank—and making a
little deposit ourselves.

No one should ever forget that athletes are entertainers, too.
Sports is entertainment, nothing more. In comparison with actors, we're a damn bargain. And yet, for some reason, people

are constantly scrutinizing, criticizing, and whining about the athletes' salaries, saying, "Hey, you're just running up and down the court in shorts and sneakers, you don't deserve that kind of money." At the same time, they're making Bruce Willis a hero.

Well, actors aren't getting their asses kicked by Kevin McHale, Buck Williams, and James Worthy every night, either. And they can make bad movies until they're eighty years old, while we're lucky if we can play until we're thirty and walk when we're fifty. Given the pounding that I've taken during my career, combined with the injuries I suffered during the 1990–91 season—a stress fracture to my right ankle at midseason and partially torn knee ligaments toward the end of the year—I know that by forty, I probably won't be able to walk normally. But that's the price you pay to be a professional athlete, and it's worth it.

But let's be real. The NBA is a business, a highly successful and lucrative business. With expansion, new television contracts with NBC and TNT, with growing sales from officially licensed NBA products like T-shirts, mugs, posters, and God-what-have-you, and with increased attendance in just about every city, all but four of the NBA's twenty-seven teams turned a profit in 1989–90. And an average of 16,759 fans attended an NBA game in 1990–91, which proved that the league's business prospects are as strong as ever. When it comes to the bottom line, the NBA is truly *FAAAAN-TAS-TIC*.

NBA player salaries pale in comparison to the revenues earned by the owners. And to my knowledge, no one's ever paid a dime to watch Harold Katz or any other league owner do one damn thing. As long as there's no end in sight for profits, there's no end in sight for the players' paychecks. So get used to it.

The highest salary I'll earn, in the final guaranteed year of my contract, is just over $4 million a year—barring a renegotiation, which is always a possibility. But look for other players to earn several times that amount.

Already Larry Bird will earn $7.1 million for the 1991–92 season, the last year of his contract. And before long, players like Patrick Ewing could sign new deals worth more than $5 million annually, which would force guys like Michael and Magic—and yes, me—to walk into the owners' offices and say,

"What's the deal?" It would create havoc. In fact, when Patrick lost his arbitration hearing with the Knicks in the summer of '91, a lot of guys were pissed. We were all hoping for a raise.

One day, maybe professional athletes will even catch up with Bruce and Arnold; I know we'll catch them if they keep making movies like *Bonfire* and *Kindergarten*.

Most fans have a distorted view of contract renegotiations. They think we're overpaid in the first place, so why should we want more? But the sports business is unlike any other industry. With an athlete's career being so short, we're forced to try and earn as much as we can before our bodies break down and our skills deteriorate. I've renegotiated my contract twice during my career, and each time the Sixers were more than willing to agree to a new deal because they knew that the franchise was increasing in value—Katz bought it in July 1981 for $12 million; in 1991 it was estimated to be worth $75 million—and that without me, the Sixers would have absolutely zero chance of winning the title and putting fannies in the seats every night. I said I deserved a raise, and they knew I was right.

Some players have used tricks in order to get a raise when talks aren't going their way. Some have faked injuries; others have put forth a halfhearted effort during games. Both of those methods of negotiations are gutless. If a player wants more money, he should just be a man about it and ask. Now, I'm not above holding out if I don't think the negotiations are making progress. That's different from faking an injury or playing half-assed basketball because at least I'm being honest about my reasons for not playing, and I'm not dragging my teammates into my problems by doing something that might affect their performances, too.

Withholding our services is the only real weapon we have in securing better contracts, and as long as we're honest about our reasons for wanting more money, then that's all a player has to do in order to make the owner see the light. Most owners don't know what they've got until it's gone.

I can sleep at night knowing that I deserve every penny I get, just like most every other player in the league—even Scott Hastings. But that doesn't keep this poor Alabama boy from shaking his head in humble amazement every day when he thinks about his financial condition. I never played basketball because I thought it was going to make me rich; I played so that I would be able to take care of my family and make them comfortable, which I could have done by making a good living at a number of other professions.

I also played for the challenge of getting better at the game, of proving wrong the people who doubted my skills—from coaches who thought I wasn't good enough to make their teams because I played "like a white boy" (whatever that means) to critics who thought that no one my size could dominate inside the paint in the NBA. Beyond that, winning was always my motivation, not money.

But make no mistake, I'll never underestimate the value of a buck. Especially a buck with my name on it.

In October 1984, I signed my first NBA contract with the Sixers, and it was for more money than I'd thought I'd ever see in my life—more than $2 million over four years, which included a $250,000 signing bonus, a quarter of a million dollars just for writing my name on the dotted line!

My salary—after the team got rid of Leo Rautins and opened up a nonminimum-salary slot for me—was $150,000 for my rookie season, a whopping amount at the time in the league, with raises to $432,000 in the second year, $650,000 in the third, and $700,000 in the final season of the deal.

Dumping Rautins, the team's 1983 second-round draft pick, was no big loss for the Sixers. He had played in only twenty-eight games during the previous season and would play only four games for the Atlanta Hawks before being waived again, this time forever. But it was a big gain for me because it allowed the Sixers to satisfy my salary demands and avoid an ugly holdout. And it would have been ugly.

Instead, everyone was happy—even though I had to agree on a weight clause that said I would be fined for weighing over 268 pounds. The clause in my current contract says I have to stay under 260. No big deal. I've known since my final year at Auburn that I play better at a lower weight, about 250 pounds, so I've never had a problem making weight in the NBA.

Besides, do you think I'd give Harold Katz a *refund* for any reason at all?

For a few minutes after I put my signature on that first contract, I was in the Twilight Zone. It was an absolutely incredible feeling. "Damn," I thought to myself, "I'm making two million dollars for playing basketball."

I was like a little kid walking to the candy store knowing that I could have anything I wanted from the shelves around me. Five years later when I renegotiated for the second time and signed my current contract—a six-year, $19-million deal guaranteed through 1994–95, with a three-year option worth another $12 million—I actually went numb for a few minutes. Never in my wildest childhood dreams did I expect to earn $2 million, $3 million, or $4 million a year doing *anything*, let alone for playing basketball.

The reality of it was scary. To think that there was almost nothing material that I could want that I couldn't afford was just about incomprehensible. The key word is *almost*.

Too many young professional athletes can't control their new-found wealth. To a lot of us, signing a multimillion-dollar contract is like winning the lottery. We see what we think is the contract's bottom line—the dollar signs—but fail to see the true bottom line: economic reality, after taxes.

Without common sense and self-control in spending and saving, those millions might as well be Monopoly money. Frivolous buying sprees, high-risk investments, and idiotic handouts to friends, family, and sometimes to people we hardly even know can reduce your bank account to a closet full of outdated clothes, a garage filled with used cars, and a portfolio composed of swampland in New Jersey and a ranch in west Texas, all before you've figured out how to unsnap your new warm-ups.

Fortunately for me and my family, I survived my period of free-spending insanity and moronic investing. But not before I made some serious mistakes and learned some costly lessons.

Until the middle of the 1988–89 season, four years into my pro career, I received an allowance of $10,000 a month from my agent, Lance Luchnick. Little did I know at the time that I would eventually lose a fortune in bad investments—but more on that later.

I called my allowance "blow it" money, because Lance was paying all of my bills. My paychecks from the Sixers were sent directly to him in Houston—a tremendous, major, stupid mistake. He wrote checks and made the payments for everything I needed, from my mortgage to credit cards and even my electric bills.

So, at the age of twenty-one—just a few years out of the projects—what did I do with my ten grand per month? Stupid shit. Basically, I blew it on anything and everything I ever wanted to buy. I called it "living" expenses. It was really "livin' large" expenses.

When you make the kind of money I made as a rookie, people treat you like gold. Especially banks. I walked past a bank and was offered credit. So what did I do? I bought anything and everything my signature could get. I bought eight or nine cars— four Mercedes-Benz models, a BMW, a couple of Porsches, and two trucks—and kept them in either Philadelphia or Alabama. A half million dollars in cars! It was ludicrous. I could only drive one car at a time, but having all of them was like a dream for someone whose mother had had to take the bus across town to work when my grandmother needed the family's only car, an old, beat-up Chevrolet Bel-Air.

I bought shit simply because I could afford it, not because I wanted it. Not many people that age who have the ability to walk into any dealership in the country and drive out with any car in the showroom can resist the temptation to do just that—especially someone who was raised without some of the basic necessities of life.

For a lot of young professional athletes, particularly young black athletes from low-income areas, economics becomes the primary reason we play sports. Once I realized that I had the talent to play in the NBA, following my sophomore season at Auburn, I used sports, in part, as a way to improve life for my family. Many of today's young players are no different, except the stakes are a lot higher. As I've said, I never dreamed of making a million dollars. But today, a rookie who's among the first few players drafted hits the lottery. He becomes an instant millionaire.

Kendall Gill, the fifth player picked in the 1990 draft, six years after I was chosen, signed a contract with the Charlotte Hornets worth $8 million over four years. With that kind of cash at stake at the end of the rainbow, it's no wonder that many young athletes are feeling more pressure—too much pressure, really—to play sports than to get an education.

It's no wonder that so many young athletes are leaving high school unprepared for college.

And it's no wonder so many college athletes leave school without coming close to earning a degree and are then left stranded in life because they weren't good enough for the NBA, NFL, or major-league baseball.

There's nothing wrong with wanting financial security. Everybody does. I've got no problems with families encouraging their children to use their athletic skills as a means of achieving monetary success. But they shouldn't push it to extremes.

When Hank Gathers died suddenly in March 1989 from a heart condition that had been diagnosed several months before his death, there was a lot of talk that perhaps he felt pressured by the financial needs of his immediate family and other relatives—all of whom might have benefitted from the big payoff in the NBA—and that Hank felt forced to play basketball when he probably should have given up the game. I honestly think that most families wouldn't force their kids to do something detrimental to their health. But no kid should have to deal with that kind of pressure, not with the odds of ever becoming a pro athlete so stacked against them.

It troubles me when young high school players come up to me and tell me they're going to be an NBA player someday. My response is always, "Probably not." They think reaching the NBA is easy, and once there that it's an easy life. They think it's just about basketball. Well, it's not. It's about hard work, discipline, and caring enough about yourself to strive to get better every day. In two words, it's *real life*. Nothing less.

If there should be any pressure on young athletes, it should be that they get an education, that they obtain a degree and focus their energy on becoming productive citizens in any number of high-paying, lucrative professions. There are only 324 jobs in the NBA, and only about fifty new players on average are good enough to join the league each year. That's not real good odds, considering the thousands of college players leaving school every year, most of them thinking, "Hey, I just know I'm good enough to play in the NBA. I just know I'm better than (fill in the blank)."

They've got a better chance of landing on the moon.

Considering the odds against them, and the relatively poor backgrounds that a lot of young athletes have experienced, it's little wonder that so many of the players who do reach the pros don't have the discipline to handle their financial windfall. It was difficult enough when the windfall was a $250,000 signing bonus. When it's a $1-million or $3-million first-year salary, it's damn near impossible. That's why so many of us struggle financially during and especially after our careers, despite the high salaries.

For many of us, the life of wealth is like living in a foreign country. We're not prepared to deal with the differences, to understand anything anyone is telling us or to know the local customs. Sooner or later, if we're lucky, we eventually learn the language, but not before making a lot of costly mistakes and maybe even embarrassing ourselves numerous times.

Besides foolish spending, there's another economic temptation that trips too many young athletes and sends us tumbling back toward the kind of poverty we left behind: the temptation to loan large amounts of money to our friends and family.

Resisting the urge to give money to the people we know and love is the toughest "just say no" this side of the temptation to use illegal drugs. It's especially tough because most athletes believe—rightfully so—that we're obligated to help our families in any way we can, particularly when they supported us through the ups and downs of our whole athletic careers.

These are the people we truly love, people we've known for all of our lives. How can we turn them down?

Also, as someone who earns more than anyone in the family ever thought possible, we're almost always fighting a nagging feeling of guilt, which often causes us to reach into our wallets whenever someone asks for a handout.

The truth is, though, that an athlete's family and friends can milk him dry, just like an unscrupulous agent, and I've seen it happen too often during my career.

It's sad. More so, though, it makes me angry when I know a guy has worked his ass off to reach the top of his profession and finally gets a multimillion-dollar contract, only to be surrounded by a bunch of assholes, most of them family and friends, who don't have enough respect for the athlete to leave him and his money, *his* money, alone.

One of the ways we get suckered by people close to us is by thinking that these people are telling the truth when they promise us that the cash is just a loan, not a gift. "Yeah, man, I'll pay you back," they say.

Bullshit.

I've made about $200,000 in "loans" to friends and family during my career that I know I'll never see again. If I hadn't learned how to say no early during my career, that figure might have become $2 *million*.

I used to have a problem telling the people that I love, "No, I can't." Sometimes, I still do. If someone I truly care about needs something material that I know I can buy without even thinking about it, how can I say no?

Sometimes it's a car, so that the person can get to work every day and not have to take a bus.

Maybe it's clothes, so that they can make a good impression at work.

Perhaps it's a house payment, enough to get through hard times.

Maybe it's money to cover debts, enough to keep someone from going under.

It might even have been money to pay for unforeseen medical expenses.

Sometimes, it was $10,000. Or maybe $5,000. To me, it was loose change. But in reality, it was enough that I soon found myself in the danger zone—not financially, but mentally. I was giving away money for reasons I couldn't even remember.

Even worse, after a period when I was giving out money like Santa Claus, people began *expecting* me to give them money, as if I were the United Negro Whatever I Need the Money For Fund. Rather than doing whatever they could to help themselves out of their problems, these people started thinking, "Hey, let's ask Charles!"

Once I realized I was being used, it became much easier to "just say no." And I did, even though it didn't go over well with people who thought that, because of my salary, I *owed* them money whenever they needed it. A lot of people in Leeds, many of whom I thought were friends, started trashing me all over town. *Charles has changed. He ain't cool anymore. He's an asshole.*

I've come to understand that money doesn't change people as much as it changes the people around them. People whom I've known all my life, people for whom I would do almost anything in the world, suddenly became jealous of my success and began asking for the most ridiculous amounts of money as soon as I joined the NBA. Basically, they thought I was a bank.

Professional athletes and entertainers are also targets for solicitors from all sorts of charitable and wannabe charitable groups, individuals, and organizations. But as usual, we've got to learn to be careful, to weed out the truly deserving from the truly ludicrous. Every day my telephone at home rings and it's someone on the other end wanting money. I get sob stories in the mail. I get sob *faxes*, for chrissakes! *My son is dying, would you send him to Disney World?* Jesus. Give me a damn break.

It would be easy to say yes to every request we receive because deep down in our hearts, we all want to be well liked, and getting involved with popular and high-profile charities is one way to insure that people who don't even know you will feel that you're a wonderful person. *Isn't that special?* But that's a good way to run yourself ragged to the point where you can hardly do your main job, kicking butt on a basketball court.

Anyway, too many athletes and entertainers donate their time and money to charities for the absolute wrong reasons: either they need another tax deduction or they think it'll make people believe they're an all-American boy, which could translate into more endorsements. These are the athletes you see on the nightly news shaking hands with sick kids, then a month later on the very same network selling some product that's not good for anyone.

Yes, I give money to charities, but how much I give and to which groups I give is nobody's business but mine, my family's, and my accountant's. I've always believed that if you do something out of the goodness of your heart, rather than simply to enhance your public image, then who has to know except you and God?

In a strange way, I've been able to capitalize on my antihero image with commercials that reflect my personality. None of the three companies whose products I've endorsed—Nike, Gillette Right Guard, and Nestlé (Chunky candy bar)—ever asked me to do anything but be myself, which is the only thing I would ever do when it comes to endorsements. I also enjoy the performance aspect of the commercials, especially when the shoots are completed and everyone's pleased—even surprised. Despite the fact that I hate the long hours, I really try to concentrate and study my lines because I don't ever want anyone thinking, "Look at him, just another dumb jock." Not that any of the shoots were easy. On the contrary:

- *Right Guard*—"Well, it's off to the foxes"—required two ten-hour workdays in Charlottesville, Virginia, as well as one helluva lot of patience. I'd be in the middle of saying my lines, and my horse would start to pee. Or the dogs would bark. By the end of the two days, I was cranky and just about ready to kill the damn dogs. It was also freezing, which did nothing for my disposition. Or my love of animals.

- *Nike*—Believe it or not, the ad featuring David Robinson—"Charles, have you ever been fined?" "Oh, no, never, no, no, no . . ."—was filmed before the spitting incident. On this shoot, I was allowed to be a little creative and rewrite the script. It had originally been written that I would just say, "Nope." During one of the first takes, I joked around with the line by shaking my head and repeating the "no" several times. It turned out well. Everyone on the set had a good time, and it turned out great. In the newest Nike commercials, I got to work with the best director I've ever known, Joe Pitka. He never over-works his people—I once worked with Spike Lee, and he had so many takes I wanted to kill him. Joe's a frustrated basketball player, though. In between every take, he wanted to play one-on-one. About the only thing I can say is that he's still living to talk about it.

• *Chunky*—The shoot took more than twelve hours, and believe me, no matter how much I love Chunky—and I do—it's hard to look happy when you bite into a candy bar for the twentieth time. When the director yelled, "Cut," I spit it out fast. I didn't get home until about two A.M., and I didn't want to see another chocolate bar for a couple of days—even a Chunky. (Did I mention how great I think they are?)

While we're on the subject of endorsements, I'd like to address the criticism that professional athletes like me, Michael Jordan, and David Robinson are receiving because kids are committing crimes over sneakers and other sportswear products we endorse. The truth is, I've never even given it a second thought.

Our message has always been clear: the shoes are good, buy them. That's all. Nothing more. No pumps or "Air" Anythings will ever turn a kid into Michael Jordan, David Robinson, or Charles Barkley. But somewhere along the way, the message got lost. It got lost because kids weren't being taught proper values at home or in school. And it got lost because people were allowing kids to feel like their image was related to the shoes they wore. That's stupid.

It's also stupid to blame athletes for the problem. But that's typical of society. We love to blame other people for our problems.

Well, this is the problem: people are raising bad-ass kids.

I won't let anyone put that on me.

When I speak to kids, I try to explain to them that I am who I am because of God-given physical gifts and hard work—not because of my Nikes. I know most of the kids think I'm full of shit, but I just hope I can reach a couple of them every time I speak. I also know that the jails have always been full of hard-headed people who wouldn't listen to those who tried to guide them the right way.

Until society comes up with stiffer penalties for criminals, there'll always be crimes. And we also have to solve some of the problems on the outside. In some cities, being in jail is better than struggling on the streets. I've spoken to some inmates who've said they committed crimes on purpose, just to get off the street. That's ridiculous.

That's why I don't worry about whether my endorsements will cause someone to kill another person for a pair of sneakers. Our ads might be a symptom of the problem, but we're not the disease.

But society, as usual, has to blame someone for its insecurities and its inability to provide everyone with the basics of life. It must blame someone for its failures. Well, I say, everyone must take responsibility for their own lives. Whether they're successful or not, they're the ones to credit or to blame. Not anyone else.

I'M NO DUMMY. I know a lot of people I meet treat me well because I make a lot of money and play basketball for a living. I'd say 90 percent of the people who speak to me on the street, in a mall, or in a restaurant fall into one of those two categories. I can tell who's for real and who's full of shit. As long as I know that, I'm safe.

Athletes and entertainers get in trouble when we start believing the stuff we hear from people who are only pretending they like us for their own selfish reasons. Too many of us believe the hype. I give Moses all the credit for teaching me the real deal when it comes to the glory of sports. "Don't believe the shit you hear," he said. "Don't believe it." That's why I keep my distance from most people and generally go my own way. I don't need anybody else around me except God, my family, and a very, very few close friends.

I've been lucky when it comes to money and my family. I decided early in my career to give them everything they needed—cars, homes, all the necessities—so that they wouldn't have to call me for money whenever the urge hit them. I figured that if they were driving around in a car that I'd purchased and living in a home for which I was paying the mortgage, then they would be taken care of financially. They would never have a need for anything and could just enjoy their lives. I also wanted to make life comfortable enough for my brothers that all they would have to concentrate on is keeping their lives together, staying away from drugs, and getting an education.

My brother Darryl, who suffered the stroke, is getting himself together, which makes me extremely happy. He's conquered his drug problem and he's got his life moving in a positive direction. My other brother, John, just received a scholarship to attend the University of Arkansas, Little Rock. To see them moving forward and out of trouble, and also being able to take care of my mother and Granny, was all I ever wanted out of life.

But family and friends aren't always the problem. Money has done funny things to some athletes. The ones who amuse me the most are the guys who dress like Giorgio Armani, Don Johnson, and Philip Michael Thomas every damn day. You know who I'm talking about. Just look around the next time you attend a game.

Among the group of agents that I was considering to represent me when I left Auburn, Lance was the only agent who hadn't given me money while I was in school. When it came down to my final selection, that worked in his favor. I thought he had been smart enough to know that I couldn't be bribed. I hadn't even met him until after I decided to leave school, after the Olympic Trials, and I chose him for the worst reason anybody could choose an agent—write this down, kids—*because he was a good guy*.

Lance was everything I wanted in an agent. He was smooth. He was young. He was cool. He had mastered the art of "street talk" and was well versed in black music and other forms of black culture—I guess you've got to be that way if you're going to be a sports agent—so he never seemed like someone who would be working for me. He seemed like he could be one of the fellas. I liked that.

He took me on the nightclub circuit in Houston, and we partied like two people who had a lot in common—when, in fact, it was all a game. We were about as different as two guys could be in terms of upbringing and values.

I was caught off guard by his act, and I bought it hook, line, and sinker.

At the time I was trying to hire an agent, I was having problems with a couple of the agents who had helped "finance" my lifestyle while I was in college. They were pressuring me to sign an agreement right away, but I had no real "interview" process, and I couldn't decide what I wanted to do, who I wanted to handle my money. Some of them were putting on a lot of pressure, being real heavy and threatening to reveal that I had taken money while I was in school if I didn't allow them to represent me.

What did I care? I was gone.

Lance was just the opposite of those guys. He didn't put any pressure on me. We just hung out, playing the streets like a couple of musicians. I soon signed with him, and as soon as I signed my first contract, I paid every one of those agents back for every dime they had "loaned" me while I was at Auburn. I wanted to start my pro career with a clean slate, without anyone saying that I owed them something. Being indebted to anyone can be a dangerous way to be, especially when that "anyone" is an agent.

Maybe the root of the problems I eventually had with Lance was that I became too friendly with him. He was a white guy who acted like he was black. Maybe I was fooled into thinking that he was my friend, someone I could trust, rather than someone with whom I had a business relationship, someone who had to be accountable for every penny of mine that crossed his desk. After all, I had to trust someone, so it might as well have been someone with whom I could have a good time. And that was Lance.

But then again, maybe I was just stupid.

Of course, I wasn't the only athlete who's ever been caught off-guard by a fast-talking agent. The line starts at Kareem Abdul-Jabbar and winds through practically every city with a major-league team. And it includes some of the most prominent athletes in professional sports, guys like Ricky Pierce, Larry Smith, Terry Catledge, and Cliff Levingston. All of them have claimed that agents cost them hundreds of thousands of dollars, at least. And all four players have blamed their financial losses on Lance.

Here's one more tale of stupidity and bad judgment to add to the list.

MY RELATIONSHIP WITH Lance didn't change during my first four years in the league. We were like running buddies, partners against the world. I was extremely happy with my first contract, which had been more than fair, at least at the time, for the fifth player chosen in the draft. Since then, things have changed so much that most rookies are paid more than guys who've been in the league for more than five years. For instance, Gill's $1.5-million salary for his rookie season was higher than that of ten of his teammates!

Rookies aren't worth the kind of money they're making these days. It isn't fair that any rookie makes more than an established player who's been busting his ass in the league for five or six years. In most cases, rookies don't play as much as the older players because they aren't ready to handle the league's talent level, which has gotten so much better than it was ten years ago that very few rookies can even play dead at the NBA level—let alone play well and contribute to their teams' success.

In 1990–91, I thought only three rookies were really worth a damn: Derrick Coleman, Dee Brown of Boston, and Gill (though I still don't think Gill was worth $1.5 million). None of the other twenty-three first-round draft choices were in the same class with those three guys, not to mention the other forty-nine rookies— guys who played in at least one game. They weren't even in the same building.

Derrick is a stud. Even as a rookie, he was one of the toughest guys who guarded me all season, which was why I averaged a below-average 25.1 points a game and shot like crap in four games against the Nets. It's also why I'll always be a Derrick Coleman fan, even on those nights when I'll look forward to playing him about as much as I look forward to talking to Rod Thorn.

Brown probably had more of an impact on his team than any other rookie. When he came into the game, it was as if the Celtics had found a fountain of youth. Soon he could become the Kevin Johnson of the Eastern Conference: a pain in the ass.

And Kendall will be an All-Star. Write it down. If the Hornets trade him, it would be one of the stupidest things they could ever do.

The jury is still out on Lionel Simmons of Sacramento, who finished second to Coleman in the race for Rookie of the Year. How he came that close, I don't know. The only thing asked of him was to come to games and shoot. He was never asked to play defense, to rebound, or to pass. Hell, he wasn't even playing under any pressure to win. Because of those conditions, his numbers—18 points per game—were inflated. On a real team, he might have averaged 10 points a game; he might also have become a better player.

Anyway, two years into my own career it was already clear that I was underpaid. I was the Sixers' second-leading scorer, trailing Moses Malone but ahead of Julius Erving, and was our leading rebounder. Lance handled my renegotiation as well as any agent could have done, getting me an eight-year deal that averaged $1.613 million a season, give or take a few cents. As far as I was concerned, I was in fat city.

Of course, he was making money, too. Big money. And at my expense.

At the time, there were no regulations concerning the amount of commission an agent could charge for negotiating a contract. In 1988, the league's players, knowing that salaries were exploding to ridiculous heights, voted to restrict fees to 4 percent, an amount that would still allow agents to pocket huge commissions. With no cap, Lance pocketed 10 percent of my rookie contract, paid to him in large increments, starting with my first paycheck. That amounted to $200,000 that I just kissed goodbye before it ever crossed my palm.

As a rookie, I didn't want to get involved in any financial matters. I just wanted to play basketball and enjoy life. I didn't want to pay bills, write checks, anything—all things that showed how careless and immature I was at the time. The only instructions I gave Lance were two simple ones: "Give me my allowance and then invest the rest."

In truth, as long as I had my $10,000 a month, I didn't care what happened to the rest of the money. I wanted it to be invested wisely so that my family wouldn't have to worry about a thing for the rest of their lives, but I didn't care how it was invested, where it was invested, or with whom it was invested. All of these were huge mistakes. Very few young athletes making long dollars are prepared to manage it themselves, so they've got to trust somebody. But my experience taught me that they've also got to pay attention to every dime, every penny that they earn, because in the end, it's the athlete who gets screwed, not the agent.

My financial "plan," as it were, was fine. If Lance had placed my money—the $250,000 signing bonus, plus about $5,000 on the first and the fifteenth of every month, minus my ten grand and his commission—into a damn savings account at 6 percent, or maybe bought some CDs and a couple of government T-bills, I would've been living large by now, even if I never signed another contract. But he didn't. Instead, Lance was putting my money, *my* hard-earned cash, into a lot of high-risk speculative ventures that to this day haven't earned me one damn dime.

I might as well have flushed it down the toilet.

Thanks to these investments, I was soon living a financial nightmare—all because I trusted the wrong person. And because I didn't pay attention to what was happening to my cash.

I confess: I screwed up, too. A lot of what happened to me was my own fault. Lance didn't take the time to discuss any of his money schemes with me, and I didn't care to ask. Major mistake.

The damage:

I was part owner of a couple of farms. I had paid about $100,000 to feed cattle on a ranch in a little town called Crizzo Springs in south Texas, and I owned about seventy-five head of Beefmaster cattle in a small town near Houston, which cost me more than $150,000.

I was also growing pecans in another dot-small Texas town, on a farm in which another $25,000 of my cash was sunk; and I was involved, to the tune of $80,000, in another partnership called the Highway 90 Joint Venture, which owned raw land near San Antonio that was supposed to be worth $1.5 million at the time my group sank $900,000 cash into it. It was appraised in 1990 for less than the $600,000 note that was taken out to buy the property.

There's more: I had about $100,000 in two hotels, one that went bankrupt and another that never broke ground; another $50,000 in a Texas bank that went bust; and another $50,000 in a horrible car dealership in New Jersey.

But even worse, my taxes were screwed up big-time. Lance had either paid my taxes late or not at all, every season since I came into the league—four years' worth of back taxes and penalties. *Get out your calculator, fella, and say a prayer.*

A lot of people were living well off my money—extremely well.

On April 3, 1988, the *Newsday* newspaper on Long Island, New York, ran a long article on Lance, charging that he had paid high school and college coaches in order to get them to convince players to sign with him. Some of the money went to the player; the coaches kept the rest. The payments violated NCAA regulations.

The article also talked about some of Lance's questionable business dealings with several NBA players, including the ones I've already named. It was ugly. As I read it, my palms sweated and I had daymares. I wondered if I had any money left at all.

When people asked me about the article, I admitted that I had taken money from agents while I was at Auburn, though not from Lance. I also said that I thought there was nothing wrong with paying players because college athletes can't work while regular students can. "Universities prostitute guys," I said.

In a sense I didn't want to believe that the article had anything to do with me. After all, I trusted Lance. He was a great guy. So I tried not to think twice about the allegations. But then, more rumors about some of Lance's deals started to circulate among the players in the league, especially those of us whom he represented, including Levingston, Pierce, Alton Lister, Vinnie Johnson, Robert Reid, and Catledge. By the best we could figure when we started comparing notes, we had all lost money on deals Lance had arranged.

The players started exchanging information. Everybody and their brother was telling me not to trust Lance; they were warning me. But I was loyal, blindly loyal.

Maurice Cheeks had also been represented by Lance for the first eight years of his career, but he switched to Lee Fentress of Advantage International in Washington, D.C., prior to the 1986–87 season. He dropped Lance because of some bad investments in condos. One reason I didn't worry about my investments was because Lance had represented Maurice, too. I guess we were just alike: naive, trusting, and unconcerned.

In mid-June, the bomb dropped. The NBA Players Association suspended Lance from representing athletes because of the findings in the article. Soon, a lot of people started panicking, including me. I started having my paychecks sent directly to me instead of Lance, and I just deposited them into a checking account that was bearing next to nothing in interest. I didn't care. At least it wasn't losing money.

Deep in the back of my mind, I still wanted to think that my finances were just fine, but it was becoming harder and harder to believe it.

That summer, a friend of my mother's recommended that we hire the accounting firm Arthur Young & Company to audit Lance's books. I was real worried about what they were going to find, and I started shifting some of my money away from Lance's clutches. I got in touch with Glenn Guthrie, a Birmingham investment banker and Auburn alumnus whom I'd met while I was still in high school. Glenn was one of the few decent boosters I'd come across. While a lot of other people were fickle—they were either your friend or a stranger depending on how many points you scored that night—Glenn was a genuine friend throughout my ups and downs.

During my junior season at Auburn, I hurt my back and had to miss several games. Glenn was the only university booster who stuck with me when I couldn't play. He was the only person who was there for me when I needed someone. Even before he had anything to do with my life, other than being a basketball fan, Glenn treated my mother and grandmother with respect. I always remembered that, especially when I picked up the telephone and dialed his number.

"Glenn," I said, "I think I've got problems. I want you to invest some money for me."

He agreed, and I sent him a check for $30,000, what I had put in my checking account. He immediately placed it in solid, tax-free investments. A couple of weeks later I sent Glenn another $100,000, and it, too, was tucked safely away.

In December, I invited Glenn to Philadelphia, along with a lawyer he hired, Tom Sullivan, to meet with me and Joel Walberg, one of Lance's partners, to pore over my most recent tax returns. Shortly after that, I asked Glenn to take charge of my finances and my career, and in March we called Lance and fired him.

By then, I soon discovered, it was too late. Basically, the shit hit the fan. The deeper we got into the audit, the more we saw my finances were a mess.

Lance claimed that it was the guys who worked for him who screwed up the investments, not him. "I gave them the money and they lost it," he said. "It's not my fault."

No matter. To me, he was responsible.

I didn't have any money from the investments that Lance had set up for me. Not one dime. I had already made over $1 million in my career, but I didn't have anything to show for it. Nothing. I was shocked, pissed, and distraught. But there wasn't one damn thing I could do about it.

Later, Sullivan characterized my investments as "nuclear waste" because they never go away.

Eventually, I tried to sue Lance in an attempt to recover my losses, but he responded by filing for bankruptcy. And I didn't pursue the lawsuit because even if I had won, he wouldn't have had the money to pay me. I consider it a wash—a costly but educational wash. In exchange for my not pursuing the law suit, Lance forfeited all claims against me.

If nothing else, I thought Lance could have apologized. It's not right. What did he gain? And was it worth it?

I'll never get any answers. Instead, Lance still denies doing anything wrong. He claims he isn't guilty of anything.

By the end of the 1990–91 season, I had pretty much gotten myself out of danger. That's how long it took us to pull me out of most of the deals, cutting our losses. I've paid off most of the debts, pulled out of all but one of the partnerships—anybody need any beef cattle?—settled my bill with the IRS, and paid my own accountants and lawyers. Total bill: $1.5 million.

Fortunately, I've never been one to worry about the past, only the future. I consider the Lance saga in my life to be over. Now I've got to go on about the business of making my family comfortable and happy. I made a fool of myself, made one big mistake, and lost a whole hell of a lot of money. Shit happens. End of story.

What truly amazes me is that despite what happened to me, athletes are still signing Lance to be their agent. He represents Keith McCants of the Tampa Bay Buccaneers in the National Football League, their No. 1 pick in the 1990 draft and the fourth guy picked overall. And he represents a few guys in the NBA. I don't understand how that happens.

If people don't learn from other people's mistakes, then they deserve anything that happens to them. Fellas, you've been warned.

I was extremely lucky to have discovered the financial mess I was in early enough in my career to be able to recover. When I think about what happened to Kareem, losing nearly all of his $59-million fortune near the end of his twenty-year career, I can only thank God that the same thing didn't happen to me. As for my current investment strategy, it's conservative. I place 90 percent of my earnings in stocks, bonds, and other low-risk, solid-gain investments. The other 10 percent is risk money, almost play money. But no, there won't be any beef cattle added to my portfolio.

I always wondered: Did Kareem play the last couple of years of his career because he truly wanted to, or because he had to?

Athletes in all sports, despite their exorbitant salaries, have to do a better job of managing their personal affairs. Too many of us become too lax when we see all those zeros next to our name. But if you don't keep tabs on your cash, monitoring every transaction that takes place, seven zeros can become one big, fat zero so fast it'll make your head spin.

My advice?

1. Don't hire an agent. Hire an attorney to negotiate your contract and pay him a fee, not a percentage. All of the salaries in pro sports are easy to find, so negotiating a deal is just a matter of comparing your skills (or if you're a rookie, where you were drafted) with guys with similar statistics. As for myself, I don't need anyone anymore to speak for me at the bargaining table. All I have to do is call Michael J.

"Say, Mike, how much are you making?"

"Mr. Katz, I want a dollar less than Michael."

2. Don't let your attorney handle your money. After they negotiate the contract, don't let them get a finger on your money.

3. Hire an investment firm, and ask them—no, *order* them—to place most of your money in sound, safe investments such as CDs and U.S. government bonds, places where your money will grow slowly over time. You're probably making so much money that you don't have to worry about quick, high-risk money-making schemes. You don't have to worry about taking $25,000 and trying to turn it into $100,000 in ten days. Stay away from shopping centers, land-speculation deals, oil wells, and any other "can't miss" investment. Under the new tax laws, there's no need to "hide" cash in shady tax shelters anymore. If anybody tells you otherwise, they're lying.

4. Stay hip to what's happening. When an athlete's money goes sour, he's the one who gets in trouble with the IRS and investment companies. He's the one who gets screwed in the end, which is why a little bit of attention will be the best investment any athlete can make.

In 1988, my mother and I were discussing the upcoming presidential election when I told her that I was going to vote for George Bush, the Republican, rather than Democrat Michael Dukakis. She was stunned. As a longtime Democrat, like most blacks, she thought that I would naturally pull the lever for Dukakis.

"But Charles," she said, "Bush will only work for the rich people."

"But Mom," I responded, "I am rich."

Thankfully, that story still makes me smile.

10

THERE ARE IDIOTS OF EVERY RACE

I MARRIED A white woman.

So what? It's nobody's business but mine and my family's.

Still, the fact that my wife, Maureen, is white has pissed off enough people in Philadelphia for standing-room-only crowds at both the Spectrum and Veterans Stadium across the street. Some of the whites in town who think I'm so great simply because I can dunk a basketball would just as soon hang me from the nearest tree. And a lot of black women in the city have hassled Maureen and taunted her in public.

All of it only proves that racism has no color.

RACISM FRUSTRATES ME.

It's silly—no, stupid—to dislike someone simply because of the color of their skin, just like it's stupid to *like* someone simply because of their skin color.

Unfortunately, people are being judged by their race all over the country, even in sports, where a lot of people judge athletes—particularly black athletes—by different standards depending upon the color of their skin. Fans, the media, and team management too often look upon black athletes as commodities, as pieces of meat who got their skills naturally, who don't suffer pain and who only play badly if they're on drugs. That goes double for black athletes who don't fit the all-American-boy mold. At the same time, most white athletes are looked upon as "family" by management and fans, and they're often given the opportunity to work for the team they played for in some capacity after their playing days are over.

Case in point: In April 1991, just five years after retiring from a very average nine-year career with the Bucks, Kings, and Knicks, Ernie Grunfeld was named New York's vice president of player personnel, the team's second-highest-ranking executive. Grunfeld had quickly moved up the ranks, joining the team as a radio announcer immediately after his retirement in 1986, then to assistant coach in 1989, and then to player personnel director in 1990, where he stayed until his latest promotion.

This isn't a knock against Ernie. He's paid his dues and is as qualified for the position as anyone else the Knicks might have dragged off the street, but guys like Billy McKinney also paid their dues. Yet after playing seven seasons with the Kings, Jazz, Nuggets, Clippers, and Bulls, and working several seasons as a scout for various NBA teams, including Chicago, Billy was fired from his job as player personnel director for the Minnesota Timberwolves in November 1990 just because he knew more about basketball than the coach, Bill Musselman. Then the Timberwolves turned around and fired Musselman at the end of the season. At the time, McKinney was still out of a job.

Even worse, former All-Stars like Bob Lanier (fourteen years in the NBA), Nate (Tiny) Archibald (thirteen years), George McGinnis (eleven years in the NBA and ABA), and several other black former players haven't been able to get jobs in the league in any capacity. It doesn't make any sense, especially when there are enough idiot GMs working for their third or fourth NBA team to start another entire league.

Thank God I have no interest in working for an NBA team when my body finally gives out. With my reputation, I wouldn't even have a shot at cleaning the toilets in the league offices in New York, let alone any other NBA job.

I firmly believe that when it comes to athletes, sports is the one area of society that brings the races together without any hint of racism. For as long as I can remember, I've played on integrated teams, and there were never any incidents that could be categorized as racist. Don't get me wrong; guys of different races have gone at each other pretty hard. There have even been fights. But that's competitiveness, not racism.

Competitors always want to do their best. And they always want to beat the other guy—no matter his color.

Racism is the easiest excuse in the world. I've had black teammates in the NBA who've grumbled about playing time, but they seem to grumble louder when they're playing behind a white guy—guys like Marc Iavaroni, Tim McCormick, and Danny Vranes. Not great players, but good players. That's bullshit. "The reason you're not playing is because the white guy's better than you," I'd say. "So shut up and stop complaining."

Sometimes, I think that if it weren't for sports, society would be all fucked up instead of only partially fucked up.

PEOPLE SHOULD BE judged by their actions, their words, and what they stand for, not for something over which they had absolutely no control—their race. I've already accomplished a lot of things in my life, and I'll continue to accomplish things long after my career is over. I'm proud of what I've been able to achieve, but one thing I didn't achieve was being black. It was God-given, not Charles-given. Why should I be "proud" of something I had absolutely nothing to do with?

Sure, members of the Ku Klux Klan will tell you that they're proud of being white, but what they're really proud of is being in the Klan. It's the only thing in their lives that they ever truly accomplished, joining a group that criticizes other people for no other reason than that they're different.

Basically, they're proud of being assholes.

In 1988, the Reverend Jesse L. Jackson became the first black American to make a serious challenge for the presidency of the United States. His success in the state primaries was largely due to the great many people—people of all races—who agreed with his position on the various issues. But there were also a lot of blacks who supported Jackson for only one reason: because he was black. That's just as stupid as voting for a candidate because he's tall or short or good-looking.

Society has so many problems these days—homelessness, the recession, and crime immediately come to mind—that people have simply stopped looking at the whole picture when it comes to the issues and problems they face every day. Instead, they pretend like we live in Disneyland where everything is as simple as "It's a Small World." That mentality is what makes so many people gather among themselves and pat themselves on the back for being black or white or Italian or Korean or anything. It's why people do stupid things for the wrong reasons—like voting for, or against, someone because of their race.

Jesse had nothing to do with his blackness. Neither did Virginia governor Douglas Wilder, nor did any of the more than two dozen black congressmen (and women) or the thirty black mayors in large cities around the country. So to vote for Jesse, or any other black political candidate, simply for that reason is ludicrous.

PHILADELPHIA IS ONE of the most racist cities I've ever seen. It's almost completely segregated, with the majority of black people living in a part of town known as North Philadelphia, which is also very poor, while whites dominate the population in just about every other part of town, but especially in Chestnut Hill, where the rich whites live. But more than that, a lot of people in the city have an attitude problem when it comes to race.

Most whites are afraid to go into the "black part of town," and blacks in the city are often harassed at public places like shopping malls in the white—excuse me, I mean the "exclusive"—parts of town.

I'm smart enough to know that because I'm a professional athlete in a town that's crazy about sports, I'm immune to the kind of racism that most blacks in Philadelphia experience on almost a regular basis. One way to stop people from reacting to the color of your skin is with the color of money. Well-paid black athletes and other entertainers in this town—guys like Randall

Cunningham, Keith Jackson, and Reggie White of the Eagles; and saxophonist Grover Washington, Jr.—are heroes. But without that big fat paycheck, all of us would just be another bunch of potential criminals to most of the whites in town. To some idiots, we'd just be another group of niggers.

You know, honey, that Charles Barkley's a helluva black basketball player. I've heard that one before, along with a few other idiotic words of wisdom from some of the bigots in Philly. Well, a word to the people in town who think that way: If you've got that mentality, I'd rather you not come to the game. I'd rather you not watch. Stay away from the Spectrum. Root for the Knicks. Stay home!

Actually, I laugh at racists—and there are racists of all colors. That's about all they're worth, a good chuckle. How can you take a racist seriously when all he's doing is using racism as an excuse for his own lack of success in life?

Because they're failures, racists look everywhere for reasons why they're in the garbage at the bottom of the barrel, everywhere except where they should look—in the mirror.

Black racists blame their problems on "the white man." *I can't get over because the white man's treating me bad.* Right.

Hard work, intelligence, and discipline are the key ingredients of anyone's success. With them, a person of any color can overcome practically any obstacle—and that includes discrimination, poverty, and almost any other condition that has nothing to do with your will to succeed.

White racists, on the other hand, blame their problems on blacks and the antidiscrimination laws that have tried to change more than a hundred years of unfair hiring practices that kept blacks, other minorities, and women from getting their fair share of the nation's jobs and other resources. *I'm better qualified, but I can't get a job because the company's got a quota of blacks and women—people less qualified than I am—that they've got to hire before they can even look at my application.* That's bullshit, too.

White racists can't get over the fact that a black man might be just as good at something as they are, if not better. They can never imagine that a black man could be smarter than they are.

The bottom line is that all racists need to feel secure about themselves—*My problems aren't my fault!*—so they get mad at someone else, the government, the system, even the dog. But mostly, they get mad at somebody who's not like them instead of facing the truth: that they're losers.

Most people have faced discrimination at some point in their lives. Blacks, whites, and a lot of other people have been treated like shit by people whose only concern was the color of the other person's skin. For some people, it happens every day. But the intelligent ones among them don't let discrimination stop them from moving toward their goals.

If they're discriminated against by a teacher, they just work harder and move on.

If they're discriminated against by someone interviewing them for a job, they just become more qualified and move on.

If they're discriminated against by their boss, they just become so good at what they do that the boss can't overlook them, then they move on.

They move on—more determined than ever.

My own experiences with racism while growing up in Leeds helped teach me early in life that there are idiots of every race. For the most part, I was too young to have experienced any of the blatant racism that was so prevalent throughout the South. By the time I was ready to go to elementary school, laws had been passed making separate public facilities—schools, bathrooms, restaurants, anything—illegal. The civil rights movement was at its peak around the country, but to a little kid in Leeds, Alabama, it seemed like it was happening on another planet. I didn't watch many of the historical events on television. I couldn't. We only had one small, black-and-white set in the entire house. It could only receive three channels, and two of them didn't come in too well.

That doesn't mean I was immune to racism, or ignorant about what was going on around me. There were only a few black students at Leeds Elementary School, the formerly all-white school I attended that was downtown, several miles from where I lived in an area along with most of the other blacks in town. Busing had just reached Leeds, so any black kid who wanted to go to Leeds Elementary could have gone there. Leeds Elementary had better facilities, more books, and more school supplies than the black elementary school, which didn't even have enough money to buy new books every year, let alone other new supplies.

Only a few of the blacks realized the impact of sending their kids to Leeds Elementary. Too bad. I'm convinced that the kids who went to that school are today, in general, better off academically and professionally than the kids who went to the all-black school. Sad, but true.

I was involved in a lot of fights and shoving matches at Leeds Elementary. My mother and grandmother had tried to prepare me for the name-calling and the taunts, but most of my days were still filled with stress because of the way I was treated at the school and then again by the kids in my own neighborhood. But I blamed the way these kids acted on their own stupid insecurities rather than on anything that had to do with me. The vast majority of the kids at the school, and the vast majority of kids in my neighborhood, were truly nice to me, so I didn't hate the school or the kids I met there. I can't help but feel, though, that the kids who were racists then are still racists—racist failures.

I was always more upset with the blacks who mistreated me than the whites. Maybe a better word is disappointed. I could never understand why they resented my attending the mostly white school, especially when they had the opportunity of going there themselves. My family only sent me there so that I could maybe have a better life than they had growing up. But rather than support that decision, people criticized my mom and Granny and accused them of "trying to be white." It was unbelievable.

There's a big difference between trying to be something different from what you are and trying to improve yourself. A lot of blacks still haven't learned the difference between the two. We spend too much time criticizing each other over whether someone is "trying to be white" by getting an education, or speaking a certain way, rather than encouraging each other and supporting those blacks who are doing whatever they can to overcome all of the obstacles in their way.

Sometimes I think we hold each other back more than the white man does.

Even though I was hurt by some of the racist assholes I went to school with when I was young, the experience was one of the best things that could have happened to me because it taught me at an early age to judge people as individuals, not as members of a particular group. There were many blacks in Leeds who didn't condemn me and my family when I went to Leeds Elementary, and there were whites at the school who tried to make me feel comfortable.

Most importantly, I learned that there are idiots of every race. And there are good people, black and white. To say that one group, or any group, is better than another is ludicrous.

It was a good thing I had received that early education in race relations because when I reached Auburn, it was time for postgraduate work.

From the beginning of my arrival at college, my life at Auburn wasn't all basketball and classes. Socially, I can only characterize my initial experiences as "interesting." The student body was 99 percent white, a major shock for a kid who lived in the black part of Leeds all his life. One of first my reactions when I got to Auburn was, "Jesus, there's no black people here."

It was strange. There were more than 18,000 students at Auburn, but only about 430 blacks. And of that group, most of us were athletes; the few other blacks were brains, damn near geniuses. If you were a black with just average intelligence and couldn't play sports, you could forget about going to Auburn. You went to Alabama.

The sea of white faces was pretty intimidating at first, even though I had attended an all-white elementary school and a racially mixed high school. I didn't know what was going to happen. I didn't know whether these farm kids would be able to deal with me and my outrageous attitude and become my friends, or whether they would turn on me because I was black.

As it turned out, I had nothing to be afraid of. I was never involved in any racial incidents at Auburn. I never had any problems there with racism or racists. Students, teachers, alumni, everyone always made me feel good about my decision to attend the school—even as I was catching hell from Sonny Smith and hating every minute of it. I understand that much of the way they treated me was because I was an athlete, but the atmosphere at Auburn was truly like one big family. That's mainly because the surrounding town—Auburn, Alabama—revolved around the school, and the school revolved around sports. Everyone within a hundred miles of the campus supported all of the school's programs—academically and athletically.

It was also an experience that added to my belief that blacks have to be able to deal with whites, and vice versa, in every situation. It doesn't matter how they feel about each other, because, in the end, neither of them is going to change colors.

It pisses me off when I hear blacks say they can't deal with a white world. Well, guess what? It's not going to change, so rather than staying to ourselves and segregating ourselves from the rest of society, we've got to learn the tricks of the trade, then use them in order to achieve success.

ONE OF THE longest-running soap operas in Philly involves the whispers surrounding my marriage.

There have been whispers about why I married Maureen ever since we got married on February 9, 1989. I've heard the garbage some people have said: "Charles just married her because she was white; he always wanted to marry a white woman." That's bullshit. I married Maureen because I loved her and I thought she'd make a great mother. That's it. But I know there'll always be snide remarks and hateful stares. That's why our few close friends in Philadelphia are so important to us. They help us put up with the crap that's around us every day. All our friends and family want is for us to be happy.

MAUREEN BARKLEY: *Charles and I met in October 1987 when he stopped me and my boss as we were leaving a Friday's restaurant in Philadelphia. He was polite. He said hello to me and my boss, but I had heard that he was a jerk. And I had seen him play and thought he was immature.*

He went into the restaurant and asked the manager who I was. Then he talked one of my girlfriends into giving him my number. Without asking me if it was okay! If she had, though, I would probably have told her, "No."

We actually talked on the telephone for about a month before going out. That allowed me to get to know him much better, which was good because I didn't think much of him at the start.

Our first date? A basketball game. He left me two tickets, so I took my brother.

There were two girls sitting in front of me who stared at me so much that I thought Charles had left four tickets for women. Actually, they were friends of his and he had told them to check me out and tell him what they thought. Nice guy, huh?

I didn't know this when we went out to lunch a few days later, so I wasn't very friendly. Eventually, Charles told my girlfriend—the one who had originally given him my number—that I was stuck up, when I was just reacting to the fact that I thought he had invited two other women to the game.

We both had a good laugh when we realized both of us were wrong. Finally, we worked everything out.

What someone does with their own life shouldn't have an impact on anyone else's life. Whether I married a woman who's black or white shouldn't matter one bit to anybody outside of our families. Sure, it was an adjustment for both groups of our parents, particularly for Maureen's parents. They were shocked when their daughter pulled a "guess who's coming to dinner" on them twenty times over. *Not only is she dating a black man, but she's dating a big black man.* They got over it, though. Now, all they're concerned about is their child's happiness.

MAUREEN: *For a long time, I didn't tell my folks that Charles was black. I didn't know how they would react, and I wasn't real eager to find out. Turns out they were uncomfortable, but not because of Charles's race. They were concerned about him spending so much time on the road. My dad asked, "What do you think they do out on the road?"*

Fortunately no one in Philadelphia has ever made any racial comments to us when I was around, or I might have had to smack someone, male or female, across the face.

MAUREEN: *People always stare. By the way they're acting some-times I don't know if they're staring at me because I'm Charles's wife, or if they're just staring at Charles.*

When I'm alone, people say things to me on a regular basis. More than I tell Charles about. It happens to me about once a month at my health club, and the comments come mostly from either black women or white men.

They'll whisper just loud enough for me to hear, "That's the bitch who's married to Charles Barkley."

Or they'll follow me into the bathroom and say, "Why don't you stick with your own kind."

They're just jealous. Charles is a good catch.

In April 1991, just after the spitting incident, a white man came up to Maureen in a bar in Philadelphia and acted like he was someone she knew. "How's Charles?" he said. "How's the baby?"

After Maureen smiled and said that everyone was fine, he spit in her face and said, "How do you like that, nigger lover?"

Maureen didn't even tell me about it until late that night because she was afraid that I might've gone out and tried to kill the guy. She was right. If I'd been there and I had my gun, I might've blown his fuckin' head off. And I wouldn't have been sorry about it one bit.

What's most scary is that the majority of people think we live in a world where everything is just fine, that racism and stupidity are gone because a bunch of black men are getting paid millions of dollars for running around in the NFL, NBA, and major-league baseball—all leagues that once barred blacks.

They think everything is just fine because a few blacks are becoming successful in business, entertainment, and politics.

But it's not true.

There will always be racism. It will always be around us. When we stop recognizing the truth, then we'll all be in deep, deep trouble. But we can't allow ourselves to become a part of it, to be suckered into arguing about race, something that people can't change about each other, something that shouldn't matter at all.

MAUREEN: *I don't know what we're going to tell Christiana about racism. We'll have to be really strong for her. And we'll have to be honest.*

Remember, racism is the racist's problem, not ours.

11
SERIOUS, SERIOUS PAIN

OH, SHIT!

Damn.

The mind can do amazing things in just a short period of time. In an instant, during the few seconds when I felt the kind of piercing pain in my left knee that every professional athlete dreads, my entire career actually flashed before my eyes.

One moment I was bumping bodies and elbows underneath the boards as a shot bounced away from the rim, and then— after the sudden pain sent me crashing to the floor, helpless and scared—I was wondering if I would ever play basketball again.

It was Sunday afternoon, March 31, 1991, and the Sixers were playing the Cleveland Cavaliers at the Spectrum in Philadelphia. Midway through the third quarter, I got caught in the lane behind my teammate Rick Mahorn as several players pushed, shoved, and grabbed each other while trying to rebound a Cleveland shot. In the confusion, Rick lost his balance and tumbled backward. Before I knew what had happened, all 255 pounds of him was landing on my knee—an otherwise healthy joint that had never suffered from anything worse than soreness and tendinitis (the ailment of choice in the NBA) during almost fifteen seasons of basketball.

I was surrounded by bodies, swallowed by bodies, but I still intended to get the rebound. I almost always got the rebound. But this time, I couldn't move backward to avoid Rick's weight.

And by the time I realized something bad was happening to me, his body had caught me like a vise. I couldn't do anything to deflect the weight of this 6'10" behemoth. Then I felt the snap or the tearing. Most of all, I felt the pain.

I screamed.

I clutched my left knee, tumbled to the floor, and rolled onto my left side. Rick was also on the floor. He was unhurt, but he was afraid—afraid to believe that he might have been responsible for what he was seeing. Even some of the Cavs stopped playing and tried to help me. As I lay there on the floor next to Rick, and as the crowd inside the Spectrum fell silent, Cleveland forward John "Hot Rod" Williams, the highest-paid player in the NBA, stooped over and tried to comfort both of us.

But nothing helped. The knee hurt. Hurt bad. And I knew the injury was worse than a minor sprain because when I got up, I couldn't put any pressure on the leg. None at all. "That's it," I thought. "I'm a cripple."

What I believed was happening to me was every athlete's worst nightmare: a potentially career-ending knee injury. Specifically, I thought I had suffered a torn medial collateral ligament, which can best be described as a knee explosion. It's as if the knee is blasted by a Scud missile. Destroyed. When the smoke clears, there's nothing left but a few shreds of muscle. And whether or not the athlete ever plays again—Bernard King is the classic comeback fairy-tale, coming back five years after such an injury to become an All-Star—he is never, ever quite the same.

As I lay there on the floor, I had two thoughts. One of them concerned Johnny Dawkins, our starting point guard, who had been lost for the season with a torn anterior cruciate during the first quarter of our fourth game of the season. That was the first time I had ever seen someone go down with the injury, and it was ugly. Not so much for the pain, but because I knew Johnny would be out for at least a full year, twelve months of painful rehabilitation and an uncertain future.

It was the same injury that had knocked guys like Bernard, Larry Krystkowiak, Eddie Lee Wilkins, and Danny Manning out for an entire year and threatened the careers of some other players. Johnny tried to get up immediately, and for a minute it looked like he could put some pressure on the leg. But then he collapsed. It was obvious that he was going to be gone for a long time.

The other thought concerned my own career, and how maybe, after seven years of constant punishing, jumping, and running in the NBA, the injury was simply the culmination of what had been happening to me for an entire year: a complete body break-down.

My body was not meant to play the way I do. I'm shorter than most of the guys who play up front in the NBA, the guys who play elbow wars every night, so I've always known that someday it would take its toll, that my body would just give in to the pounding it took eighty-two nights during the regular season and in the playoffs. But that was okay; it was the sacrifice I had decided to make in order to provide my family and friends with everything they needed, to be able to pay them back for the things they provided for me when I was growing up in Leeds. Seeing my mother, my grandmother, and my two brothers happy and excited about life after all of the poverty and pain we all had suffered through, it's worth the sacrifice to me, worth the pain.

And there has been pain. Plenty of it.

It began during the 1989–90 season—my sixth year in the pros—when my back started hurting almost nightly, when I suffered a slightly sprained knee and finished the year with an injury to my right shoulder that required off-season surgery. That operation was the first time anyone had ever taken a knife to me in my life. I had missed only three games during the season and had taken on much more of the team's scoring and rebounding responsibilities. Everybody wants to be a star, but being the "one" on a one-man team depressed me and made me wonder if the Sixers could ever win the NBA title.

The pain continued in 1990–91 when I suffered a minor stress fracture in my left ankle, an injury that made me miss seven more games in January. At the same time, tendinitis started making my left shoulder hurt almost as badly as my surgically repaired right one had been hurting at the end of the previous season. So finally, when my knee felt the weight of Rick's big wide butt, it was like the last straw.

Every athlete knows that if anything happens to his knee, it's probably bad. Nothing good comes from knee pain. Even a sprained knee is ligament damage, which is never easy to over-come, physically or mentally. It's just a matter of the severity of the injury—whether it's just bad, or whether it's hell.

Such fear comes from the fact that an athlete's legs are his life. For me, they're the heart of my strength. They allow me to hold my position in the trench warfare in the lane against guys bigger and stronger than me. They allow me to jump quicker than almost anyone else, which is the key to my rebounding success. And they allow me to have the endurance to run around, through, and over my opponent in the fourth quarter after I've pounded his ass into the ground for three periods.

That's why my mind raced through so many options as I lay on the court, and after I was helped into the locker room and examined by team physician Dr. Jack McPhilemy.

As I waited to learn the fate of my knee, I knew that I didn't want the 1990–91 season to end with me on the sidelines and my teammates trying to take on the league by themselves. I knew—and so did they—that it would have been a disaster.

Without me, the Sixers were the Orlando Magic—on a real bad night.

Probably the worst part about that night at the Spectrum was that my grandmother was in the stands. She had come to visit and was sitting with Maureen when the injury occurred. As much as I was afraid of the eventual diagnosis, I knew that she felt worse sitting in the stands and worrying. So after I was taken into the locker room, I sent one of the locker-room guards out to bring her to my side.

Almost everyone I really cared about was with me as Dr. McPhilemy examined the knee. On one hand, I was optimistic because the pain was not excruciating. But I knew that pain was not a true barometer of the severity of the injury, particularly with me because I've always had a high pain threshold; if I couldn't play with pain, I wouldn't be playing at all.

After a few minutes of tugging, pulling, and twisting my knee, Dr. McPhilemy told me that I had suffered a second-degree sprain. He said that while I had, in fact, torn the knee ligaments, they were only slightly torn, not shredded like Johnny's.

"How long before I can play again?" I asked.

"About a month."

"Shit."

There were only ten games left in the regular season. A month on the sidelines would have meant that I wouldn't be able to return until the second round of the playoffs—if there was a second round for the Sixers. That's not how I wanted my season to end, not this season, which had already been one of the toughest years of my career. So I resolved right then that if the tests— I was scheduled to undergo an MRI (magnetic-resonance imaging) the next day, which would determine the full extent of the damage—confirmed Dr. McPhilemy's original diagnosis, I would return in two weeks.

I didn't tell anyone, but I was going to return before the end of the season. No matter what.

I've always been a fast healer, so I knew I had a shot at my goal. I made up my mind that if there was any way at all, God willing, I would be back before the end of the regular season. That was my promise to myself.

I DIDN'T WANT the 1990–91 season to end for me like the previous year had ended, facing shoulder surgery, a long and uncertain rehabilitation period, and an even more uncertain basketball future.

My shoulder had actually started to hurt midway through the 1988–89 season when I took a hard shot while trying for a rebound. I thought the pain was the result of a deep bruise, maybe even a strained muscle. But rather than have it examined by a doctor, I iced it down and continued to play through the pain until the end of the season. During the summer of '89, I tried to cure the pain on my own by strengthening the shoulder with a weight-lifting conditioning program and coach. It was the first time in my life that I'd ever worked out with weights. By the end of the summer, I'd lifted so much weight with my sore shoulder that I almost felt like my body was tilting to the right.

I finally went to a doctor just before the start of the 1989–90 season and was told that I had ruptured a muscle in my shoulder, an injury that required either rest, in order to heal on its own, or surgery. For me, the choice was easy: none of the above. The season was about to start, so it was too late for surgery and there was no way that the Sixers' management was going to let me sit out the first few weeks of the year, so I didn't even ask. I just played.

As you would expect, the shoulder never got better. By the middle of the season, it was killing me, to the point where I shouldn't have been playing. But we were in the midst of trying to win our first Atlantic Division title in seven years, the first of my career, and I wasn't about to jeopardize our chances by missing several games. So I played.

It was a major mistake. Playing another thirty games and taking a few more hard shots turned my shoulder into hamburger. I was in excruciating pain. Late in the season, every time I shot the ball it felt like someone stabbed me in the shoulder with a knife. After games and practices, I was iced down and treated by our trainer, Tony Harris. He massaged the shoulder every day. Tony was the only person who knew how much I was really hurt, and I made him keep it a secret.

Why?

Because there are so many nitwits in the world who think that if an athlete says he's hurt, then he's lazy. I remembered how the team—management and players—had treated Andrew Toney when he tried to tell everyone his feet were hurting. No one believed him, and we all treated him like a dog. So I thought it was best to just keep playing.

By the end of the season I could hardly do anything with my right arm. I was just flinging the ball toward the basket, especially at the free-throw line. I wasn't scared about the pain, only mad at the Philadelphia fans who were giving me a hard time because of my pitiful free-throw shooting. I shot only 60 percent from the line in the playoffs against Cleveland and Chicago, well below my career percentage (.760) for the playoffs.

Most of the other areas of my game didn't suffer at all—I still averaged 24.7 points and 15.5 rebounds in ten playoff games— but when I missed a free throw, I was booed like I had shot someone's grandmother.

Did I think of telling anyone about the injury? Hell no. I just took my medicine because, by then, I already knew about fans and how they treated me in Philadelphia. I could score 30 points and grab 15 boards in a game, but if I missed a free throw in the final minute of a close game—a game that was close because I had been busting my ass all night—I was a jerk. They would turn on me in a heartbeat.

The 1990 first-round Cleveland series, which lasted the full five games, took a major toll on my shoulder. The Cavs beat the shit out of me; it was part of their game plan. Starting forward Winston Bennett came out like he had specific instructions from coach Lenny Wilkens to pound on me, then Hot Rod Williams came in to finish me off. With my shoulder the way it was, I couldn't do much about the punishment, except dish out some of my own. That was the reason for the kind of body shots I used to bounce Craig Ehlo around the court. (Those shots led to the league's new "Barkley Rules," which said that any player who committed what the referee considered to be a flagrant foul was automatically ejected.)

It seems that everybody wants to dish out against me, but nobody wants to take it. When my shoulder was pounding, the Cavs took every opportunity to beat me up. But when I started cheap-shoting them back, they started crying.

I averaged 35 points in the first two games of the series and helped finish off the Cavs with 18 points and 19 rebounds in the deciding fifth game at the Spectrum. But by the time we went to Chicago for game one of the conference semifinals, the Bulls knew I was hurting.

So did I.

It's just something an athlete knows. We know our bodies better than most people know their families. Throughout the five games of the series with the Bulls, I finally realized that something was seriously wrong with my shoulder. I figured that I would have to undergo an extensive rehabilitation period during the summer. When I was told by two doctors following the play-offs that I needed surgery, I got scared. "Oh, shit," I thought. "Will I ever be good again? Will I ever be the same?"

I believe that once an athlete's body is sliced by a surgeon's knife, he's no longer whole. He's no longer the invulnerable athlete he always thought he was. I'd never had surgery and I was scared. I thought about the procedure twenty-four hours a day until I finally went under the anesthetic on June 25, 1990, and I almost changed my mind about it several times.

I also felt alone, particularly concerning the Sixers. Among management, Tony was the only person who was there when I needed him all summer—before and after the surgery. To the Sixers, I was just another piece of raw meat. If I couldn't play, they didn't give a damn about me. I should have known that already after watching how the team traded and released so many loyal players through the years. Now I for damn sure knew it.

My fear concerning my shoulder didn't pass for several weeks after the surgery. For a long time, I couldn't move my arm on my own. It was strapped to my body, worthless. I wondered if the surgeon had done something wrong.

Although my arm was immobile, the doctors didn't waste any time in starting my rehabilitation. The surgery was on a Monday afternoon. At seven A.M. Tuesday morning, somebody walked into my room and asked me if I was ready for my workout.

"Are you nuts?" I asked.

They meant it. I couldn't move my arm, so the doctors moved it for me, pulling at it like they were yanking the drumstick from a turkey. I screamed, cursed, and yelled like a wild dog. Moments like that should be the only time that you're allowed to use drugs legally because you just can't make it without them. I felt pain like I had never felt before.

It was three weeks before I started to see light at the end of the tunnel. That's how long it took before I could move my arm on my own, without help and with pain I could tolerate. Still, I was worried. I wasn't trying to get well enough to become a bus driver; I had to play professional basketball and I didn't know if my arm was going to let me do that again.

It was my faith in God that got me through. I figured that He was testing me, presenting me with a situation where He could see what I was made of. But several weeks later, when I left my home and family and departed for training camp, I still didn't know the answer.

I REALLY DIDN'T know what to expect of myself or the team when I arrived at the Franklin and Marshall College in Lancaster, Pennsylvania, the Sixers' traditional training site, and started preparing for the 1990–91 season. My first thought was that we would have to face up to the fact that we just weren't good enough to be contenders—that for this year at least, it just wasn't going to happen. Despite the fact that we had won fifty-three games the year before and reached the second round of the playoffs, I had some serious doubts about the season.

I didn't know if Johnny Dawkins, a fifth-year pro out of Duke, would be able to run the team as well as the guy we traded in order to get him, Maurice Cheeks.

I didn't know if guard Hersey Hawkins, our 1988 first-round draft pick—after we got him from the L.A. Clippers in exchange for Charles Smith—and a potentially explosive scorer, was finally ready to live up to the nickname I had given him: Franchise, Jr.

I didn't know if Manute Bol was worth what we had traded in order to get *him:* a first-round draft pick.

I didn't know if Rick Mahorn's sore back would hold up for another season.

I didn't think our bench—guys like Ron Anderson, Kenny Payne, Derek Smith, and our rookie, Brian Oliver from Georgia Tech—was good enough to match up with the teams at the top.

And most importantly, I didn't know if anyone on the team would step forward and help me out on a consistent basis.

I couldn't carry the load by myself any longer. I couldn't keep us in games and win them, too. It's just impossible. All I ever asked of my teammates was to keep us in the game, then I promised I would try to win it in the fourth quarter. But there's no way I could do both: no player can, not even Michael, the NBA god. But too often in the past, my teammates played like I was supposed to do it all every night. That attitude pissed me off.

But my feelings changed drastically during training camp. For once, it seemed my teammates came to camp ready to play, and within a few practices I started to believe that we could kick some people's butts. Maybe even win the title. My shoulder didn't feel good, despite all the rehabilitation I had gone through. But because I wasn't at full strength, everybody—at least those guys who were healthy; Derek was playing on a bad knee and would be cut before the end of camp—knew that they would have to play much harder. And they did.

For once, I actually felt good about an upcoming season. I was psyched. I thought we were the second-best team in the East behind the Bulls, and that with a few breaks we could reach the NBA Finals. That's what was going through my mind as I shook Michael's hand at center court in Chicago Stadium just before the opening tap for the first game of the 1990–91 season. Little did I know that in a few weeks my feeling of confidence would be gone. Or that every moment of frustration I felt on the court during the season would be matched by an event of insanity off the court.

WE BEAT THE Bulls, 124–116. I scored 37 points and grabbed 10 rebounds, but we won with our depth. Believe it or not, our bench beat up on the Bulls' reserves. It was an all-around performance that showed that we could be a true force throughout the year. Not that we wouldn't struggle. Our starting center, Mike Gminski, opened the season with an elbow injury that affected his shooting touch. With him struggling, I wasn't getting much scoring help up front, which allowed teams to focus their defenses on me. So what else was new?

We squeaked by New Jersey in the second game of the season when Derrick Coleman grabbed my airball desperation 3-pointer at the buzzer as the ball reached the rim. There was no way it was going in, but the referee ruled that Derrick had grabbed the ball while it was above the rim—the play was called goaltending and the shot tied the game. We won in overtime, 112–110.

Afterward in the locker room, I joked to a group of reporters that it was the kind of game that would drive some players to do crazy things.

"This is the kind of game that if you lose, you go home and beat your wife and kids," I said. "Did you see my wife jumping up and down at the end of the game? That's because she knew I wasn't going to beat her."

Nobody in the locker room made much of the remark. Most of the guys who cover the team know me; they know when I'm serious and when I'm joking. What I said that night was a damn joke! Okay? You would have thought I was a damn criminal after the uproar that was created later in the month when several papers printed the remark—my biggest mistake was telling the reporters to do so: "Piss off those women's groups," I said that night—and the shit hit the fan.

When the remarks were finally printed, I was lectured (again) by Harold Katz, who warned me that I was making things harder on myself by my conduct. I didn't agree. I think too many people look to create controversy at my expense. I'm the controversy of the month. The following day, I was lectured (again) by Horace Balmer, the NBA's director of security. (I've probably seen him more times since I came into the NBA than I've seen my own family.) And women's groups around the country acted like I was a mass murderer. There were pickets outside the Spectrum on a couple of game nights and letters of complaint came flooding into the team's offices. The reaction pissed me off so much that after I wrote a letter of apology to a Philadelphia group called Women in Transition, which helps battered women, I decided to take some action of my own: I boycotted the media.

I thought the Philadelphia beat reporters had betrayed me, so beginning on November 27, after a loss to New Jersey at the Meadowlands, I promised them that until Christmas all of my postgame remarks would go like this: "(Winning team) played great, (losing team) played bad. (Star player) had a great game." That was it. End of interview.

It was a riot. For the first few nights, most of the writers stood there with their mouths open and their notebooks empty. They couldn't believe it. Stop the presses! "Charles Barkley Has Nothing to Say!" They didn't know what to do with themselves. Some of them acted like they couldn't write their stories without my comments. I knew my silence wouldn't last long, but it was my way of letting the writers know that when I cooperate with them, it's with the understanding that they'll have the brains to know when I'm serious and when I'm not.

Brains and the media. Maybe I'm asking too much.

THE SIXERS ARE a collection of strong personalities, from the owner to the players. Among my teammates, Manute may be the funniest and most intelligent guy I know. But he also has a short fuse, which is why he and I got into a wrestling match in the locker room later in the season. And before Rick and I were teammates, we hated each other. Then we found out that we were just alike. Otherwise, the Sixers are a bunch of guys who are serious about their jobs, even though they may not be the most talented group in the world.

In between, there's Jim Lynam, our head coach. He's the best coach I've ever played for, but at times last season we had major disagreements that would have led to problems if we didn't respect each other as much as we do.

On November 14, at home against the Atlanta Hawks, Jimmy benched me with 4:34 left and the team leading by only 4 points—all because I took a jumper from just inside the 3-point circle. Jimmy thought it was a bad shot. So what? I'd been hitting my outside shots lately, so I figured, why not?

If the shot goes in, nobody says one damn word. We were ahead, 98–91, so it would have pretty much iced the game and I would've been a hero. But the shot didn't fall and Jimmy lost it.

After Dominique Wilkins buried a 3-pointer at the other end, Jimmy called time-out (which didn't surprise me) and replaced me with Hersey (which did). I was stunned. He said I took a bad shot. I didn't agree, but that didn't matter. What mattered was this: taking me out of a close game in the fourth quarter was stupid. Besides, if Jimmy always took someone out of the game for taking a bad shot, we wouldn't have anyone on the floor most of the time. If he was going to do that to me, he should do it to everyone.

I sat on the bench and fumed. And when Jimmy called me to come back into the game, I ignored him. I sat there and watched the Hawks pull to within 2, 100–98, while he called my name four times before I finally stood up. I was still mad as hell.

I scored 5 straight points after returning to the game and we won, 112–104. Afterward, I told Jimmy, "I did what I wanted to do and that's basically it." I got mad, it passed—no big deal.

(Later in the year, Jimmy and I had another major disagreement, but this time I was right. We were playing the Knicks in March and the score was close in the beginning of the third period when I got a technical for arguing a call. Nothing new, right? Well, Jimmy benches me. Takes me out of the game like he's punishing me for getting a technical. Hell, if he benched me every time I got a T, Jayson Williams—a rookie forward who got almost zero playing time—would get more minutes than I do. Anyway, Jimmy leaves me out of the game for a few minutes. When he calls for me to go back in, we're down by 10!

"This is bullshit!" I yelled. I was standing right in Jimmy's face. "You take me out and now you expect me to bring us back? This is bullshit! Don't ever do that again!"

I didn't appreciate what he did to me, and as far as I was concerned, that was it. I went back into the game, but we eventually lost, 102–94. Afterward, I was told that I was going to be fined $5,000 for the outburst.

That, too, was bullshit. Five thousand dollars for voicing my opinion? Maybe I shouldn't have talked to Jimmy like that in front of the team. Maybe I should have pulled him aside instead of saying what I had to say like I did. Maybe I was wrong. But a $5,000 mistake? Please.)

After that game against the Hawks, we won two of our next three games, losing only to the Knicks in New York. We had lost Johnny Dawkins by now, and our next-best point guard, Rickey Green, didn't play against the Knicks because of a bruised knee, and just about everyone else on the team had the flu. We were blown out 106–79. It was just one of those nights in the NBA when one team had no business taking the floor, especially against a team like the Knicks—a bad team with just enough talent to fool themselves into thinking they're as good as they were on this particular night. Patrick Ewing, Gerald Wilkins, and Kiki Vandeweghe were all high-fivin' like they had won the NBA title when they wouldn't come any closer to winning the NBA than the Albany Patroons.

Down in our locker room, no one was broken up about the loss. I had missed 10 of my 14 shots, but I was truly more concerned about getting healthy. A reporter asked me if it had been a tough night. "There are no bad nights in the NBA, and don't let anybody tell you any different," I said. "The best thing about tonight was that we all got paid."

We won our next three—against Sacramento, Cleveland, and the Hawks—before the loss to the Nets, after which I started my Steve Carlton act. I thought that was as low as my season would get, both on and off the court. I was wrong.

And yet the 1990–91 season was far from seven months of gloom and doom. In fact, some of my favorite moments came when they meant the most—against the Celtics, the team everyone thought was going to give the Bulls a real run for the conference title in the East. Bullshit. If the Celtics couldn't stop me—and with both Larry Bird and Kevin McHale old and hobbled by injuries, they've almost completely given up trying to; Kevin Gamble was the new sacrificial lamb—how were they going to stop Michael Jordan? Only in their dreams.

I actually love the Celtics because they've got good people. Larry taught me a lot about the game, particularly how to mentally psyche out an opponent. In his prime, Larry talked a lot during games. He called you a chump when he scored and called you a sucker when he took the ball away from you at the other end. That was pure mental intimidation. It was a great ploy, one that I added to my repertoire early in my career. When most people hear the words *cocky* and *arrogant*, they think of me. I think of Larry Bird.

Our first appearance against Boston that year was a show, a night when the party began long before the final buzzer. From the moment I walked into the arena at 6:29 P.M.—Jimmy said we had to be there by six-thirty, and I've never been one to break any rules—I was psyched. It was a rare night when the Spectrum was full. When Sixers fans decide to get off their butts and come to the game, the Spectrum can be one of the best arenas in the league for the home team, right behind Chicago Stadium and the Arco Arena in Sacramento.

In other words, the Celtics didn't have a chance. I hit 16 of my 23 shots for 37 points, crushed their front line for 13 rebounds, and damn near earned a triple double with 8 assists as we pounded the pitiful Celtics, 116–110, in a game that really wasn't that close. What was most impressive was that the Boston game was our fourth game in five nights—just another example of the kind of asinine schedule created by our friends in the league office. You can usually take that fourth game and flush it down the toilet. But Boston is incentive enough to overcome any amount of battle fatigue and soreness. Hell, I would've gotten out of a wheelchair to play the Celtics. If it had been the Orlando Magic? Call 911 because I would have been dead.

By the end of December, we had finally found a rhythm. We were getting consistent contributions from a lot of guys, which was the primary reason we had the fourth-best record in the league (19-8) after beating Washington, 106–105, in overtime at the Baltimore Arena. That game was typical of our victories: fifteen of our wins had been by fewer than 10 points. But I didn't care. When you win, no one asks by how much or why.

It was also typical in that I was getting some help. Hersey scored 26 points, which is just about what he should average in this league; Rickey Green added 16 points and 5 assists; Ron Anderson had 14 points off the bench, and even Manute was a factor with 5 rebounds and 4 blocked shots in 21 minutes of chaos. In four straight games, Manute had done the one thing he does well: get in the way. He blocked 16 shots during that stretch and altered more others than a Patriot missile.

Talk about a strange guy. When I first saw Manute in 1985, he was a rookie with the Washington Bullets, and I thought he was a circus freak. He's 7'7", about seven feet of which is stilts. He's a Dinka tribesman from the Sudan, which must have the tallest doorways in the world because everyone in the tribe is supposed to be as tall as Manute. I didn't think he'd last very long in the league before somebody snapped him in two like one of Bo Jackson's bats. But five years later, he was still stealing money, still standing in the middle of the lane and turning basketball into a different game altogether. Bol-ball. And it's ugly.

I've always liked him because he has a great outlook on the game. He's always having fun on the court, even though he's also extremely competitive. He also talks more shit during a game than Chuck Person could ever dream of saying. Whenever he blocks someone's shot, Manute yells, "Get that weak shit outta here!" Or if I was the victim, it was, "Take that, Barkley man!" Anybody else would have pissed me off with that, but when I turned around and saw Manute, all I could do was shake my head and laugh.

I always knew that he was a great person, but I didn't know he was so intelligent. He's one of the smartest people I've ever known, and truly funny off the court. For us, he was a breath of fresh air. And he can take as well as he gives—usually. One day after practice, Manute started giving me a hard time about growing up in the projects. That was my cue.

"When I was a kid, at least I could go downstairs to the refrigerator and get my food," I began. "When you were a kid, you had to go out and hunt food down.

"You're what we would look like on the Nutri/System diet. You're the 'after' picture."

One day later, though, he and I fought before a practice in Atlanta when he lost his temper. It started over another one of our verbal exchanges—I probably know more "lion" and "jungle" jokes now than anybody on the planet—but it escalated when Manute couldn't take it as well as he was dishing it out, and he let his temper get the best of him. We wrestled on the floor of the locker room until I got on top of him and clamped him down. It embarrassed him that I had him tied up like that; a lot of people were around and he didn't like being shown up. Then we almost didn't make it out onto the floor for practice because he slapped me upside the head and said, "Come on, let's go." He really wanted to fight!

We got into it for a few moments and had to be restrained by our teammates. But when the fight was over, we forgot about it. We even went out for a few beers later that night. Manute and I didn't let our bad feelings linger more than a couple of days. He's a great friend, but friends sometimes need their asses kicked, too.

As much as I like Manute, I don't think the Sixers made a good trade to get him from Golden State. During the 1990 off-season, we sent our 1991 first-round draft pick to the Warriors for Manute.

Now, correct me if I'm wrong, but isn't a first-round draft choice supposed to be someone the team expects to be a contributor to your team for at least six or seven years? Isn't a first-round draft choice supposed to be a strong player, someone who can do at least two things, such as score and rebound, or pass and play defense? Isn't a first-round draft choice supposed to be a young talent?

Well, Manute isn't any of those things. He's a one-dimensional player who doesn't give you anything except blocked shots. Sure, we needed a shot-blocker, someone who could intimidate our opponent. He gave us that during the 1990–91 season, blocking an average of 3.01 shots per game, and that doesn't count the number of shots he changed every night. (He even slapped away an amazing 10 shots one night in February against the Sacramento Kings.) But on those nights when he didn't help us defensively, he didn't help us at all because offensively he's not worth anything, except for an occasional dunk or awkward 3-point attempt. When he was on the floor, he had to be surrounded by players who could score, and we had to use a lot of traps to force the other team in his direction.

All of this meant that we were essentially playing four-on-five at the offensive end of the floor. We traded a first-round draft choice—which turned out to be the 16th player picked overall, Chris Gatling of Old Dominion—for a twenty-eight-year-old flyswatter who scored only 1.9 points a game. Hell, my grandmother could score 2 points a game, as long as she wasn't double-teamed.

Then again, maybe it was best that we didn't have a first-round pick given our recent history in the draft. In the seven years between 1984 when I was drafted and the 1990 collegiate draft, the Sixers picked seventeen players in the first two rounds. Eleven of those guys were still in the league at the end of the 1990–91 season, but only three of them—Brian Oliver, a 1990 second-round pick from Georgia Tech, Kenny Payne, a 1989 first-round pick, and myself—are still on the Sixers. That's more proof of the Sixers' disloyalty to its players. It seems that ever since I arrived, they would rather trade away good players than allow them to develop in Philadelphia.

Brian was our first pick in the 1990 draft, a real steal in the second round who fell that far because of a stress fracture in his ankle that hampered him during his senior season. He's going to be a good player; he can pass and score, and he can direct the team. And he's kind of cocky. Guards have to have that kind of attitude, especially point guards. All the great ones are a little bit cocky, from Magic Johnson, John Stockton, Terry Porter, and Kevin Johnson in the West to Isiah Thomas, Dee Brown, Mark Jackson, and Sherman Douglas in the East. Brian will do well because of that.

The most difficult part of Brian's rookie season was that he tried too hard. In practices he could do all the right things, but in games he wasn't the same smart, relaxed player. He'd try to steal every pass. He'd try to guard every guy like it was the final seconds of the seventh game of the NBA Finals and the Sixers were leading by 1, trying to get into their jock. And he'd try to make every great pass imaginable.

Like most rookies, Brian never seemed to accept the fact that the NBA isn't college, where he was much better than the other guys on the floor. In the NBA, everybody on the floor is just as good as he is. That's what he'll have to learn. He barely shot 40 percent for the season, so Jimmy couldn't use him down the stretch when we needed points. He played only 11 minutes a game and was looking over his shoulder for most of the season as the team brought in guys like Mario Elie, Jim Farmer, and Tony Harris (no, our trainer didn't suit up) for short stints at his position. Fortunately for him, Brian came on in the last few games of the season. He scored 34 points in the last three games and showed that he could be a solid player in the Sixers' future.

When things were going bad for Brian, I tried to keep his spirits up. Moses Malone did that for me; I try to do the same for the young players coming along now, because a player who doesn't have any confidence in himself might as well be dead.

THE 1991 SEASON totally changed for us in late December and early January. That's when we started showing some dangerous signs. Suddenly, my teammates stopped giving me the kind of support I needed in order for us to be a strong team; and we made yet another stupid trade that set us back at least another season. It all started like this:

We took our 19-8 record out west for five games against the Lakers, Phoenix, Seattle, Utah, and Denver. We came home with four losses, no true starting center, and a shitload of frustration and anger.

In the first three games of the series, I felt like I was playing on an island—all alone against the natives. Our bench, the guys whose only job is to keep us in the game when the starters rest, averaged only 23 points against the Suns, Lakers, and Sonics, which forced the starters into trying to mount comebacks, something that's damn near impossible on the road. And it wasn't as if the starters were on fire, either. Hersey was averaging double figures, but had none of the explosive spurts that he's always been capable of creating. And while Gminski was playing more consistently after a slow start, he was obviously affected by the trade rumors that had been flying around the league for several weeks.

We were becoming more and more of a one-man show again, and it was starting to piss me off.

Then, boom! On Friday, January 4, I walked into the locker room at the Salt Palace in Salt Lake City and saw nothing but long faces. That's when I looked around and didn't see Mike. Jimmy told us that he had been traded to Charlotte for Armon Gilliam, a twenty-six-year-old, fourth-year power forward from UNLV who had been the second player taken in the 1987 draft; and 6'11" center Dave Hoppen, who was also twenty-six, but who had played for four teams since being picked by Atlanta in the third round of the 1986 draft. In other words, he couldn't play. Four NBA teams can't be wrong.

When I heard the news, I was stunned. Trades are a part of the business, but it's always tough to lose a good friend. And that's what G-Man had been to me during our three years together. In the days just before the trade he was going nuts. On the road, we stayed up at night talking, and all he talked about was the fact that he thought he was going to either the Lakers or Golden State. He was very sensitive about all the talk—too sensitive. He wanted to stay right where he was because he and his wife, Stacy Anderson, had just built a new home in Villanova, which he started after signing a four-year, $7-million contract in 1989.

That kind of contract usually tells you that the team is making a commitment to you. Except if that team is the Sixers. In Philadelphia, there's no such thing as commitment.

Armon has averaged almost 16 points during his career, but as we soon found out, he's not a strong rebounder or a shot-blocker. Hell, he's not even a consistent scorer. And without G-Man, we were suddenly without a center—again. That left us in a vulnerable position from which we never recovered, because Manute was useless as a starter and Rick's bad back kept him from being mobile enough to play against true centers every night.

Every great team has a good center—not necessarily a great center, but someone who's tall, quick, and strong enough to rebound and be a presence in the middle; and someone who can score when needed. G-Man was not a shot-blocker, but he could score. And if the Sixers had been patient enough to allow him to recover from his elbow injury, we would have been a better team at the end of the season. Instead, we went into the toilet.

By the time we went into Milwaukee on January 11, our team rebounding stank and everyone was confused about their roles. That left more of the burden to me to make everything right. But just then, everything started to go wrong.

Late in the victory over the Bucks, I landed on Hersey's foot and felt something pop in my left ankle. I knew it wasn't broken, but the pain was tremendous. I had played 42 minutes that night, scored 37 points, and grabbed 12 rebounds. But I know my body, and I knew I was through for the evening, maybe much longer. I'm one of the quickest healers in the league, so when I got up two days later and the pain was as bad as it had been on the night of the game, I knew something was wrong.

That's when I started to think stress fracture. The next day in Philadelphia I underwent a bone scan that revealed what the doctor called "hot spots," three areas that he said represented slight fractures caused by the stress of my weight coming down on the ankle incorrectly in Milwaukee. In other words, a stress fracture. Even worse, a possible *three* stress fractures.

When I heard the words, the first thing that came to mind was Andrew Toney.

He isn't the only player who had his career cut short by stress fractures, but I know what Andrew went through, and it was hell. I was deathly afraid that the same thing might happen to me, so I decided that the only person on the team I would trust was Tony, our trainer. If anyone else who worked for the team had anything to say, I didn't want to hear it.

I refused to follow anyone's timetable but my own, which was really none at all. The most frustrating thing about a stress fracture is that you can't do anything about it but rest. One reason I agreed to have a cast placed on the foot was so there would be no doubt in anyone's mind that I was hurt. I didn't want to hear any shit from Harold Katz or anyone about coming back until I felt I could return without doing any permanent damage.

There was one problem, though. I'm a terrible patient, particularly when the team is losing.

I felt bad for my teammates. They were playing their asses off and still losing. A lot of them weren't used to their new roles and responsibilities. Hersey missed one game with a pulled quadriceps muscle, but when he came back, he tried to do a lot more than normal. After four games—four straight losses—he was physically and mentally exhausted. He reminded me of myself during the 1988–89 season when I had to carry a sorry team by myself. After every game that year, I thought I was going to die. By the end of the season, all I could do was go through the motions. When I looked at Hersey, I saw myself.

At the same time, I knew I couldn't do anything to help. I was running and jumping for short periods, but I was also having some serious, serious pain, the kind that frightened me more than it hurt because it was a shooting pain right in the area where the injury was supposed to be, not a dull, almost constant pain. I can tolerate pain, but the sharp pain worried me. A lot.

Two weeks after the injury, I underwent another test and found out what I already knew: the injury wasn't getting any better. An MRI showed that the three hot spots were still there, which meant that they were still healing. I sent the results of the tests to my personal physician in Birmingham, Alabama, Dr. James Andrews, the same doctor who worked miracles with Bo Jackson when Bo suffered a hip injury in January 1991 that a lot of so-called experts said would end his career. By September, Bo was playing for the Chicago White Sox, the team that signed him after the Kansas City Royals waived him like idiots.

A few days after Dr. Andrews got the test results, he said it was in my best interest not to play. He told me to sit out a few weeks and not come back until the ankle felt better. Two opinions; two thumbs down. For once, I listened.

On Friday, January 25, the Celtics came to town. It was one of the most surprising nights of the season. The guys crushed the Celtics, 116–94. Hersey left everything he had on the floor, scoring a career-high 38 points with 6 assists and an unbelievable

9 steals, also a career high. Rickey Green had 27 points, 9 assists, and zero turnovers in 35 spectacular minutes. Everyone else went along for the ride, pressing and trapping the Celtics into committing 21 turnovers. The game marked the halfway point of the season and left us with a respectable 23-18 mark that would have been much, much better if it weren't for the injuries and adversity that hit us. But even so, we were happy to be where we were—still in contention for the homecourt advantage in the first round of the playoffs. The Spectrum was a party.

My best moment of the night, though, came after the game when McHale caught me in the hallway and offered some advice: "Don't play," he said. "Just don't. It's not worth it. It's not worth the risk."

No one knew better than Kevin when it came to stress fractures and risks. During the 1986–87 season, he suffered a stress fracture in his right foot but played on it anyway and waited until after the season to have surgery. He missed the first fourteen games of the next season, and two years later, he still wasn't the same player.

"I screwed up my game for two years and my foot's still not healed," he said. "It might not ever get well."

For the next several days, I thought long and hard about what Kevin had said to me. I had missed seven games altogether (the team was 2-5 without me) and hoped to be able to return on Friday, February 1, against the Suns. But the foot was still sore, especially after a couple of practices, and while the pain was no longer constant—the ankle only hurt after I played—Tony told me on Wednesday that he thought it was best if I continued to rest it. He gave me two hours of treatment after practice, then suggested that I sit out the next four games, which led into the All-Star break. That would have given me another twelve days to rest and rehabilitate before playing in another game.

I told him that I'd sit out the games through the break, but in my heart I had other ideas. That night, I went home and kept the foot in a bucket of ice all evening. The following morning, there was some pain, but not enough to keep me out of practice. And after the ninety-minute session, I told everyone that I felt better. In truth, I still felt awful, and I was still worried about

doing permanent damage, but as long as the pain wasn't un-
bearable, I had made up my mind that no matter what Kevin,
Tony, and everyone else was saying, I was going to play the final
four games before the All-Star break, starting with our game
against Phoenix on February 1.

Why?

Because we couldn't afford to fall out of the playoff race. Or
at least if we did, it wouldn't do us any good. If the Sixers had
kept their 1991 first-round draft pick, I might have sat out more
games, since losing would have moved us higher in the draft and
given us a better shot at getting a great player. If we missed the
playoffs altogether, our pick would be in the lottery with a shot
at No. 1 and someone like Larry Johnson of UNLV, Billy Owens
of Syracuse, or Georgetown's Dikembe Mutombo. It would have
been worth it then to sit out a few more games and pray for the
lottery. But the geniuses in the Sixers' front office had ruined
that dream by giving up our No. 1 pick for Manute. Think about
it: Larry Johnson for Manute. Billy Owens for Manute. Dikembe
Mutombo for Manute.

I decided that if there was any chance that I could come back
and help us stay in the playoff race, that's what I would do because
making the playoffs, even if we lost in the first round, would be
better than losing games for nothing.

I also knew I had the five-day All-Star break coming. I was
going to fly to Alabama and rest both my body and my mind
with my family. Being with them always energizes me, and I
was looking forward to the chance to see them—and to heal.

Let's face it, returning to action for me was a no-win situation.
Besides the prospect, and probable reality, of an early-round
playoff exit, I had to consider my own career. If I tried to play,
I could suffer an even more serious injury and be out for the
entire year. That was a real possibility, one that I thought about
for a long time on February 1 as I sat in the locker room at the
Spectrum and got dressed for the game with Phoenix. Just before
tip-off, though, I put it out of my mind and never considered it
again.

I played 32 minutes against the Suns. I had 24 points, 12
rebounds, and 8 assists as we beat them at home. My ankle hurt

like hell, but I vowed that from then on—through the final thirty-nine games of the regular season and hopefully, the playoffs—no one would know about the pain.

Three more games and I would be able to rest. Three more games and I would be home.

FIVE DAYS LATER, I was minding my own business, sitting in my hotel room at the Marriott in Troy, Michigan, resting for that night's game with the Pistons, the next-to-last game before the break. I had been voted by the fans to start for the East team in Charlotte, but the announcement was made while I was out with the ankle injury. I had already decided that I wasn't going to risk my career by playing in a meaningless exhibition game.

Besides, I had done my duty to the league. In 1990, I played in the game despite a groin injury that needed rest. (Okay, so I was threatened with a three-game suspension by the NBA, which might also have been a factor in my decision.)

And besides, Larry Bird had already said that he wasn't going to play, either, because of an injury—an injured back that had kept him out of action since January.

And besides . . .

Then the telephone rang.

It was Rod Thorn from the league office with some friendly advice: Play in the All-Star game, or else.

Or else what?

"Suspension."

This is bullshit. What about my injury?

"If you're well enough to play now, it's the league's position that you're well enough to play in the All-Star game."

What if I get hurt and can't play for the rest of the season? Don't you think Harold Katz would be pissed?

"We've already talked to Harold. He understands."

NO WONDER I came to Charlotte with an attitude. About the only good thing about the weekend was that my family flew in from Leeds and surprised me. Almost everyone except my grandmother was there, including my mother, my brother Darryl, and his wife, Melanie. Seeing all of them made me feel better about being held hostage by the league office over a damn exhibition game, instead of being able to rest my injury. Makes sense, huh?

I tried to make the best of it, even though I wasn't going to bullshit any of the reporters who were sitting around the table with me at the Friday press conference by telling them I was happy to be there.

No, I was going to be myself, whether the people in the league office liked it or not:

So, Charles, are you happy to be here?
"Do I look happy?"

Not particularly.
"Hell, no, I'm not happy. And you know, if I would've sat out Wednesday's game against the Bullets, I probably wouldn't have to be here with you guys. But I wouldn't do that. It would have been cheating my teammates. The bottom line is that I was told to play. Now that I'm here, I'm glad to be here."
(Okay, so I lied.)

Would you be willing to take a pay cut if it would help the team sign a better player?
"Hey, I was the first player who ever offered to take a pay cut before the media started pulling Magic's and Michael's chains about it. But no one listened to me. I made the offer several years ago, and it still stands."

Do you think your mouth gets more attention than your basketball performances?
"Before my career's over, I'll finally get the credit I deserve. Then again, I'll probably be dead and gone before people will say, 'That fucker was awesome, wasn't he?' Now, people try to come up with all kinds of different reasons why the 76ers are successful. You guys figure it out. In order for us to have been respectable for the last six or seven years, there's been one consistent factor. Think about it."

Detroit general manager Jack McCloskey was upset that Hersey Hawkins was named to replace the injured Isiah Thomas on the East team. He said it was a "dark day" for the NBA.

"Now why did you ask me that? I came down here in a good mood. I don't want to hear that bullshit. Detroit's already got a couple of guys on the team. Hersey deserves to make the team. It's a dark day because he lives in Detroit. If it's such a dark day, then turn the damn lights on."

My business manager, Glenn Guthrie, damn near had a heart attack when he saw me wearing a cap that read "Fuck Iraq" across the front before the press conference. The war in the Persian Gulf was in full swing, and as a professional athlete, I wanted to use my visibility to call attention to the guys who were putting their lives on the line so I could go out and earn $3 million a year playing basketball. The people who protested the war pissed me off. Protests were the last thing the servicemen needed to see when they saw the news from home. They needed to see that we weren't just living our lives without thinking about them. They needed to see that we were with them when they took off for bombing missions or waited in bunkers as Scud missiles flew over their heads. They needed to see caps that said "Fuck Iraq."

Glenn begged me to take it off, at first saying that the TV cameras wouldn't shoot me while I was wearing it—"Good," I said, "maybe they'll leave me alone"—then saying it wouldn't be good for my image to be seen in a cap covered with profanity. Obviously, he was desperate if he thought telling me that my image would suffer was enough to get me to take it off.

I finally stopped torturing Glenn and took it off just before I went into the ballroom. But for me, the cap set the tone for the whole weekend. I've always felt that sports is nothing more than entertainment. It's supposed to be something that can take your mind off your job, your money problems, family problems— anything that's putting pressure on you and making life difficult. That's why I'll never take myself so seriously that I'll compromise my integrity by being someone other than who I am, no matter how much it costs me. That's why I'll always have fun on the court, why I'll always pump my fists, encourage my teammates, and thump heads after a big play. All because I'm having so much fun.

At the same time, I think fans take sports too seriously. When

I see the kind of hatred for me and my teammates that I see on the road, when I hear the kinds of vulgar, asinine statements from the stands that I hear in opposing arenas, and when I hear about people getting mad because they bet their paycheck on a game and lost—it all makes me want to throw up.

Sports is fun and games. It's entertainment, no more serious than a movie or a broadway show. But war is real life. And what the soldiers were doing in Saudi Arabia was a billion times more important than anything I was doing that weekend in Charlotte, North Carolina.

That was the feeling I had as I sat in the locker room just before we took the court for the All-Star game. If nothing else, I wanted to entertain the guys who could watch, to give them something to relax over. For two hours, I wanted to help them take their minds off Sadamn Insane.

While I was getting dressed, NBA commissioner David Stern came into the locker room and walked toward where I was sitting. With the way I was feeling about the league forcing me to play, it was not a good time for me to see him, let alone talk to him. I wanted to tell him that I didn't think it made sense for me to be there when I should have been resting my foot. But before I could say anything, he spoke.

"Charles," he said, "I just wanted to say that I'm glad you're here. Thanks for coming, and have a great game."

What was I going to say? He caught me off guard. It made me feel good that the commissioner would go out of his way to say something to me—especially when the Sixers hadn't said a damn word. It was nice of him. David makes a lot of money, even more than I do. So I went into the game with a good feeling. I wanted to play hard and play well. I started the game with a goal: to grab 20 rebounds. I didn't give a shit about anything else. Scoring, blocking shots, nothing. I figured that if I could accomplish that, it might help the guys in Saudi Arabia to know that someone was working hard to entertain them.

After tip-off, it seemed like a lot of players had the same idea that I had about the game. Most All-Star games are run-and-gun games with a lot of dunking and not much defense. But our strategy on the East team was to use our height advantage—the West had so many guards that Clyde Drexler and Chris Mullin, guys who play on the perimeter for Portland and Golden State, had to play up front at some point in the afternoon—to win the game on the boards.

The physical play rubbed off on everyone. The guys were making a concentrated effort to play hard, competitive defense. The two starting centers—Patrick Ewing for the East and David Robinson for the West—were trying to block everything.

It was a completely different kind of All-Star game. Instead of a lot of fancy assists, there were a lot of turnovers. The two teams turned the ball over 51 times. But no one cared because everybody was playing so hard. And despite the turnovers, guys were focused.

It was just the kind of game I love.

It was so nice to finally play with some guys who were thinking as fast as I was, and who were seeing the game at the same pace I do. Most of the guys who are All-stars don't think on the same level as their teammates; they see the game differently, faster, like they can see things before they happen. That's what makes them All-Stars, not just their physical talent.

One of the most frustrating things about the Sixers is that so many times I'll see things that my teammates don't see: an open passing lane, the ball-rotation on a shot, the bounce of a rebound, an open shot just waiting to be taken. It drives me crazy. I know I'm usually on a different page from almost everyone else on the team. I know what we should be doing on a particular play, but sometimes they're a step or two behind, and nobody is there long enough to develop the same sense I have.

In Charlotte, I found myself thinking so far ahead of the game a couple times that I thought I was playing by myself. But then I found out that Bernard King was on the same page, and he'd be looking for me out on the break and giving me the pass right where I could pick it up and score. Or I'd see that Patrick was on the same page, throwing an outlet pass to halfcourt that no one on the Sixers would even have seen.

It was like a basketball orgasm! During the game, I turned to some reporters who were sitting near the bench and said, "If I played with some of these guys, I'd win the championship every year."

Although I didn't know it at the time, the All-Star game would be the highlight of my season. I got my 20 rebounds—22, to be exact—and added 17 points. (Of course I didn't get through the afternoon without some controversy. In the middle of the third period, I crashed over Kevin Johnson when he tried to set a pick on me. Little guys should know better. I acted like I didn't see him, but I did, and I went through him just like I would have if he'd been Karl Malone. It's called physical intimidation and it's a part of the game. He didn't try it again, did he?)

I never once thought during the game about the MVP award— it usually goes to the high scorers; besides, the media vote for the award and I knew I wasn't very popular with those guys— so I was genuinely surprised when they announced my name at the end of the game. I was a little disoriented as a crowd of people from the league surrounded me to take me to midcourt. Someone—I don't know who—handed me a baseball cap. It was perfect.

It read: "Operation Desert Storm."

I don't put too much significance on personal rewards. But this one gave me an opportunity to speak my mind. I told the crowd to support the troops, and to forget about sports as anything other than entertainment. For once, I think everyone agreed with me.

Before I left the arena that afternoon and headed for the airport with my family, I was already thinking about the second half of the season. We were only four games above .500 and were 9½ games behind Boston in the Atlantic Division. I knew that all of us would have to pick it up if we expected to win anything before the season ended. It had been a very disappointing year so far, and I was afraid it wasn't going to get any better. I was afraid it was going to be another wasted year.

I asked my teammates to do me one favor for the rest of the year: just keep the games close. "I'll win 'em for us," I said. "You guys just keep us in the game. I can't do both, but if you take us into the fourth quarter with a lead, I'll win it."

Every team has someone they go to down the stretch, and on the Sixers it's me. It's my job. But the burden of having to make big shots throughout the game was too much. It's too much for anyone. The Bulls won the championship when guys like John Paxson, Horace Grant, Bill Cartwright, and Cliff Levingston off the bench started playing their asses off for three periods and then let Michael do his thing in the fourth. If the Sixers are going to win anything before I retire, it won't be because I played any better than I have during my career. It'll be because my team-mates gave me some support. Period.

Then something strange and amazing happened.

They did.

For the next several weeks, we played some of the best bas-ketball we'd played all season. During one seven-game winning streak we beat the Lakers and Trail Blazers, the two best teams in the Western Conference, and we did it without my having to score more than 32 in any game. We did it because Hersey and Armon were scoring more than 20 points nearly every night; because Andre Turner—it seemed like he'd been cut by prac-tically every team in the league before we signed him—was living up to his nickname, Little General, by piling up assists and burying the outside shot when Armon and I were double-teamed; because Manute was blocking shots like a madman (at one point, he had 25 blocks in six games); and because everybody was pitch-ing in defensively, where our trap was becoming one of the best in the league.

Three of the seven victories during our run were at home, but I didn't give a damn if they were played on Mars. Everything was clicking and we were gaining ground in the standings. We'd given up on trying to catch Boston, but we wanted to finish fourth in the Eastern Conference so that we would have the homecourt advantage in the first round of the playoffs against the fifth-place team, which would probably be the Milwaukee Bucks.

Of course, some teams seem to have a hex against other teams—and for no explainable reason, for us it was the pitiful Knicks.

New York has Patrick, one of the best centers in the game. And it has the best crowds in the league; there's not a player in the NBA who doesn't like playing in Madison Square Garden. But the Knicks probably had the most disappointing team in the league, and it wasn't always the players' fault. The team's front office was a nuthouse. By the end of the year they had had four different coaches since Hubie Brown was fired in the middle of the 1986–87 season, not counting the new guy, Pat Riley. Hell, they've had more general managers (four) than the Sixers have had coaches (three) since I came into the league. They've also made several dumb moves—like I should talk, considering the team I play for—like bringing in Kiki Vandeweghe and losing guys like Johnny Newman and Sidney Green to free agency and expansion without getting anything for them in return. Instead of addition by subtraction, the Knicks front office seems to believe in subtraction by subtraction.

But still, the Knicks kicked our asses five times in six games in 1990–91. It was unexplainable, except that I didn't play in four of the games, and once, on March 13, we were coming off a double-overtime win over the Hawks in Atlanta the night before. Despite the losses, the Knicks were not one of the teams on my All-Respect List. After the 102–94 loss at the Spectrum in March, a reporter pointed out to me that they were just 3½ games behind us in the playoff race. The Knicks were hot, he said. Was I worried?

"Are you kidding me?" I said. "They'd have to become a raging inferno to catch us."

I was right. The Knicks usually played like they hated each other, refusing to pass the ball to the open man and making more selfish plays than anyone else in the league. They finished eighth in the standings in the East and went out with a whimper against the Bulls in three straight games in the first round. How they beat us four straight times, I'll never know.

But then again, if we were anything in 1990–91, we were consistently inconsistent. We lost games to the Knicks, the Nets, and the Washington Bullets during the same month in which we showed a lot of character in beating the Blazers, the Bulls—who by now were *the* team to beat in the league, having won 9 straight and 20 of 21 games when we beat them 95–90 at the Spectrum on March 22—the Spurs, and the Pistons, all of the best teams in the league.

Why?

Rebounding. When we won, it was because everybody pulled together and kicked ass. We weren't the most talented team in the league, so we had to play damn near perfect basketball to win. We were going into most games at a disadvantage because we didn't have a true center. Manute was being exposed. Teams started to beat him with quickness and passing, knowing that he couldn't recover fast enough to block a shot on the weak side. And Rick was getting killed. He's not a center. He's never been a center. And for Harold Katz to think that he could play center every night was ridiculous.

Worse than that, there was a real feeling of uncertainty growing in the locker room. Despite the fact that we were playing well and were beating some good teams, a lot of guys on the team started to think that they were going to be traded. Not during the season—the trading deadline passed on February 21—but after the season, and while the end of the year was still a long way off, guys started playing for their livelihoods rather than for the team. Why be loyal when the team doesn't return the favor?

Sometimes a player will walk a very thin line when it comes to how well he plays. Nobody wants to lose, but one of the reasons that a player doesn't play as well as he's capable of playing is pressure. When a guy feels like he's going to be thrown away like a used jock—even if it's not true—he puts a lot more pressure on himself trying to prove he belongs. And it doesn't work. That's what happened to Rick, Andre Turner, and Armon during the last few weeks of the season, and it was one of the reasons we couldn't sustain our momentum down the stretch.

We knew how much we were striding the line when we went into New Jersey on March 26. And we knew that the Nets were one of the teams that could give us trouble, so we were particularly concerned about going into the Meadowlands and getting out with a win. Instead, the team left with a 98–95 loss, and I left with something that I'll carry with me my entire life: From now on, March 26, 1991, will always be remembered as the day of "the spitting incident," the day Charles Barkley spit on a little girl.

For the next forty-eight hours, I was as miserable as I've ever been in my entire life. But it didn't seem to matter to anyone. From that moment on, Charles Barkley was an asshole. No matter what I said, no matter what I've done for children during my career, one moment when I lost my mind seemed to cost me everything.

I expected to get booed on the road. Hell, I've been booed

by some of the best fans in the league, people who came up to me after the game and said, "Hey, Charles, you're a great guy. Nothing personal. I'm one of your biggest fans." But I didn't expect that I would get booed at home. Yet that's what happened after I returned from my one-game suspension and I was introduced at the Spectrum on March 29 for our game against Charlotte.

I was stunned.

I was pissed.

I was hurt.

I was everything anyone could imagine.

I focused my emotions into a pretty good game—26 points, 13 rebounds, and 5 assists in just 29 minutes—but I played in a fog, still thinking about what had happened during the previous three days. We pounded the sorry Hornets, 124–107, but I don't remember much about the night other than the boos.

For once I showed some restraint. I was ready to trash the fans; I had killed myself for this team and had worked for numerous charities in Philadelphia throughout my career. If anyplace was going to give me a break—knowing that I was truly sorry for what had happened—I thought it would have been the people in my own city. But like I've said before, there are some real assholes among sports fans. Most of them are great people, but a few aren't. Those are the ones who booed me in Philadelphia on the night of my return.

But I didn't say anything that night. For once, I kept my mouth shut. When reporters approached me after the game, I made a short speech: "On the advice of my public-relations counsel, Rick Mahorn, I'm not talking. Have a nice Easter."

It was just as well. I was in enough trouble. I didn't need an entire city trying to burn my house down because I called them all assholes.

It should be easy to see now why, as I lay on my side on the floor of the Spectrum two nights later, clutching my injured left knee, I wondered if the roof of the arena was going to crash down and just finish me off completely. But that was before I promised myself that I would be back in two weeks—not a month like the doctors had said—in time to play at least three games before the playoffs.

Everybody I knew—my business manager, my family, even some of my teammates—was telling me to kiss off the rest of the season and concentrate on getting healthy. We all knew that the season was hopeless, that without a center we weren't going to go anywhere in the playoffs except on vacation. Glenn Guthrie begged me to forget about playing. He said it wasn't worth the risk that I might tear the medial collateral ligament completely and be faced with a full year of rehabilitation, all for nothing.

I listened to him, but I had no intention of quitting. Because that's what it would have been, flat-out quitting. I didn't feel like I owed the Sixers anything, but I owed my teammates everything. I owed them anything I could do to help us win the championship. Even if we didn't have a shot.

That's why I vowed to come back—for my teammates and myself.

Sitting out all those games this year was one of the toughest things I've ever been through. I've never liked being hurt, and I wasn't used to having to watch my teammates struggle through games knowing that there wasn't anything I could do about it. It was frustrating, and I hated it. That's why I sat in the press box during the seven games I missed because of the knee injury; sitting on the bench during seven games in January was just too hard for me. I was too close to the action, close enough to touch it, but for me it was like touching air—there was nothing there.

I didn't enjoy it at all. I had never missed more than nine games in a row during my NBA career and had missed more than three games in an entire season only once. Sitting there, I got frustrated when someone made a bad play, and I went crazy when a referee made a bad call. (At least now I know that I could never be a coach; I might strangle someone.)

Basically, it was hell, and it was just too hard on me. So, after my knee injury, I sat twenty-two rows above the floor in the hockey press box. From there it seemed like another game, almost like those weren't my teammates out there but just another team. I still got upset, but knowing I was too far away for anyone to hear anything I said made it easier to keep my mouth shut.

Not that it was easy. Not at all. We were already a team that needed to play well in order to win, so losing me a second time was all we needed to fall apart. And in my first game out, the guys were awful. We were killed at home by the Bucks, the team we were trying to catch for fourth place in the playoff standings. We still had a chance to catch them—we trailed them by three and a half games with nine games left in the season—but after watching how we played that night, I knew we had no shot. Even Hersey said after the game that the guys had "looked like we just didn't care." He was right.

We salvaged some pride the next night in Indianapolis by beating the Pacers, 107–104, but maybe the highlight of the season came four days later in the least likely place—Chicago Stadium.

I broke my not-sitting-on-the-bench rule for that one, a nationally televised game against the Bulls. There was no reason in the world for us to win this game. The Bulls were 32-5 at home, and we had plenty of our own problems. I was just beginning to bend my knee, Rick was limping around with a badly bruised heel, and Kenny Payne, my backup, had twisted his ankle in practice on Friday. Only nine players suited.

What helped us was a gift: the Bulls didn't take us seriously. The night before, the Knicks had beaten the Pistons to give Chicago the Central Division title, and after the Bulls took a 41–26 lead in the second quarter the whole town started to celebrate.

But worse than that, something happened that made us think that the Bulls didn't have any respect for us. And the offender was my friend Michael Jordan.

Just before tip-off, Michael walked over to our assistant coach Fred Carter and whispered in his ear. Fred and Michael go all the way back to Michael's rookie year when Fred was still an assistant in Chicago, so they're buddies. "Why didn't you come play golf with me this morning?" Michael said.

Fred was stunned. He ran over to us and told us that Michael had played golf at seven A.M. on the morning of the game. Even I was stunned. The best player on the planet out on the golf course just seven and a half hours before tip-off! If I'd done that, I would have been crucified, and rightly so. I told my teammates that Michael had showed no respect for his profession and no respect for us by playing golf instead of preparing himself to play.

More than two weeks later, just before the start of our second-round series with the Bulls, Michael tried to play it as a joke, a psyche job to get Hersey out of his game. He said that he told Fred about playing golf because he knew Fred would run right over and tell us—"Telling Fred's just like telling the whole team," Michael later said—and that maybe Hersey would become overanxious because he would be thinking Michael was tired from an early-morning round of golf.

Well, it backfired. Hersey lit Michael up for 31 points, and the rest of my teammates got psyched up, too. Armon, who usually wouldn't rebound to save his life, was a monster; Ron Anderson, our best long-range shooter, found his touch. Together, they helped us pull to within a point at halftime, and from there it was a war.

Ron scored 28 points before fouling out with about a minute left in the fourth quarter. That left all of the scoring burden to Hersey. He played well during regulation, scoring 23 points, but OT was going to be different, and I wanted to make sure that he knew it.

Why did I start calling Hersey "Franchise, Jr."? Because if the Sixers are ever going to become contenders, he's going to have to take his game to the next level—real soon. The 1990–91 season was Hersey's third in the league, and by then everyone knew he had talent. He could score 30 points a night if he wanted to, but for all his talent, he's just not aggressive. He doesn't grab the game by the throat like he should. He waits for his spots instead of creating them.

If Hersey Hawkins had Andrew Toney's attitude, he'd be illegal.

There wasn't anything I could do in street clothes as the team broke from the huddle to start the overtime period in Chicago, except make sure that everyone stayed focused and knew what they were supposed to do. That's why I grabbed Hersey as he started to walk onto the court.

I got up in his face and started yelling. I had almost lost control. "If you want to be an All-Star, this is the kind of situation when you've got to step up and take over," I yelled. "You're a star, so play like one!"

Hersey was kind of stunned. "I'll see what I can do," he said.

"No," I yelled. "Just *do* what you can do."

I couldn't believe what I saw next: Hersey with an attitude. He scored 8 of the team's 11 points in the extra period. He scored on drives, and on jumpers from all over the floor. For five minutes, I was watching the closest thing I'd ever seen to Andrew. We won, 114–111.

That was our peak. We lost three of the next four games, including embarrassing losses to the Bullets and the pathetic expansion Minnesota Timberwolves at home, and fell out of the race for any homecourt advantage for the playoffs. At the same time, I wasn't seeing the kind of improvement in the knee I'd hoped for.

On April 15, I tested my lateral movement. I could run straight ahead and backward, I could shoot jump shots and land comfortably, but basketball is played from side to side, and if I couldn't move laterally, the Sixers might as well have filled my spot with the Rocky statue that stands in front of the Spectrum. After doing a few drills, the knee started to hurt like hell. I was distraught because I had thought I might actually be able to play the next night against the Knicks at Madison Square Garden. Instead, it looked like I might not be able to come back at all until the playoffs.

One thing I knew for certain was that whenever I came back, I was going to be hurting. I was not going to be 100 percent. The knee was not going to be pain free. So my comeback became a matter of how much pain I was willing to endure in order to play. I knew the consequences, and as the end of the season came closer, the possibility that I might reinjure the knee or tear the ligaments completely became a real possibility. But as I sat in the Garden and watched us lose again—108–99 in OT—I decided that if the knee was strong enough to survive, then I would have to be strong enough to play through the pain.

Two days later, I told Jimmy that I was ready to play that night, at home against the Celtics. I had been fitted for a brace that would protect my knee against an injury caused by bumping into someone else. But it couldn't protect the knee against itself, against its own weakness. It was a chance I wanted to take in order to try and get ready for the playoffs; I needed some games for my conditioning and for my head. With three games left in the regular season, I needed to know if I could play.

I asked Jimmy to keep it quiet. I didn't want a lot of fanfare or publicity about my return, so not even all of my teammates knew what was happening until I started getting dressed before the game.

The locker room was unusually quiet. No one wanted to say much of anything to me, especially as I sat in the corner and strapped on the brace, which ran from midcalf to midthigh. Everyone welcomed me back; they said the team needed me down the stretch if we were going to be ready for the playoffs. A couple of guys, though, asked me if I knew what I was doing. They said it wasn't worth it. Rick, who was starting to sense that he wasn't going to be around after the season, told me I was crazy to risk tearing up my knee for a team that doesn't give a damn about loyalty to its players. "You're nuts," he said.

Said Ron, "I think we were all just keeping an eye on the knee."

Everybody was uptight during pregame warm-ups. No one said a word to me out on the floor. The knee was stiff and painful. I shot a few free throws, but without bending my knee; I figured it only had a certain number of bends in it for the night, so why waste them on meaningless free throws? No one came near me as I jogged up and down the sidelines. And when I passed Celtics coach Chris Ford I gave him a hug—he welcomed me back and told me to be careful. No one thought twice about it.

The first few minutes of the game were unreal. I felt like everything revolved around my knee. My first couple of shots were bricks; I was thinking about the knee instead of playing. I had made an agreement with Jimmy that I would play the first six minutes of every quarter before coming out. At the end of the first period, I had zero points and zero rebounds.

In my mind, the first quarter was only a test. I wanted to see how much I could take. When I came out for the second quarter, the tests were over. It was game time.

On our first possession, I drove inside and scored. Then I hit a jumper. Finally, I crashed through bodies for two dunks, both times hanging on the rim and enjoying the feeling of playing again.

The Spectrum exploded, and finally, my teammates relaxed.

I lost all concern for the knee. I was playing again, and nothing else mattered. I played 24 minutes and scored 21 points with 6 rebounds, and we crushed the Celtics 122–97.

But none of that mattered. What mattered was the feeling I got from my teammates. There were more hugs, head-butts, high-fives, butt-slappings, and belly-butts that night than there were probably during the entire rest of the season combined. Anyone who doesn't think that I care for my teammates, or who thinks my teammates don't like me because I criticize them sometimes, should watch a tape of that game.

When I dove for a loose ball and crashed into the scorer's table in the second half—"Dumb. Just dumb," Rick told reporters after the game—and so many of my teammates ran over to see if I was okay, you couldn't have told me that this was a group of guys who hated each other.

When I left the floor late in the game with Brian on one side of me and Manute on the other, both of them with their arms around me, you couldn't have told me that we didn't respect each other.

And when we came into the locker room after the game and everyone started teasing me with raunchy jokes and cutting me down for my bricks at the start of the game, you couldn't have told me this wasn't a team that could do well—and maybe even win a championship—if management just left everyone alone.

We lost the final two games of the season—in Miami and Cleveland—to finish with a record of 44-38, fifth best in the East and the eleventh-best record in the league. Considering that we had won fifty-three games the year before and forty-six games in 1988–89, our record was disappointing. But given all of the injuries, the stupid Gminski trade, and all of the off-the-court distractions that marked the season, it was almost a miracle.

There was only one scare during my three-game return. In the middle of the third period against the Cavs, we were running the "fist-up" play in which I set a baseline screen for the guard cutting through the middle. Brian was the guard, and as he ran past me, our knees collided. It sent a sharp pain through my leg and I damn near screamed.

I tried to keep playing, but couldn't. Too much pain. I left the game and didn't return at all that night. I knew I hadn't done any serious damage because I could still put weight on the knee.

That didn't keep me from giving Brian a hard time about it. "Listen, rook," I said. "You stay away from the guys in the red. Those are the good guys."

A few hours later, I limped onto the team plane and had to ice my knee all the way back to Philadelphia. But I wasn't too concerned. I knew that the pain wasn't going to go away. That was a given that I had accepted from the moment I came back. I also knew that the Bucks, our first-round opponent, were going to try and wear me down by beating on me with a bunch of different guys, including my good friend Larry Krystkowiak, who was activated for the playoffs after missing most of two seasons after tearing his medial collateral ligament. I had also accepted that. I knew that I had four days to get ready for the playoffs, and if the knee didn't swell, I was going to be fine.

The team? I didn't know.

BUT I SHOULDN'T have worried. As I said all year, the Bucks were a mirage.

I said that when they won their first eighteen home games of the season and everyone started saying they were unbeatable in the Bradley Center. And I said that when they were 24-8, with one of the best records in the league. "New contenders!" everyone said.

Bullshit.

The Bucks were a soft, guard-oriented team that allowed its big men to take jump shots and told its guards to rebound. Right. As the season went on, their weaknesses were exposed.

We may not have had more talent than they did, but we had more guts, and that was enough to sweep their butts right out of the playoffs in three games. We beat them by being quicker on defense and more aggressive in every area of the game. It wasn't any more complicated than that.

The only negative part of the series had nothing to do with the Bucks. One asshole fan behind our bench began shouting obscenities at us just before the start of overtime in game two in Milwaukee. Several things started coming toward us from the stands: Coins. A cup of beer. Even a cup of ice that just missed us. I know that after the spitting incident I promised never to get involved with a fan again, but I'll always defend my teammates, so I responded to the ice by throwing a couple of cups of water at the guy in the stands.

About a week later, I received a citation from the Milwaukee Police Department, charging me with disorderly conduct. The fine was $100. I couldn't believe it. Some asshole throws beer at me and I get a ticket! I wanted to fight it. Paying the fine would be an admission of guilt, and I wasn't guilty of anything but protecting myself and my teammates from people who shouldn't be allowed at games. Hell, that guy should have gotten a ticket before I did. But Glen Guthrie and my family convinced me that fighting the ticket wasn't worth it.

If the city of Milwaukee gets its jollies from giving Charles Barkley a ticket, screw 'em!

SOMETHING HAPPENED TO us between Milwaukee and Chicago. Maybe we stopped believing in ourselves. Maybe we were just flat-out tired, I don't know. All I know is that between the first-round series against the Bucks when we played our asses off, especially on defense, and the conference semifinal series against the Bulls, we went limp.

We came out in game one like we weren't there. The Bulls pushed us around on defense, ran around us on offense, and outhustled us all over the floor. While I was scoring 34 points, Armon, Hersey, and Ron—our other scorers—were tentative and pitiful. Almost scared. They made just 7 of their 30 shots in the game. Like I said, not even there.

The Bulls dared us to beat them from the outside. They double- and sometimes triple-teamed me, which meant that *somebody* was open. But nobody wanted to shoot. Instead of taking the open shots, guys were taking extra dribbles, right into the defense, or making too many passes.

We're not a great team. We're a very good team. There's a difference. Great teams can play with their heads up their asses some nights and still win. Good teams have to play hard every night, especially in the playoffs. We acted like we were a great team against the Bulls, and they made us look like the Nets.

What bothered me most about game one was that we didn't play hard. If we play hard and lose because the other team just plays better, well, there's nothing you can do about that. But when you don't play hard, you're not even giving yourself a chance to win. That's what we had against the Bulls: no chance.

But I wasn't surprised. ("I'd be surprised if we had a black president," I said the next day, "but nothing on a basketball court surprises me.") We hadn't been consistent all season, so why should we start now?

I also said after the game that I wasn't going to criticize my teammates. The year before, all hell broke loose when I did the same thing that Magic Johnson and Michael Jordan had done: evaluate their teammates in a truthful manner. But when Charles Barkley criticizes his teammates, he's a jerk. I stopped trying to figure this shit out a long time ago.

So this year, I said I was going to keep my mouth shut. Or at least partly closed. "I did my part," I said after game one. "Hopefully, everybody else will follow through."

They did, but it wasn't enough. Our primary weaknesses, rebounding and the lack of a center, were our downfall. The effort was there in game two, but the Bulls were simply the better team. We were outrebounded 42–27, and their two centers, starter Bill Cartwright and backup Will Perdue, averaged 19.5 points in the first two games, while Rick (6 shots, 2 points in the two games) and Manute (12 points) didn't give us anything.

That's when I started getting frustrated, when I started thinking, "What's the point of trying?"

If Harold Katz wasn't committed to building a contender, then maybe it was time for me to go elsewhere. Maybe it was time to leave Philadelphia.

It didn't help that everybody in the city was suddenly a basketball expert. Guys flipping fries at Burger King were suddenly coaches. One guy called up my radio show after game two and said that Jimmy Lynam and Fred Carter were bad coaches because they hadn't taken advantage of Manute as an offensive force. Jesus Christ! Give me a damn break! The guy scores 10 points in one game and now he's Kareem Abdul-Jabbar?

PHILADELPHIA INQUIRER COLUMNIST BILL LYON, IN A COLUMN WRITTEN AFTER THE SIXERS WON GAME THREE, 99–97: *Barkley might be able to do more were he whole, but he lugs around a bad back, bum knees, a throbbing shoulder, and a knee brace that, by description, feels like a small child is clinging to him.*

We were all on our last legs. We knew it, and so did the Bulls. But game three was our final chance to salvage anything out of the series. We could overcome an 0-2 deficit, but an 0-3 deficit was insurmountable. Michael helped us out by forgetting about his teammates; he took 34 shots that night. Only one other Bull, Scottie Pippen, took more than 9 shots, and the rest of the team was obviously frustrated.

We got great play—for once—from Armon, who started at center in order to give us some offense from the position and outscored Cartwright 25–9. He also, surprisingly, came up tough on the boards with 11 against a guy who's four inches taller. He even yelled at me, unbelievably, after I yelled at him midway through the third quarter.

"Grab some damn rebounds," I said.

"Don't yell at me," he yelled back.

I was kind of surprised, but it was good to see. Every good player has a little bit of asshole in him.

We still needed a last-second hero to win it. And even though we would lose the series in five games, that one play at the end of the game might do more for us in the long run than anything else that happened during the season.

With 14.9 seconds to play we were down by two with the ball and a time-out. I know Michael Jordan like a book, so when Jimmy Lynam called a play for me to get the ball at the top of the key and drive right, I knew exactly what would happen.

With Michael guarding Hersey in the right corner, I knew he would cheat toward me when I started to drive. I figured that would give Hersey just enough of an opening to bury a shot, so I told him to spot up in 3-point territory. And I told him to watch for the ball.

The play worked to perfection. I took three dribbles right and there was Michael, right on cue. I threw a bounce pass to Hersey and he didn't hesitate. He caught the ball and shot it all in one motion. Good thing—Michael had recovered from his mistake and damn near blocked it. Hersey shot it just over Michael's outstretched hand and nailed it.

I hope that shot gives Hersey the confidence he needs to become a better player. Because we need him to do just that.

THE FINAL TWO games of the series were more of our worst, a sorry production all around. We got kicked 101–85 in our own building on Mother's Day to fall behind 3-1, which all but ended our season. I couldn't hold my frustration in any longer during the game. Once, I was running the break and fired a pass to Armon—Mr. Macho Armon Gilliam had 8 points and 8 rebounds in the game—and watched the ball hit him in the back of the head because he wasn't looking. I turned away and hung my head. I was disgusted. You always look at a guy when he's dribbling in your direction; that's elementary basketball.

Later in the game, Hersey missed an easy lay-up and I just slumped my shoulders and shook my head in disbelief. I was so frustrated that I lost my mind: I took off my knee brace near the end of the first half, threw it under the bench, and played the rest of the game without it.

Trainer Tony Harris yelled at me. The team physician told me not to do it. I didn't hear either one of them. Or I didn't want to hear them.

I don't know exactly why I did it. Just like everything else, it was bothering me. It just seemed like the right thing to do. Maybe the only thing I could do. I was desperate.

By the time the final buzzer sounded, I had had enough. I was ready to go. *Adios.*

I was through with the Philadelphia 76ers.

The way I saw it, the team had two problems: management and players.

The atmosphere among the players had deteriorated because nearly everyone thought that they were either going to be traded or cut right after the season. Rick and Ron thought they were history (Rick, of course, was right), and given Katz's lousy track record on personnel moves—nineteen different players were on the roster in 1990–91—I couldn't blame them for feeling that way. It's tough to play hard and play well under those conditions, and most of the time we did neither.

Under these conditions, I didn't think we would ever win a title. And I believed that the only way the Sixers would be able to change that was to do something drastic: trade Charles Barkley.

After game four, I sat in front of my dressing area and was depressed. I drained a few beers and just sat there staring at the floor. I had decided that I was going to ask Harold to trade me while I was still in my prime and worth a lot to another team. I told reporters that I had made a decision about my future with the team, but that I wouldn't tell them until the series was over. Not that I didn't give them enough clues as I rambled on, groping for the right words that said everything I felt:

"There's a lot of uncertainty. Guys have to feel secure. You wouldn't write good stories if you always felt you were going to be traded. . . . I don't feel cheated, but sometimes you get frustrated. You have to be consistent. You have to know what guys are going to give you every night. If you want to be good or great, you've got to work every single day. I didn't get where I am having one good game, one bad game, one good game, one bad game."

When someone asked me about taking off my knee brace, I almost laughed. My knee was, by then, the least of my worries:

"The worst thing that could happen is that I would tear my knee up. They could stitch it up and I would be ready next season. The question is, where would I be bandaged up next season?"

I went out to dinner after the game with my family and Glenn Guthrie. I told them I was ready to leave, that maybe it was the best thing for me and the Sixers as well. I thought of teams I'd like to play for. The Clippers had a lot of talent; they could afford to lose a few players and still be a solid team. And I'd love competing in the same city as Magic. Let's see where Jack Nicholson would go then! I also thought about the Miami Heat; they were also a good team that could afford to give up a couple of players and maybe even a first-round draft pick for me. With Sherman Douglas (even though he was going to be an unrestricted free agent, I thought he'd be back), Rony Seikaly, Glen Rice, and me, nobody would be calling them an expansion team anymore.

Not everyone agreed. I was told that people would think I was leaving a sinking ship. That's crazy. Kareem was traded, and the Sixers themselves damn near traded Doc to Utah. So why in the hell wouldn't they trade me? It might be the best thing that ever happened to the franchise.

When we left the restaurant, I was wavering. I didn't know what I was going to do or say. I just didn't know.

Two nights later was only a formality, although it was our best game of the series. We did almost everything right in game five and were tied, 92–92, late in the fourth period. But then it was just Michael, Michael, Michael, Michael . . .

He was in the midst of a run of 12 straight points in the last minutes of the game. We couldn't stop him and we couldn't respond. We lost 100–95. But I couldn't ask for anything more from my teammates. They played hard and stayed in the game until the very end when it would have been just as easy to check it in and play like dogs. We did everything well, except rebound. We were killed on the boards (52–29), and without a center we were helpless.

It was during the game that I decided to give Harold one more chance. All I wanted to do was win an NBA title. I'd just as soon do it in Philadelphia, with the Sixers. For that to happen, Katz was going to have to make changes. Not wholesale changes like he had done before, but additions, more pieces to the puzzle.

We needed a center. Not a great center, but a legitimate center who can rebound, block some shots, and play good defense against the opposing team's seven-footer. We needed more shooting off the bench. Ron needed help. And we needed size. Size with quickness.

I had actually made up my mind before Christmas that I was going to meet with Harold at the end of the season and say, "I need some help." I decided to wait until the end of the season because the team didn't need any more distractions.

Now, after the Bulls series, I needed some convincing. I wasn't sure that Harold and I were on the same page. If he could convince me that he would fill our needs, then I would stay in Philadelphia. But only if he could convince me.

ONE WEEK LATER, I walked into Harold's office at the Spectrum, sat down with Harold and Jimmy, and waited to hear what they had to say. If either one of them had said the Sixers were already good enough to win the title, I was gone. I was ready to tell them that I didn't want to waste my time working out all summer, then come to training camp in the fall and find the same guys and get beat in the first or second round of the playoffs again. That's not my goal.

I love Philadelphia. I want to finish my career in the city. But I'd rather lose in another city where I would have less pressure on me.

I was proud, though, when Jimmy stepped in and said that he agreed with my assessment of the team. He said this team right now was not good enough to win the championship. Harold agreed, and he promised that before the start of training camp for the 1991–92 season, he would get me some help. That's all I wanted to hear.

What I didn't want to hear, though, was Harold's thoughts about me. He said he had no problems with my performance. ("You shouldn't," I said. "I'm one of the five best players on the planet.") But he said he would like to see me score about 4 or 5 fewer points and average more rebounds than I did during the 1990–91 season, which was just over 10 a game. He said he'd like me to average about 14 rebounds a game.

Now, I love rebounding. It's my passion, always has been. But I'm a realist, too. I averaged more rebounds when I played power forward, which had me closer to the basket. But because of my quickness and ball-handling skills, I can better help the team at small forward, which is why Rick and later Armon, manned the team's power forward position. I was confused.

"Let me get this straight," I said. "You want me to guard guys out on the perimeter, but still get more rebounds. You want me to get out on the break, but still get more rebounds. You want me to chase guys who are shooting jumpers from the top of the key, but still get more rebounds. It's just not possible.

"It's wishful thinking, and I've got no problem with that. You're entitled to your opinion. But it's just not possible. When G-Man and Rick were doing a great job on the boards and I was out on the wing, everyone was happy with my rebounding. But then you trade G-Man and move Rick into the middle where he can't play, and we get killed on the boards because Armon won't rebound, then you ask, 'Why isn't Charles rebounding?' Think about it. Charles is doing the same thing he was doing before the trade. What's different? Think about it.

"It's just not possible."

But after nearly two hours, I decided to put my faith in God and Harold Katz, and to hope that by the start of the 1991–92 season, the Philadelphia 76ers would be stronger, quicker, and better than before.

Why God?

Because Harold needed all the help he could get.

IT WASN'T LONG before the changes began. And in typical Sixers style, they began with the kind of unprofessionalism that the team has been known for when it comes to the way it treats its players. On July 1, Rick and I were in the Poconos working at a Sixers youth camp when he called home and listened to his answering machine. There was a message from the Sixers: "Call as soon as you can."

When Rick returned the call, he was told that the team was not going to renew his contract, that they needed room under the salary cap in order to make more moves and that they just couldn't afford the $1.6 million he was supposed to get paid for the 1991–92 season.

That was it. Hang up the phone. Bye.

I understood that something had to be done, but it's tough to lose a friend, and Rick was one of the best friends I had in the league. He helped me keep my sanity. I was disappointed in the way the Sixers handled the move; after eleven years in the league, after playing out of position for the Sixers for most of last season and missing only two games despite a bad back, I thought he deserved better than to be told over the telephone that the Sixers didn't want him anymore. That was rude and unprofessional, but that's the Sixers.

Three weeks later, I found out why Katz let Rick go: to sign Charles Shackleford, a 6'10" center/forward who was basically thrown away by the Nets—*the Nets!*—after just two years with the team. In 1989–90, his second year with the team, "Shack" averaged only 8.2 points and 6.8 rebounds in seventy games. He missed twelve games with various injuries, and he was arrested for possession of marijuana. Not exactly the type of player I had in mind. And if the Nets couldn't use him, it's hard to imagine how he can be our starting center.

Charles played last season in the Italian league, where he led a team called Phonola Caserta to the championship. The league said he averaged 15.8 rebounds playing center over there, but I don't know if their numbers can be trusted.

Katz also signed Mitchell Wiggins, a tough, competitive guard who played five seasons for the Houston Rockets but was banned from the league in 1987 for testing positive for cocaine. He got himself clean and was reinstated by the league 2½ years later. In 1989–90 he played for the Rockets, but they didn't want him after the season. He's supposed to back up Hersey Hawkins and help Ron Anderson with our scoring off the bench.

As I went to training camp for the 1991–92 season, I don't know if I was encouraged or pissed. The Sixers didn't discuss any of the moves with me. I think I've earned the right to advise management about personnel moves—just like Magic, Michael, and Larry. It's frustrating to think that Harold doesn't think I know more about the game than he does, or at least that I know enough to help him make decisions about the team.

If he'd asked me, I don't know if I would have told him to sign Charles Shackleford and Mitchell Wiggins. And even now, I'm not sure whether they'll help—especially Shack. I won't know until I get to Lancaster, Pennsylvania, and see them play. For me, it was a summer of "wait and see."

I truly hope it works out. I hope Shack can average 10 boards a game, about 10–15 points a game, and a couple of blocks, too. I hope Mitchell is another Ricky Pierce, the league's best reserve guard.

All I want is a real, legitimate shot at winning the NBA championship. That's all. After watching Michael win it last year, and seeing how much it meant to him, I decided that winning a championship was all I had left to play for.

And I want to win it in Philadelphia. I want the Sixers to win the championship, and I want to help them do it.

I don't want to be traded.

I don't want to play for the Clippers or the Heat.

I want to be a Sixer.

For now, at least. By the middle of the 1991–92 season, if Harold's moves don't work, maybe I'll do something drastic.

Maybe I'll change my mind. Again.

12

SO, CAN DRUG DEALERS BE ROLE MODELS, TOO?

*"Just because I dunk a basketball doesn't mean
I should raise your kids."*
"But you're paid to act like a professional."
"I'm paid to kick ass on the basketball court."

I'LL START AT the beginning, and I'll only say this once: Professional athletes should not be role models.

During the 1990–91 season, I hosted a talk show on radio station WIP in Philadelphia. I was getting paid to run my mouth. I loved it.

The show gave me the opportunity to express my opinion on everything from zone defenses to the war in the Persian Gulf, and to address some of the criticisms and controversies that hounded me throughout the year. I took questions from listeners at home and in their cars, and from people in the audience at the restaurant that hosted the show. The live-audience format allowed anyone in the city to confront me face-to-face with whatever problem they might have had concerning my behavior, anything I might have said or done, rather than just talk about me behind my back—which is an asshole's favorite pastime.

Toward the end of the year, a woman grabbed the microphone and started tearing into me for being a poor role model for young people who look up to professional athletes, and who aspire to follow in our footsteps. She whined and moaned, saying that as a member of the Sixers who made millions of dollars for playing basketball, I was obliged to be a goody two-shoes.

My biggest problem with this whole question of whether athletes and entertainers should be role models for young kids, especially young black kids, is this: How the hell does an athlete qualify for the job?

If the only qualification for being a role model is that you have to be able to dunk a basketball, then I know millions of people who could become role models. That's not enough. Hell, I know drug dealers who can dunk. So, can drug dealers be role models, too?

While nobody would even think of calling a drug dealer a role model, that's exactly what they've become for a lot of kids. It's an unfortunate fact of life that a lot of kids who live in impoverished areas look up to drug dealers because they're the only wealthy people they come in contact with. And they've got all of the material things these kids think they need in order to be known around the 'hood as a success—fancy cars, expensive clothes, and mobile phones.

These are the marks of success, the only way to be "down" in a place where most everyone is simply down-and out, trying to survive.

It's only natural that a lot of kids become involved with drugs, which they see as the quickest way to material success. Faster than going to school. Faster than getting a job at McDonald's. And even faster than petty crime. It's a way to get a piece of the rock. That's why children as young as eight, nine, and ten years old are joining forces with drug dealers, working in entry-level jobs like runners and lookouts in cities throughout the nation. Probably not too far from where you live. Drugs have become everybody's problem—not just black people's problem, or poor people's problem.

It's your problem. It's my problem. And it's going to cost us more than a generation of our youth. It's going to cost us an entire generation of people who should be growing up to be productive, hardworking citizens. They should have been our mailmen, our construction workers, our contractors, our architects, our fashion designers, our businessmen (and business-women), our doctors, attorneys, politicians, and even our athletes and entertainers.

Instead, too many of them will either be in jail or dead because of drugs, or the gang-related violence associated with drugs.

And do you know what? As much as I think they're scum, I don't even blame the dealers themselves for the problem. They've chosen to become criminals, and truth is, they'll prob-ably all be dead before they're thirty. Good riddance.

But I don't give them all of the blame.

I also blame the parents who don't teach their kids proper values, and who don't tell their kids that respect and success in life have nothing to do with material wealth. Too many of them just sit on their asses all day, doing nothing to make life better for themselves or their children. Some of them are committing more misdeeds—like abandoning their families, taking drugs, abusing spouses, and generally being massive, lazy failures—than all of the professional athletes and entertainers put together. And they do them right in the home, and in front of their kids. There are even parents who condone their kids' involvement in drugs because of the money the child brings home. I've spoken to policemen in various cities who said that after they've arrested a youngster for being a lookout for drug dealers, then called the parent to come pick up the child, that the mother has been more upset about the fact that the police confiscated the child's money—money earned from the drug trade—than they were that their child had been arrested.

It's a shame.

Respect and success are earned with hard work, education, discipline, and an ability to move toward becoming a productive citizen at any number of professions and endeavors. Material wealth is fine. Everyone wants to live comfortably and be able to afford some of the nicer things in life. If that's how you define success, there's more than one way to attain it. But everyone starts the same way—by getting an education and finding a damn job!

That's my main point. It's asinine to make someone a role model simply because of what they've accomplished as an athlete or entertainer. Parents should be the child's primary role models. Even single parents don't have to succumb to the pressures of having to provide for their kids by themselves. It's hard. I know it's hard. But there are ways for them to better themselves to the point that they can eventually improve their lives—even if it's just one day at a time.

And it would be worth every bit of the effort, because when a child sees his or her parent working, working and working some more in order to provide the necessities of life; and when a child sees that parent reading newspapers, books, and magazines; and when a child hears that parent talking about school and praising the child's grades, it all means more—much more— than anything Charles Barkley, Magic Johnson, or even Michael Jordan could ever say or do to influence the child's life.

So, if you want to blame someone for the problems of our youth, blame the parents who are shirking their duties and using poverty as an excuse.

It's not my job to take on their responsibilities. Not my job at all.

On the other hand, I don't mind being an example for young people of someone who overcame living in the projects and being abandoned by his father to become a success. And I take exception to anyone who says that my behavior in any way detracts from that truth.

Those people's values are screwed up. I'm a good person. I'm honest. I work extremely hard to provide for my wife, my daughter, and the rest of my family. I take good care of them, and I worry about being able to protect them, especially from some of the loonies out there who resent the kind of money athletes make, and who think I'm supposed to be different from what I am. I've met a lot of real knuckleheads since I came to the NBA, a lot of people who look like they might want to make a name for themselves by assaulting Charles Barkley. I've also received death threats over the telephone—that's why I change my number on a regular basis—and in letters that come to the Sixers' office.

People in the public eye really have to watch out for themselves. The way society is today, with people mugging, hitting, and killing each other for everything from jackets to Rolex watches to drugs, there's a lot of danger. And I'll do anything—*anything*—to keep my family safe.

That's why I own a gun.

I've never pulled the gun on anybody, and I would never use it on someone—unless I had to. But if my life was threatened, or my wife or my family, I would not hesitate. I hope I never have to pull my gun on anyone, but I want to have the freedom to have it. And I do.

I'm proud to own a gun. It's my right. And I wouldn't think that exercising your rights could get you labeled a bad role model—those words again. But it happens.

I was on my way back from conducting an antidrug clinic for about five hundred kids in Atlantic City in August 1988, at the West Side Complex, a community center and elementary school. It was a great time; the kids were enthusiastic, and they listened to what I had to say: that I was no stranger to peer pressure, that I had once followed the crowd and gotten into trouble. I told them to make something of themselves by being strong individuals, not weak followers. Afterward, I hung around for about forty minutes and signed autographs. By the time I stepped into my car, I felt good. Real good.

I was driving on the Atlantic City Expressway—okay, I admit I was speeding, but it's not like I was doing 100 or anything—when I got pulled over by a New Jersey state trooper. In the midst of her questioning, she decided—it couldn't have been because I'm a famous athlete, could it?—to search the car for drugs. She found the gun lying on the back seat.

That's when she hauled me into the police station and I was charged with carrying a weapon and failing to have a New Jersey permit. They didn't seem to care much that the gun was registered in Pennsylvania, where I happen to live. They were just so happy to have arrested Charles Barkley.

A few weeks later the charges were dropped, and in September a judge ruled that the trooper didn't have probable cause to search my car. Which I could have told them.

I was vindicated, but not before the media had a field day with me, dragging me through the mud and screaming about how I had again done something unworthy of a "role model."

My having a gun has nothing to do with me being a role model, and for people to make judgments about me because of it is asinine.

But the way I feel is that the only person I have to be a role model for is my two-year-old daughter, Christiana. Nobody else. And nobody else has that responsibility to her, either. Her mother and I are her role models. Not Michael Jordan. (Even though she screams his name whenever he comes on television.) Not Chris Evert. Not Jackie Joyner-Kersee. Not Monica Seles, Steffi Graf, or Zina Garrison or any other female athlete. It's Charles and Maureen Barkley's job to raise their child, no one else's.

It's our job to care for her, protect her, and encourage her to become whatever she wants to be in life. It's also our job to tell her the truth—whether it's about the racism she might face by being the child of an interracial marriage, or the odds and obstacles she might face in trying to achieve some goals.

Like becoming a professional athlete.

If she tells me she wants to be a professional tennis player or golfer, I'll tell her the same thing I tell every other kid who says they want to be the next Michael Jordan, Karl Malone, Buck Williams, or heaven forbid, the next Charles Barkley: Forget it.

Most young athletes—I don't care if they're Mr. All-Everything on their junior high or high school teams—have absolutely no shot of becoming a professional athlete. Zero. None. The statistics are only 1 in 10,000. Some odds. Out of every ten thousand high school basketball players, only one will reach the NBA. Out of that same group there'll probably be maybe a hundred doctors and lawyers, about a dozen scientists, a few hundred businessmen and businesswomen, and countless people who simply become successful hardworking members of their communities. And one NBA player.

I never discourage any young person from pursuing their dreams, even if it's to become a professional athlete. But it can't be their only dream. Kids have to have many dreams, enough to ensure that at least one of them will come true. The Fortune

500 is filled with people who dreamed of becoming a professional athlete. I'll bet that most of those CEOs were talented basketball, football, or baseball players in high school and college. I'll bet a lot of them looked up to the professional athletes of their time, guys starring in the majors, and in the young NBA and NFL. And I'll bet that they wanted to be just like their heroes.

But they were smart. Being just like their heroes wasn't all that they wanted. And when they realized that they weren't going to play for the New York Yankees, Boston Celtics, or Green Bay Packers, they went on to pursue their other dreams. They got their education, took a job, found something they enjoyed doing, and chased it like they were chasing a fumble or a loose ball. When they tackled their competition or scored big in the board-room, they pretended they were Dick Butkus or Roger Staubach. And when they took their best shot at the negotiating table, they were Elgin Baylor. They found other ways to pursue their com-petitive passion—such as weekend leagues—or they picked up sports like golf and tennis, anything that allowed them to retain their athletic spirit. But it was only a diversion. Their primary efforts went into their work, their livelihood, their obligation to their families.

Because of the odds against ever reaching the NBA, NFL, or major-league baseball, it makes no sense to place pro athletes on a pedestal, to tell kids that they should aspire to become just like us when about one hundredth of one percent of all high school football and basketball players will ever play in the pros. One damn tenth of one percent! That's about as close to impos-sible as you can get.

One of the main causes of the crisis among black Americans these days is that we allow too many of our kids to think they're going to be professional athletes when their chances are almost nil. We feed a fruitless dream, forgiving our kids for spending more time at the playground than in the classroom, and worrying more about their scoring average than their grade point average. That's stupid.

Kids today need an education and religion a whole lot more than they need to be encouraged to be professional athletes. They need to be sent to the library instead of the sporting goods store, to the museum instead of the gym, and to church instead of the street corner to hang out with the fellas.

Sure, I left college without getting my degree, but as I've said many times, the only reason I went to college at all was to be able to get a job that would allow me to take care of my family. I didn't care what kind of job it was, only that it would pay me enough to be able to help my mother and grandmother. When I left Auburn after my junior season, it was because I had achieved what I set out to do: get a job. Luckily, God blessed me with the physical gifts and the desire to become an NBA player. That became my job.

But in the spring of 1984, at the time I decided to leave Auburn, about a thousand other college basketball players were also leaving Division I schools. Most of them thought they were good enough to play in the NBA, and almost all of them had already fantasized about spending the money they thought they were going to get from their first NBA contract. In their minds, they were driving cars whose names they couldn't spell, wearing clothes designed by people whose names they couldn't pronounce, and drinking expensive champagne they didn't even like because, hey, they were headin' for the NBA. Because that's what people had been telling them ever since they first dunked in junior high school—everybody from their folks to their friends to their coaches and their relatives.

They're all full of it.

Check it out: only forty-one of all of the college basketball players who came out of school at the same time I did—and this was one of the best classes in NBA history—played even one season in the NBA. Seven years later, just nine of those twenty-four first-round draft picks were still in the league at the end of the 1990–91 season. Altogether, only twenty-four of the guys I came into the league with were still in the league at the end of the 1990–91 season. *Figure it out. One in ten thousand.*

By the end of the 1992–93 season, when I'll be thirty years old and probably crippled, there'll probably be only a handful of my rookie classmates left in the league. The rest of them will be trying to figure out what to do with the rest of their lives. Almost all of us—except the guys like Hakeem Olajuwon, Mi-

chael Jordan, Sam Perkins, John Stockton, and myself, guys who
were lucky enough to sign megadeals during our careers—will
be trying to figure out how to earn a living.

Some odds, huh?

At the same time, most of the nonathletes I went to college
with are working in jobs that will give them security for as long
as they're able to get up in the morning and go to the office.
That's because they got an education and didn't place their
dreams of success into something as risky as trying to be a professional athlete. In other words, they didn't bet their lives on a
lottery ticket.

Nothing in the world worth having is free. Nothing is easy.

In athletics I've seen it all. Guys with great talent who didn't
make it because they didn't have a brain in their head. And guys
who reached the NBA by working their butts off, even though
they didn't have more than a few ounces of talent to their names.
That shows that no matter what profession you choose to pursue,
it's all about hard work. Nothing more. Or less.

I'm writing this just before the start of the 1991–92 season,
and I'm tired. After seven years in the NBA, my body aches
every day, and I'm starting to look forward to the end of my
career.

I hope I'll be able to play more than four more seasons before
my body breaks down completely. But I think I'll only be able
to play at my current level for another three seasons, through
1993–94. I just don't think my body will take more than that.
But I can promise you one thing: until I'm forced to, I'm never
going to let down. I'll never turn the engines off.

I enjoy being on top of my profession. Anyone can be mediocre—especially near the end of their careers when a lot of guys
are just cruising for the paychecks. But it takes lots of hard work,
energy, and effort to stay at the top. And that's where I want to
be.

As MUCH AS it seems that I get frustrated about the Sixers, about
Harold Katz's terrible moves, and about our dwindling chances
to win the championship, I'm committed to Philadelphia. I truly
want to finish my career as a 76er.

Although getting traded wouldn't be the worst thing in the world that ever happened to me, I don't want to go to another team. But I don't want to be on a losing team, either.

When I was so discouraged during the playoffs at the end of the 1990–91 season, to the point that I came close to demanding a trade, it was only because I truly wanted the team to be a contender and I wasn't convinced that Harold had the same goal in mind.

Sure, I've got an obligation to the Sixers, but I also have an obligation to myself. Instead of criticizing me for blasting the team like I did last year, people should have commended me for wanting to win so badly—a lot more than some of the clowns who've come through this city since I've been here. I don't know why people expect me to sit around and lose in the first or second round of the playoffs every year and not complain.

If that's what you want, then find another team to root for because that's not me. I'll never remain quiet when I've got something to say.

Already, some of my critics are starting to evalute my career based on whether or not the Sixers ever win a championship. That's bullshit, but it's the kind of bad rap that goes with being a superstar. When people blame everything on you, when they take shots at you, that's when you're really good.

Right now, I envy Michael Jordan. For years, people claimed he was the reason that Chicago couldn't win the title. They never said anything about the guys he played with, guys who are no longer there. It's true, Michael could not win a championship by himself, which is why, as he cried in the locker room after the Bulls beat the Lakers for the 1991 title, he gave so much credit to Horace Grant, Scottie Pippen, Bill Cartwright, John Paxson, Cliff Levingston, and the rest of his teammates. They're the ones who had to play well in order for the Bulls to win. No one-man team will ever win the NBA title again. It takes a lot of help. The league is just too good.

Now, no one can ever take shots at Michael Jordan again. That's what I envy. From now on, he's not just "Michael Jordan, the great player." He's "Michael Jordan, world champion."

Would I be disappointed if I retired without ever winning a championship?

Of course I would. I think about it every single day. But I'm not stupid enough to say my career would have been a failure if the Sixers don't win it all. I've got more common sense than that. I'll never really complain about my life. Or my pain.

God never puts more on a person than he can handle. Most of my controversies have been mad-made, not God-made. But all of my trials and tribulations have made me a better person. Everyone makes mistakes in his life, and I'll probably continue to make mistakes. To me, each of them is a test.

God tests us all every day. The devil tests us every day. Every day we wake up, there will be someone out there to test our faith in God, and in ourselves.

That's the real key to life—understanding that no matter the test, it's always a matter of you against yourself. It's not you against anyone else, because no one can make you do something that you don't want to do.

Until I die, I'm going to do whatever it takes for me to stay who I am—not who anyone else wants me to be.

CHARLES BARKLEY'S CAREER STATISTICS

COLLEGIATE RECORD

Year	G.	Min.	FGA	FGM	Pct.	FTA	FTM	Pct.	Reb.	Pts.	Avg.
81–82—Auburn	28	746	242	144	.595	107	68	.636	275	356	12.7
82–83—Auburn	28	782	250	161	.644	130	82	.631	266	404	14.4
83–84—Auburn	28	794	254	162	.638	145	99	.683	265	423	15.1
TOTALS	84	2322	746	467	.636	382	249	.652	806	1183	14.1

NBA REGULAR SEASON RECORD

| Sea.—Team | G. | Min. | FGA | FGM | Pct. | FTA | FTM | Pct. | Rebounds | | | Ast. | PF | Dq. | Stl. | Blk. | Pts. | Avg. |
									Off.	Def.	Tot.							
84–85—Philadelphia	82	2347	783	427	.545	400	293	.733	266	437	703	155	301	5	95	80	1148	14.0
85–86—Philadelphia	80	2952	1041	595	.572	578	396	.685	354	672	1026	312	333	8	173	125	1603	20.0
86–87—Philadelphia	68	2740	937	557	.594	564	429	.761	380	604	994	331	252	5	119	104	1564	23.0
87–88—Philadelphia	80	3170	1283	753	.587	951	714	.751	385	566	951	254	278	6	100	103	2264	28.3
88–89—Philadelphia	79	3088	1208	700	.579	799	602	.753	403	583	986	325	262	3	126	67	2037	25.8
89–90—Philadelphia	79	3085	1177	706	.600	744	557	.749	361	548	909	307	250	2	148	50	1989	25.2
90–91—Philadelphia	67	2498	1167	665	.570	658	475	.722	258	422	680	284	173	2	110	33	1849	27.6
TOTALS	535	19880	7596	4403	.580	4694	3466	.738	2417	3832	6249	1968	1849	31	871	562	12454	23.3

Three-Point Field Goals: 1984–85, 1-for-6 (.167), 1985–86, 17-for-75 (.227), 1986–87, 21-for-104 (.202), 1987–88, 44-for-157 (.280), 1988–89, 35-for-162 (.216), 1989–90, 20-for-92 (.217), 1990–91, 44-for-155 (.284). Totals, 182-for-751 (.242).

NBA PLAYOFF RECORD

Sea.—Team	G.	Min.	FGA	FGM	Pct.	FTA	FTM	Pct.	Rebounds Off.	Def.	Tot.	Ast.	PF	Dq.	Stl.	Blk.	Pts.	Avg.
84-85—Philadelphia	13	408	139	75	.540	63	40	.635	52	92	144	26	49	0	23	15	194	14.9
85-86—Philadelphia	12	497	180	104	.578	131	91	.695	60	129	189	67	52	2	27	15	300	25.0
86-87—Philadelphia	5	210	75	43	.573	45	36	.800	27	36	63	12	21	0	4	8	123	24.6
88-89—Philadelphia	3	135	45	29	.644	31	22	.710	8	27	35	16	9	0	5	2	81	27.0
89-90—Philadelphia	10	419	162	88	.543	108	65	.602	66	89	155	43	36	0	8	7	247	24.7
90-91—Philadelphia	8	326	125	74	.592	75	49	.653	31	53	84	48	23	0	15	3	199	24.9
TOTALS	51	1995	726	413	.569	453	303	.669	244	426	670	212	190	2	82	50	1144	22.4

Three-Point Field Goals: 1984-85, 4-for-6 (.667), 1985-86, 1-for-15 (.067), 1986-87, 1-for-8 (.125), 1988-89, 1-for-5 (.200), 1989-90, 6-for-18 (.333), 1990-91, 2-for-20 (.100). Totals, 15-for-72 (.208).

NBA ALL-STAR GAME RECORD

Season—Team	Min.	FGA	FGM	Pct.	FTA	FTM	Pct.	Rebounds Off.	Def.	Tot.	Ast.	PF	Dq.	Stl.	Blk.	Pts.
1987—Philadelphia	16	6	2	.333	6	3	.500	1	3	4	1	2	0	1	0	7
1988—Philadelphia	15	4	1	.250	2	2	1.000	1	2	3	0	2	0	1	1	4
1989—Philadelphia	20	11	6	.545	8	5	.625	3	2	5	0	0	0	2	1	17
1990—Philadelphia	22	12	7	.583	3	2	.667	2	2	4	0	1	0	1	1	17
1991—Philadelphia	35	15	7	.467	6	3	.500	8	14	22	4	5	0	1	1	17
TOTALS	108	48	23	.479	25	15	.600	15	23	38	5	10	0	6	4	62

Three-Point Field Goals: 1987, 0-for-2, 1988, 0-for-1, 1990, 1-for-1 (1.000). Totals, 1-for-4 (.250).
Named to All-NBA First Team, 1988, 1989, 1990, 1991. . . . All-NBA Second Team, 1986 and 1987. . . . NBA All-Rookie Team, 1985. . . . NBA All-Star Game MVP, 1991. . . . Led NBA in rebounding, 1987. . . . Recipient of Schick Pivotal Player Award, 1986, 1987, 1988.